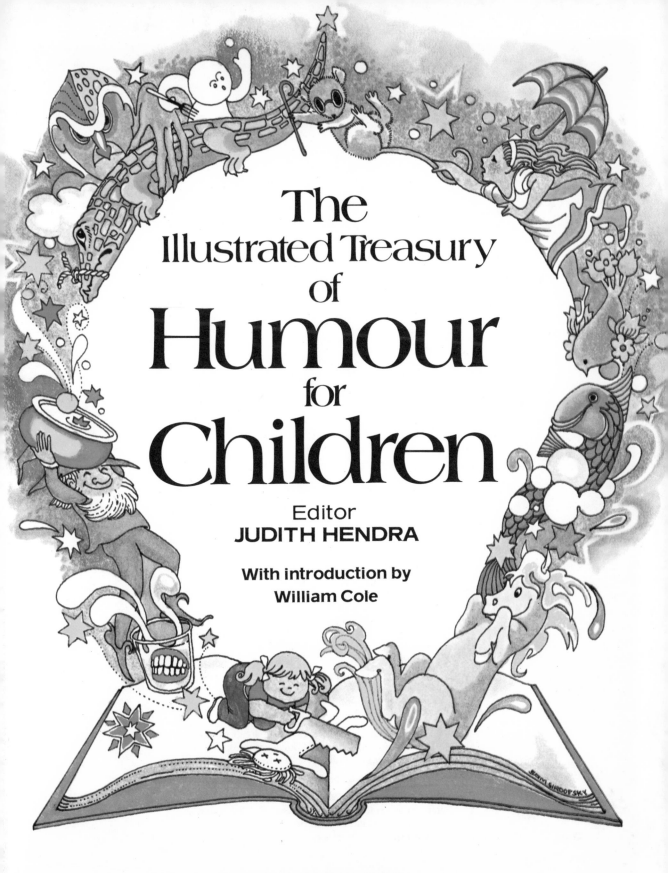

The
Illustrated Treasury
of
Humour
for
Children

Editor
JUDITH HENDRA

With introduction by
William Cole

HODDER AND STOUGHTON
LONDON . SYDNEY . AUCKLAND . TORONTO

To Tony, Kathy, and Jessica, with much love.

British Library Cataloguing in Publication Data

The illustrated treasury of humour for children.
1. English wit and humour
I. Hendra, Judith
827′.008   PN6175

ISBN 0-340-27456-5
First published in Great Britain 1981.

Published by Hodder and Stoughton Children's Books,
(a division of Hodder and Stoughton Ltd),
Mill Road, Dunton Green, Sevenoaks, Kent TN13 2YJ.

Printed in Great Britain by Sackville Press Billericay Limited.

CONTENTS

iii

LIST OF ILLUSTRATORS

ACKNOWLEDGMENTS

Grateful acknowledgement is made to the following publishers, authors, and other copyright holders for permission to reprint copyrighted materials. While all reasonable efforts have been made to find the holders of copyright materials, any omissions or errors will be corrected in future editions, and copyrights properly acknowledged.

Hilaire Belloc: "Henry King" and "Matilda." Reprinted from CAUTIONARY VERSES by Hilaire Belloc. Published by Gerald Duckworth and Co. By permission of the publisher.

John Ciardi: "Children When They're Very Sweet" from THE MAN WHO SANG THE SILLIES by John Ciardi. Copyright © 1961 by John Ciardi. By permission of J. B. Lippincott, Publishers.

William Cole: "Sneaky Bill," Copyright © William Cole 1977. By permission of the author.

Walter de la Mare: "The Eel" from STUFF AND NONSENSE by Walter de la Mare. By permission of the Literary Trustees of Walter de la Mare and The Society of Authors as their representative.

Arthur Guiterman: "The Ambiguous Dog" from THE LAUGHING MUSE by Arthur Guiterman, published by Harper and Co., 1915. Reprinted by permission of Louise H. Sclove.

O. Henry: "The Ransom of Red Chief," copyright 1907 by Doubleday & Company, Inc., from THE COMPLETE WORKS OF O. HENRY. Reprinted by permission of the publisher.

Mary Ann Hoberman: "Brother" from HELLO AND GOOD-BY by Mary Ann Hoberman, published by Little, Brown and Company. Copyright © 1959 by Mary Ann Hoberman. Reprinted by permission of Russell & Volkening, Inc., as agents for Mary Ann Hoberman.

Wilbur G. Howcroft: "My Wise Old Grandpapa" from THE FARM THAT BLEW AWAY by Wilbur G. Howcroft, published by the Hawthorn Press Proprietary Ltd. (Australia). Reprinted by permission of the publisher.

Sean Kelly: "The Knockmany Giant," Copyright © 1980 by Sean Kelly. By permission of the author.

X. J. Kennedy: "Exploding Gravy" from ONE WINTER NIGHT IN AUGUST and Other Nonsense Jingles by X. J. Kennedy. Copyright © 1975 by X. J. Kennedy. Published by Atheneum Publishers. Reprinted by permission of Curtis Brown, Ltd.

Rudyard Kipling: "Beginning of the Armadillos" from JUST SO STORIES by Rudyard Kipling. Reprinted in Canada by permission of the National Trust and Macmillan London Limited.

Spike Milligan: "You Must Never Bath in an Irish Stew" from SILLY VERSE FOR KIDS by Spike Milligan, published by Dobson Books Ltd. Reprinted by permission of Dennis Dobson.

Don Marquis: "Prudence" from ARCHY AND MEHITABEL by Don Marquis. Copyright 1927 by Doubleday & Company, Inc. Reprinted by permission of Faber and Faber Ltd.

Ogden Nash: "The Kitten," "The Pig," "The Shark," "The Jellyfish," "The Termite," "The Parent," from VERSES FROM 1929 ON by Ogden Nash. Published by Little, Brown and Co. Copy-

INTRODUCTION

An introduction to a book is where someone says, "Book—meet reader. Reader—meet book—I hope you like each other." I can say, as one whose work (and play) has been putting together about fifty collections of humor and poetry, that this is a good book to meet. A *VERY* good book. All it's supposed to do is make you laugh—not always a big, loud laugh, but sometimes an inside laugh, a kind of "humpf!" that you say to yourself.

I like the poetry best, but poetry has always been my favorite; there are so many surprises in the way poets rhyme things! (Not that poetry *has* to rhyme—some of the funniest poems don't.) A lot of this poetry, by the way, was written by kids. Where do you think those jump-rope rhymes come from? From children like you, many many years ago. Kids probably wrote some of the riddles and knock-knocks and other silliness in this collection.

One thing I find interesting is that some of the stuff in this book was written two hundred years ago, and other stuff was written last year. And the old stuff is as funny as the new! Your great-great-grandfather was probably as funny as your father (if your father is funny—as I'm sure he sometimes is). Funny's funny, no matter when. Samuel Clemens, who wrote a hundred years ago, still makes me laugh, and Oliver Herford and Wallace Irwin, from a half-century ago, knock me out.

This is the kind of book you can open up anywhere and find surprising things like Simple Simon who tried to roast a snowball, and the rotten kid the kidnappers paid his family to *take back* again, and the man who walked out in the morning and found that he had left his feet asleep in bed. There's miles of ridiculous stuff concerning giant turnips, good-mannered sharks, and exploding gravy. Things to make you laugh out loud, or snort, or just get a pleasant feeling. There's even a section of poems and stories about naughty children. That may seem surprising, but there's nothing wrong with a small amount of naughtiness. I once put together a book of poems about naughty kids, and in the introduction I wrote:

> . . . life would be boring, and life would be grim,
> If children were all goody-goody and prim.
> For children will tickle, and poke, and wiggle,
> And just when they're not supposed to, they'll giggle;
> And they are inclined to make too much noise
> (This is true of the girls—but, goodness! The boys!)

This is a book you don't have to study from; it's not trying to teach you one single thing—it's just for the fun of it. There may even be a few things here that you don't think are funny. Somebody else, however, will break up over them. That's how it goes. As Ogden Nash, our best writer of humorous verse, once wrote:

> In this foolish world there is nothing more numerous
> Than different people's senses of humorous.

William Cole

William Cole has edited over fifty anthologies—many of them collections of humorous verse for children. He often writes poetry himself, and you will find his poem about a greedy boy on page 108. He is a friend of many of the contemporary writers in this book—some of them have written verse especially for his collections.

Nursery Nonsense

A horse and a flea and three blind mice
Sat on a curbstone shooting dice.
The horse he slipped and fell on the flea.
The flea said, "Whoops, there's a horse on me."

Me, myself and I—
We went to the kitchen and ate a pie.
Then my mother—she came in,
And chased us out with a rolling pin.

Baby and I
Were baked in a pie,
The gravy was wonderful hot.
We had nothing to pay
To the baker that day
And so we crept out of the pot.

If all the world were apple pie
And all the sea were ink,
And all the trees were bread and cheese,
What would we have to drink?
It's enough to make an old man
Scratch his head and think!

SIMPLE SIMON

Simple Simon met a pieman
  Going to the fair;
Says Simple Simon to the pieman,
  "Let me taste your ware."

Says the pieman to Simple Simon,
  "Show me first your penny."
Says Simple Simon to the pieman,
  "Indeed I have not any."

He went to take a bird's nest,
  Was built upon a bough;
The branch gave way and Simon fell
  Into a dirty slough.

Simple Simon went a-fishing,
  For to catch a whale;
All the water he had got
  Was in his mother's pail.

He went to ride a spotted cow,
  That had a little calf;
She threw him down upon the ground,
  Which made the people laugh.

Once Simon made a great snowball,
  And brought it home to roast;
He laid it down before the fire,
  And soon the ball was lost.

He washed himself with blacking ball,
  Because he had no soap;
Then said unto his mother,
  "I'm a beauty now, I hope."

He went for water in a sieve,
  But soon it all ran through.
And now poor Simple Simon
  Bids you all adieu.

THE OLD WOMAN AND HER PIG

An old woman was sweeping her house, and she found a little crooked sixpence.

"What," said she, "shall I do with this little sixpence? I will go to market and buy a little pig." And so she went to market and bought a little pig. As she was coming home, she came to a stile, and the piggy would not go over the stile.

She went a little further, and she met a dog. So she said to the dog, "Dog! Bite pig; piggy won't get over the stile, and I shan't get home tonight." But the dog would not.

She went a little further, and she met a stick. So she said, "Stick! Stick! Beat dog; dog won't bite pig; piggy won't get over the stile, and I shan't get home tonight." But the stick would not.

She went a little further, and she met a fire. So she said, "Fire! Fire! Burn stick; stick won't beat dog; dog won't bite pig; piggy won't get over the stile, and I shan't get home tonight." But the fire would not.

She went a little further, and she met some water. So she said, "Water! Water! Quench fire; fire won't burn stick; stick won't beat dog; dog won't bite pig; piggy won't get over the stile, and I shan't get home tonight." But the water would not.

She went a little further, and she met an ox. So she said, "Ox! Ox! Drink water; water won't quench fire; fire won't burn stick; stick won't beat dog; dog won't bite pig; piggy won't get over the stile, and I shan't get home tonight." But the ox would not.

She went a little further, and she met a butcher. So she said, "Butcher! Butcher! Kill ox; ox won't drink water; water won't quench fire; fire won't burn stick; stick won't beat dog; dog won't bite pig; piggy won't get over the stile, and I shan't get home tonight." But the butcher would not.

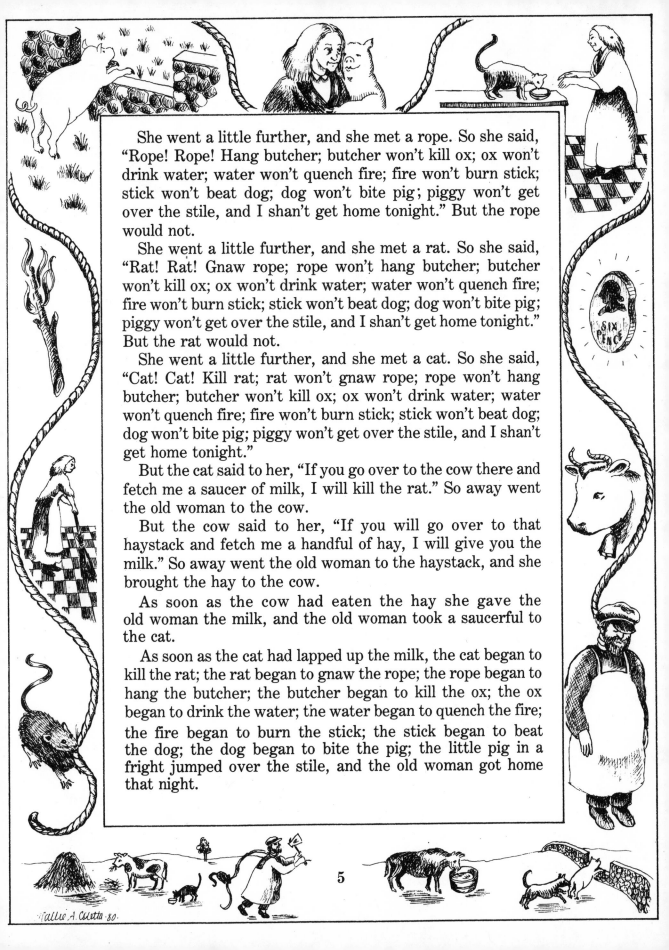

She went a little further, and she met a rope. So she said, "Rope! Rope! Hang butcher; butcher won't kill ox; ox won't drink water; water won't quench fire; fire won't burn stick; stick won't beat dog; dog won't bite pig; piggy won't get over the stile, and I shan't get home tonight." But the rope would not.

She went a little further, and she met a rat. So she said, "Rat! Rat! Gnaw rope; rope won't hang butcher; butcher won't kill ox; ox won't drink water; water won't quench fire; fire won't burn stick; stick won't beat dog; dog won't bite pig; piggy won't get over the stile, and I shan't get home tonight." But the rat would not.

She went a little further, and she met a cat. So she said, "Cat! Cat! Kill rat; rat won't gnaw rope; rope won't hang butcher; butcher won't kill ox; ox won't drink water; water won't quench fire; fire won't burn stick; stick won't beat dog; dog won't bite pig; piggy won't get over the stile, and I shan't get home tonight."

But the cat said to her, "If you go over to the cow there and fetch me a saucer of milk, I will kill the rat." So away went the old woman to the cow.

But the cow said to her, "If you will go over to that haystack and fetch me a handful of hay, I will give you the milk." So away went the old woman to the haystack, and she brought the hay to the cow.

As soon as the cow had eaten the hay she gave the old woman the milk, and the old woman took a saucerful to the cat.

As soon as the cat had lapped up the milk, the cat began to kill the rat; the rat began to gnaw the rope; the rope began to hang the butcher; the butcher began to kill the ox; the ox began to drink the water; the water began to quench the fire; the fire began to burn the stick; the stick began to beat the dog; the dog began to bite the pig; the little pig in a fright jumped over the stile, and the old woman got home that night.

THE THREE BILLY GOATS GRUFF

Once upon a time there were three billy goats who wanted to go up to the hillside to eat the green grass there and make themselves fat. And the name of all the three billy goats was "Gruff."

On the way up to the hillside was a bridge over a stream, and under the bridge lived a great big ugly Troll, with eyes as big as dinner plates and a nose as long as a poker.

So first of all the youngest billy goat Gruff came to the stream and started to cross the bridge.

Trip, trap, trip, trap, went the bridge, for the little billy goat Gruff was not very heavy. And the great big ugly Troll roared out:

"Who's that tripping over my bridge?"

"Oh, it's only me, the smallest billy goat Gruff. I want to go up to the hillside to eat grass and make myself fat," said the youngest billy goat in his tiny voice.

"Wait, I'm coming to gobble you up," said the Troll.

"Oh, no, don't eat me, I'm much too little. The second billy goat Gruff is coming right behind me, and he's much bigger than I am," said the youngest billy goat Gruff.

"Oh, very well then, be off with you," said the Troll.

A little while later the second billy goat Gruff came up to the stream and started to cross the bridge.

TRIP, TRAP, TRIP, TRAP, went the bridge, for the medium billy goat Gruff was fairly heavy. And the great big ugly Troll roared out:

"Who's that tripping over my bridge?"

6

"Oh, it's only me, the second billy goat Gruff. I want to go up to the hillside to eat grass and make myself fat," said the second billy goat Gruff in a medium sort of voice.

"Wait, I'm coming to gobble you up," said the Troll.

"Oh, no, don't eat me, I'm only middle-sized. The big billy goat Gruff is coming right behind me, and he's much, much bigger than I am," said the second billy goat Gruff.

"Oh, very well then, be off with you," said the Troll.

And so a little while later, the big billy goat Gruff came up to the stream and started to cross the bridge.

TRIP, TRAP, TRIP, TRAP, went the bridge, for the big billy goat Gruff was very heavy.

"Who's that tripping over my bridge?" roared the great big ugly Troll.

"OH, IT'S ONLY ME, THE BIG BILLY GOAT GRUFF. WHAT DO YOU WANT?" said the big billy goat Gruff in a very loud voice.

"Wait, I'm coming to gobble you up," said the Troll.

"Come on up, then," said the big billy goat Gruff. "I'm not afraid of you."

Up climbed the Troll from under the bridge and the big billy goat Gruff put his big head down and ran at the Troll with his big horns. "Bump," went the big billy goat Gruff. And "Splash" went the great ugly Troll, right into the water. And he was never heard of again.

So the three billy goats Gruff went up to the hillside together. There they ate grass and grew fat and lived happily ever after.

ANIMAL NONSENSE

A peanut sat on a railroad track,
His heart was all a-flutter;
The five-fifteen came rushing by—
Toot! Toot! Peanut butter!

Grandfa' Grig
Had a pig,
In a field of clover;
Piggie died,
Grandfa' cried,
And all the fun was over.

A rabbit raced a turtle,
You know the turtle won;
And Mister Bunny came in late,
A little hot cross bun!

Piggy on the railway, picking up the stones,
Up came an engine and broke Piggy's bones.
"Oh!" said Piggy, "that's not fair—"
"Oh!" said the driver, "I don't care."

Monkey was a-settin' on a railroad track,
Pickin' his teeth with a carpet tack;
The train came suddenly around the bend,
And the monkey reached his journey's end.

On mules we find two legs behind,
   And two we find before.
We stand behind before we find
   What the two behind be for.
So stand before the two behind,
   And behind the two before.

Up in the North, a long way off,
The donkey's got the whooping-cough.

Said the monkey to the donkey,
"What'll you have to drink?"
Said the donkey to the monkey,
"I'd like a swig of ink."

A centipede was happy quite
Until a frog in fun
Said, "Pray, which leg comes after which?"
This raised her mind to such a pitch,
She lay distracted in a ditch,
Considering how to run.

THE ELEPHANT

The elephant has a great big trunk;
He never packs it with clothes.
It has no lock and it has no key,
But he takes it wherever he goes.

THE GRASSHOPPER
AND THE ELEPHANT

Way down south where bananas grow,
A grasshopper stepped on an elephant's
   toe.
The elephant said, with tears in his eyes,
"Pick on somebody your own size."

A APPLE PIE

A APPLE PIE

B BIT IT

C CUT IT

D DEALT IT

E EAT IT

F FOUGHT FOR IT

G GOT IT

H HAD IT

J JUMPED FOR IT

K KNELT FOR IT

L LONGED for IT

M MOURNED for IT

N NODDED for IT

O OPENED IT

P PEEPED IN IT

Q QUARTERED IT

R RAN for IT

S SANG FOR IT

T TOOK IT

UVWXYZ

ALL HAD A LARGE SLICE
AND WENT OFF TO
BED

One old Oxford ox opening oysters.
Two toads totally tired trying to trot to Tilsbury.
Three thick thumping tigers taking toast for tea.
Four finicky fishermen fishing for finny fish.
Five frippery Frenchmen foolishly fishing for frogs.
Six sportsmen shooting snipe.
Seven Severn salmon swallowing shrimps.
Eight eminent Englishmen eagerly examining Europe.
Nine nimble noblemen nibbling nectarines.
Ten tinkering tinkers tinkering ten tinder-boxes.
Eleven elephants elegantly equipped.
Twelve typographical topographers typically translating types.

Hallie A. Colletta '80.

There was an old woman called nothing at all,
  Who lived in a dwelling exceedingly small.
A man stretched his mouth to its utmost extent,
  And down at one gulp house and old woman went.

There was an old woman who made green cheese,
  By beating up spinach and curds with a spoon;
And when she had done it, with very great ease,
  Tossed it up to the sky, and declared 'twas the moon.

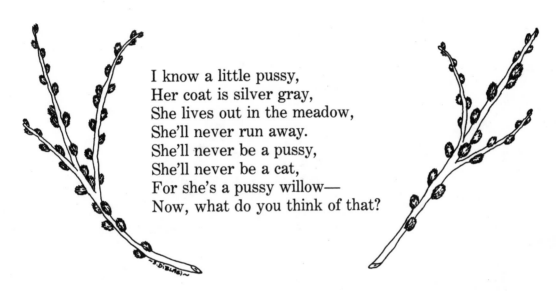

I know a little pussy,
Her coat is silver gray,
She lives out in the meadow,
She'll never run away.
She'll never be a pussy,
She'll never be a cat,
For she's a pussy willow—
Now, what do you think of that?

Have you seen the elephant
  Counting out his money?
Have you seen a limpet
  Eating bread and honey?
Or a striped hyena
  Hanging out the clothes,
With a native oyster
  Snapping off his nose?

Have you seen the crocodile,
  With a pocket full of rye?
Or a nest of water-rats
  Baked in a pie?
Or some sixty lizards
  Who'd just begun to sing?
Or a tabby cat, as a dainty dish
  Set before the king?

Fuzzy Wuzzy was a bear,
  A bear was Fuzzy Wuzzy.
When Fuzzy Wuzzy lost his hair
  He wasn't fuzzy, was he?

There was an old crow
  Sat upon a clod;
That's the end of my song.
  That's odd.

ST. IVES

As I was going to St. Ives,
I met a man with seven wives.
Every wife had seven sacks.
Every sack had seven cats.
Every cat had seven kits.
Kits, cats, sacks, wives,
How many were going to St. Ives?

THE TALE OF A TURNIP

Once upon a time there was a little old farmer, and a little old woman his wife, who lived happily together with a little girl their granddaughter, and a spotted dog called Spot, and a black cat called Minnie, and a little mouse who lived in a secret place in the barn.

One fine day in the spring the little old farmer said to the little old woman his wife, "Today is a good day for planting." So he went to the barn and chose a sturdy looking seed, a turnip seed, and went out to the field with it. When he had dug a hole, he put the seed in the ground and covered it over with earth. And he said to the seed, "Grow."

And the seed grew fast. First a small shoot appeared, then some green leaves, and then you could see the turnip itself. And it grew and it grew and it grew until it was the biggest, most beautiful turnip the little old farmer and the little old woman his wife had ever seen. And the little girl and Spot and Minnie and the mouse thought so, too.

So one day the little old woman his wife said to the little girl their granddaughter, "Today I'm going to put the biggest pot I have on the fire, and I'm going to ask your grandfather to pull up the turnip so that we can have turnip soup for supper." And when the little old farmer heard this, he went straight out to the field to pull up the turnip.

The little old farmer held onto the top of the turnip and he pulled. He pulled and he pulled and he pulled. And still he pulled, and still the turnip wouldn't come up. So he called out to the little old woman his wife, "Wife, come and help me pull up this turnip."

So the little old woman his wife came running out to the field to help the little old farmer pull up the turnip. She caught hold of the little old farmer, and they pulled and they pulled and they pulled. And still they pulled, and still the turnip wouldn't come up. So the little old woman called out to the little girl their granddaughter, "Granddaughter, come and help me pull up this turnip."

So the little girl their granddaughter came running out to help the little old farmer and the little old woman his wife pull up the turnip. She caught hold of the little old woman, who caught hold of the little old farmer, and they pulled and they pulled and they pulled. And still they pulled, and still the turnip wouldn't come up. So the little girl their granddaughter called out to the spotted dog called Spot, "Spot, come and help me pull up this turnip."

So the spotted dog called Spot came running out to help the little old farmer and the little old woman his wife and the little girl their granddaughter pull up the turnip. He caught hold of the little girl their granddaughter, who caught hold of the little old woman, who caught hold of the little old farmer, and they pulled and they pulled and they pulled. And still they pulled, and still the turnip wouldn't come up. So the spotted dog called Spot called out to the black cat called Minnie, "Minnie, come and help me pull up this turnip."

So the black cat called Minnie came running out to help the little old farmer and the little old woman his wife and the little girl their granddaughter and the spotted dog called Spot pull up the turnip. She caught hold of the spotted dog called Spot, who caught hold of the little girl their granddaughter, who caught hold of the little old woman, who caught hold of the little old farmer, and they pulled and they pulled and they pulled. And still they pulled, and still the turnip wouldn't come up. So the black cat called Minnie called out to the little mouse who lived in a secret place in the barn, "Mouse, come and help me pull up this turnip."

So the little mouse who lived in a secret place in the barn came running out to help the little old farmer and the little old woman his wife and the little girl their granddaughter and the spotted dog called Spot and the black cat called Minnie pull up the turnip. He caught hold of the black cat called Minnie, who caught hold of the spotted dog called Spot, who caught hold of the little girl their granddaughter, who caught hold of the little old woman, who caught hold of the little old farmer, and they pulled and they pulled and they pulled. And *this* time—up came the turnip!

But the little old farmer was so surprised that he fell right back on the little old woman his wife, who fell right back on the little girl their granddaughter, who fell right back on the spotted dog called Spot, who fell right back on the black cat named Minnie, who fell right back on the little mouse who lived in a secret place in the barn. And *he* fell right back on the ground. But none of them cared, because they were all so pleased to see the biggest, most beautiful turnip they had ever seen. And that night they all had turnip soup for supper.

MR. FINNEY'S TURNIP

Mr. Finney had a turnip
  And it grew behind the barn;
And it grew and it grew,
  And that turnip did no harm.

There it grew and it grew
  Till it could grow no longer;
Then his daughter Lizzie picked it
  And put it in the cellar.

There it lay and it lay
  Till it began to rot;
And his daughter Suzie took it
  And put it in the pot.

And they boiled it and boiled it
  As long as they were able;
And then his daughters took it
  And put it on the table.

Mr. Finney and his wife
  They sat them down to sup;
And they ate and they ate,
  And they ate that turnip up.

17

THE TEENY-TINY WOMAN

Once upon a time there was a teeny-tiny woman who lived in a teeny-tiny house in a teeny-tiny village. One day the teeny-tiny woman put on her teeny-tiny bonnet, and went out of her teeny-tiny house to take a teeny-tiny walk.

And when this teeny-tiny woman had gone a teeny-tiny way, she came to a teeny-tiny gate; so the teeny-tiny woman opened the teeny-tiny gate, and went into a teeny-tiny churchyard.

And when this teeny-tiny woman had got into the teeny-tiny churchyard, she saw a teeny-tiny bone on a teeny-tiny grave, and the teeny-tiny woman said to her teeny-tiny self, "This teeny-tiny bone will make some teeny-tiny soup for my teeny-tiny supper."

So the teeny-tiny woman put the teeny-tiny bone into her teeny-tiny pocket, and went to her teeny-tiny house.

18

Now, when the teeny-tiny woman got home to her teeny-tiny house, she was a teeny-tiny tired; so she went up her teeny-tiny stairs to her teeny-tiny bed, and put the teeny-tiny bone into a teeny-tiny cupboard.

And when this teeny-tiny woman had been to sleep for a teeny-tiny time, she was awakened by a teeny-tiny voice from the teeny-tiny cupboard, which said, "Give me my bone!" And this teeny-tiny woman was a teeny-tiny frightened, so she hid her teeny-tiny head under the teeny-tiny clothes, and went to sleep again.

And when she had been to sleep again a teeny-tiny time, the teeny-tiny voice cried out from the teeny-tiny cupboard, a teeny-tiny louder, "Give me my bone!"

This made the teeny-tiny woman a teeny-tiny more frightened, so she hid her teeny-tiny head a teeny-tiny farther under the teeny-tiny clothes. And when the teeny-tiny woman had been to sleep again a teeny-tiny time, the teeny-tiny voice from the teeny-tiny cupboard said again, a teeny-tiny louder, "GIVE ME MY BONE!"

And this teeny-tiny woman was a teeny-tiny bit more frightened, but she put her teeny-tiny head out of the teeny-tiny clothes, and said in her loudest teeny-tiny voice, "TAKE IT!"

Alas, alas for Miss Mackay.
Her knives and forks have run away;
And where the cups and spoons are going,
She's sure there is no way of knowing.

I asked my mother for fifteen cents
To see the elephant jump the fence.
He jumped so high that he touched the sky
And never came back 'til the Fourth of July.

I asked my mother for fifteen cents
I asked my father for fifteen more.
He grabbed me by the seat of my pants
And pushed me out the door.

Hannah Bantry, in the pantry,
Gnawing at a mutton bone;
    How she gnawed it,
    How she clawed it,
When she found herself alone.

Robin the Bobbin, the big-bellied Ben,
He ate more meat than fourscore men;
He ate a cow, he ate a calf,
He ate a butcher and a half,
He ate a church, he ate a steeple,
He ate the priest and all the people!

I do not love thee, Doctor Fell,
    The reason why I cannot tell;
But this I know, I know full well:
    I do not love thee, Doctor Fell.

Mother, may I go and swim?
Yes, my darling daughter.
Hang your clothes on yonder limb,
But don't go near the water.

Father, may I go to war?
Yes, you may, my son.
Wear your woolen comforter,
But don't fire off your gun.

The daughter of the farrier
Could find no one to marry her,
    Because she said
    She would not wed
A man who could not carry her.

The foolish girl was wrong enough,
And had to wait quite long enough;
    For as she sat
    She grew so fat
That nobody was strong enough.

Animals

Give nuts unto the monkey,
    and buns unto the bear
Ne'er hint at currant jelly
    if you chance to see a hare!
Oh, ne'er delight to make dogs fight,
    nor bantams disagree,—
Be always kind to animals
    wherever you might be.

        J. Ashby-Sterry

THE KITTEN

The trouble with a kitten is
THAT
Eventually it becomes a
CAT.

Ogden Nash

AN ALPHABET OF QUESTIONS?

Have Angleworms attractive homes?
Do Bumblebees have brains?
Do Caterpillars carry combs?
Do Dodos dote on drains?
Can Eels elude electric earls?
Do Flatfish fish for flats?
Are Grigs agreeable to girls?
Do Hares have hunting hats?
Do ices make an Ibex ill?
Do Jackdaws jug their jam?
Do Kites kiss all the kids they kill?
Do Llamas live on lamb?
Will Moles molest a mounted mink?
Do Newts deny the news?
Are Oysters boisterous when they drink?
Do Parrots prowl in pews?
Do Quakers get their quills from quails?
Do Rabbits rob on roads?
Are Snakes supposed to sneer at snails?
Do Tortoises eat toads?
Can Unicorns perform on horns?
Do Vipers value veal?
Do Weasels weep when fast asleep?
Can Xylophagans squeal?
Do Yaks in packs invite attacks?
Are Zebras full of zeal?

Charles Edward Carryl

THE AMBIGUOUS DOG

The dog beneath the cherry-tree
Has ways that sorely puzzle me:

Behind, he wags a friendly tail;
Before, his growl would turn you pale!

His meaning isn't plain and clear;
Oh, is the wag or growl sincere?

I think I'd better not descend;
His bite is at the growly end.

Arthur Guiterman

JUNGLE INCIDENT

The tiny son of Marawambo
Met a tiger in the Congo.
The tiger screamed and acted wild,
But Marawambo's son just smiled.
"Mr. Tiger, old and fat,
You're nothing but a great big cat—
Scat!"
And that was that.

Russell Gordon Carter

23

THE GIRAFFE

See the Giraffe; he is so tall
There is not room to get him all
Upon the page. His head is higher—
The picture proves it—than the Spire.
That's why the natives, when they race
To catch him, call it steeple-chase.
His chief delight it is to set
A good example: shine or wet
He rises ere the break of day,
And starts his breakfast right away.
His food has such a way to go—
His throat's so very long—and so
An early breakfast he must munch
To get it down ere time for lunch.

Oliver Herford

THE PIG

The pig, if I am not mistaken,
Supplies us sausage, ham, and bacon.
Let others say his heart is big—
I call it stupid of the pig.

Ogden Nash

24

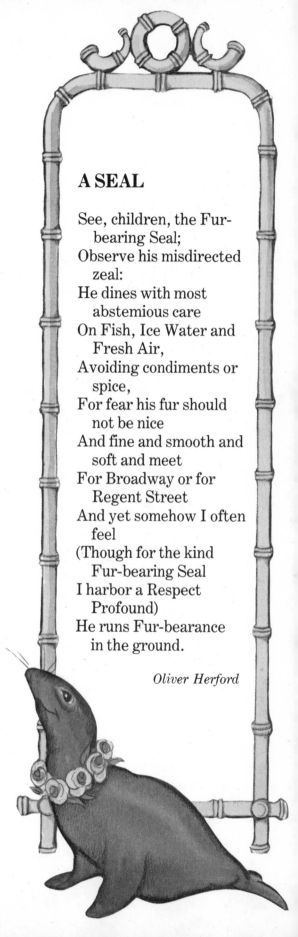

A SEAL

See, children, the Fur-
    bearing Seal;
Observe his misdirected
    zeal:
He dines with most
    abstemious care
On Fish, Ice Water and
    Fresh Air,
Avoiding condiments or
    spice,
For fear his fur should
    not be nice
And fine and smooth and
    soft and meet
For Broadway or for
    Regent Street
And yet somehow I often
    feel
(Though for the kind
    Fur-bearing Seal
I harbor a Respect
    Profound)
He runs Fur-bearance
    in the ground.

Oliver Herford

THE COMMON CORMORANT

The common cormorant or shag
Lays eggs inside a paper bag.
The reason you will see no doubt
It is to keep the lightning out.
But what these unobservant birds
Have never noticed is that herds
Of wandering bears may come with buns
And steal the bags to hold the crumbs.

ANIMAL LIMERICKS

There once was a stately giraffe,
Whose motto was "Nothing by half!"
 His old friend, the tapir,
 Said, "Cut me a caper—
It's a year since I've had a good laugh!"

So, to please him, the gracious giraffe
Jumped over a cow and her calf;
 But when the old tapir
 Told folks of this caper,
They said: "That's just some more of your chaff."

"He's a dignified chap, that giraffe,
And we know he does nothing by half;
 We can understand how
 He might jump o'er a cow,
But he'd *never* jump over a calf!"

Margaret Vandergift

There once was an arch armadillo
Who built him a hut 'neath a willow;
 He hadn't a bed
 So he rested his head
On a young porcupine for a pillow.

Carolyn Wells

There was an old man who said, "Hush!
I perceive a young bird in this bush!"
 When they said, "Is it small?"
 He replied, "Not at all!
It is four times as big as the bush!"

Edward Lear

There once was a barber of Kew,
Who went very mad at the zoo;
 He tried to enamel
 The face of the camel
And gave the brown bear a shampoo.

Cosmo Monkhouse

There was an old man with a beard
Who said, "It's just as I feared!
 Two owls and a hen,
 Four larks and a wren,
Have all built their nests in my beard!"

Edward Lear

One day I went out to the zoo,
For I wanted to see the old gnu,
 But the old gnu was dead.
 They had a new gnu instead,
And that gnu, well, he knew he was new.

G. T. Johnson

A wonderful bird is the pelican;
His bill can hold more than his belican.
    He can take in his beak
    Food enough for a week;
But I'm darned if I see how the helican!

Dixon Lanier Merritt

There was a young man who was bitten
By forty-two cats and a kitten,
    Cried he, "It is clear
    My end is quite near,
No matter, I'll die like a Briton!"

There was an old person of Ware,
Who rode on the back of a bear:
    When they asked, "Does it trot?"
    He said, "Certainly not!
He's a Moppsikon Floppsikon bear!"

Edward Lear

At the zoo I remarked to an emu,
"I cannot pretend I esteem you.
    You're a greedy old bird,
    And your walk is absurd,
But your curious feathers redeem you."

There was a young lady of Niger
Who smiled as she rode on a tiger;
    They returned from the ride
    With the lady inside,
And the smile on the face of the tiger.

A handsome young noble of Spain,
Met a lion one day in the rain.
    He ran in a fright
    With all of his might,
But the lion, he ran with his mane!

A cheerful old bear at the Zoo
Could always find something to do.
    When it bored him to go
    On a walk to and fro,
He reversed it, and walked fro and to.

A cat in despondency sighed,
And resolved to commit suicide;
    He got under the wheels
    Of nine automobiles,
And after the last one he died.

Oh, she sailed away on a lovely summer day
On the back of a crocodile.
"You can see," said she, "he's as tame as he can be.
I'll float him down the Nile."
But the croc winked his eye as she waved
   them all goodby,
Wearing a happy smile.
At the end of the ride the lady was inside
And the smile on the crocodile.

THE CROCODILE

How doth the little crocodile
  Improve his shining tail,
And pour the waters of the Nile
  On every golden scale!

How cheerfully he seems to grin,
  How neatly spreads his claws,
And welcomes little fishes in,
  With gently smiling jaws!

Lewis Carroll

If you should meet a crocodile,
  Don't take a stick and poke him; ·
Ignore the welcome in his smile,
  Be careful not to stroke him.
For as he sleeps upon the Nile,
  He thinner gets and thinner;
And whene'er you meet a crocodile
  He's ready for his dinner.

Don't try to tease that crocodile
Or try to please that crocodile,
  Don't prod or poke
  Or try to stroke,
Lest he should seize—that crocodile.

I HAD A HIPPOPOTAMUS

I had a hippopotamus; I kept him in a shed
And fed him upon vitamins and vegetable bread;
I made him my companion on many cheery walks
And had his portrait done by a celebrity in chalks.

His charming eccentricities were known on every side,
The creature's popularity was wonderfully wide;
He frolicked with the Rector in a dozen friendly tussles,
Who could not but remark upon his hippopotamuscles.

If he should be afflicted by depression or the dumps,
By hippopotameasles or the hippopotamumps,
I never knew a particle of peace till it was plain
He was hippopotamasticating properly again.

I had a hippopotamus; I loved him as a friend;
But beautiful relationships are bound to have an end.
Time takes, alas! our joys from us and robs us of our blisses;
My hippopotamus turned out a hippopotamissis.

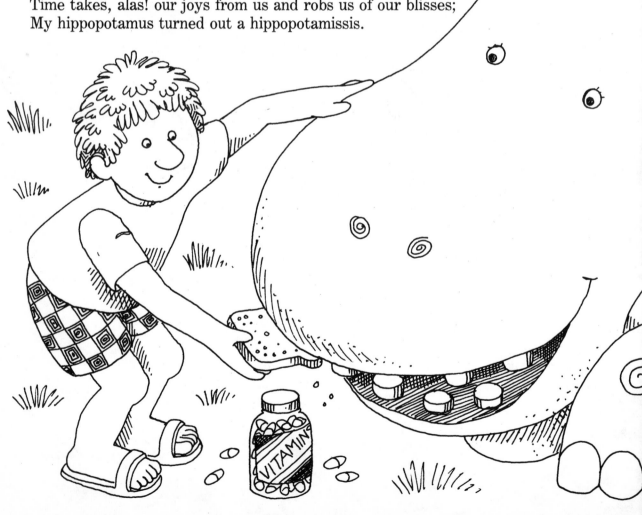

My housekeeper regarded him with jaundice in her eye;
She did not want a colony of hippopotami;
She borrowed a machine-gun from her soldier-nephew, Percy,
And showed my hippopotamus no hippopotamercy.

My house now lacks the glamour that the charming creature gave,
The garage where I kept him is as silent as the grave;
No longer he displays among the motor-tires and spanners
His hippopotamastery of hippopotamanners.

No longer now he gambols in the orchard in the Spring;
No longer do I lead him through the village on a string;
No longer in the mornings does the neighborhood rejoice
To his hippopotamusically-modulated voice.

I had a hippopotamus; but nothing upon earth
Is constant in its happiness or lasting in its mirth.
No joy that life can give me can be strong enough to smother
My sorrow for that might-have-been-a-hippopota-mother.

Patrick Barrington

AN OSTRICH

This is an Ostrich. See him stand:
His head is buried in the sand.
It is not that he seeks for food,
Nor is he shy, nor is he rude;
But he is sensitive, and shrinks
And hides his head whene'er he thinks
How, on the Gainsborough hat some day
Of some fine lady at the play,
His feathers may obstruct the view
Of all the stage from me or you.

Oliver Herford

ADVICE TO CHILDREN

For a domestic, gentle pet,
A hippopotamus I'd get—
    They're very kind and mild,
I'm sure if you but purchase one
You'll find 'twill make a lot of fun
    For any little child.

Select one of a medium size,
With glossy fur and soft blue eyes,
    Then brush and comb him well.
With wreaths of flowers his forehead deck,
And from a ribbon round his neck
    Suspend a silver bell.

If it should be a rainy day,
Up in the nursery he will play
  With Baby, Tot and Ted;
Upon the rocking-horse he'll ride,
Or merrily he'll run and hide
  Beneath a chair or bed.

And when he wants to take a nap,
He'll cuddle up in Totty's lap,
  As quiet as a mouse.
Just try it, and you'll soon agree
A hippopotamus should be
  A pet in every house.

Carolyn Wells

OLD NOAH'S ARK

Old Noah once he built an ark,
And patched it up with hickory bark.
He anchored it to a great big rock,
And then he began to load his stock.
The animals went in one by one,
The elephant chewing a caraway bun.
The animals went in two by two,
The crocodile and the kangaroo.
The animals went in three by three,
The tall giraffe and the tiny flea.
The animals went in four by four,
The hippopotamus stuck in the door.
The animals went in five by five,
The bees mistook the bear for a hive.
The animals went in six by six,
The monkey was up to his usual tricks.
The animals went in seven by seven,
Said the ant to the elephant, "Who're ye shov'n?"
The animals went in eight by eight,
Some were early and some were late.
The animals went in nine by nine,
They all formed fours and marched in a line.
The animals went in ten by ten,
If you want any more, you can read it again.

American Folk Rhyme

THE STRANGER CAT

A little girl with golden hair
Was rocking in her grandma's chair,
When in there walked a Stranger Cat.
(I'm *sure* there's nothing strange in that.)

It was a cat with kinky ears
And very aged for its years.
The little girl remarked "O scat!"
(I *think* there's nothing strange in that.)

But presently with stealthy tread
The Cat, which at her word had fled,
Returned with cane, and boots and hat.
(I *fear* there's something strange in that.)

"Excuse me," and the cat bowed low,
"I hate to trouble you, you know,
But tell me, have you seen a rat?"
(I *know* there's something strange in that.)

The little girl was very shy—
"Well, really, I can't say that I
Have seen one lately, Mr. Cat."
(I'm *sure* there's something strange in that.)

"Oh, haven't you?" the Cat replied;
"Thanks, I am deeply gratified.
I really couldn't eat a rat."
(We *all* know what to think of that.)

And then the cat with kinky ears
And so much wisdom for its years
Retired, with a soft pit-a-pat
(And that was all there was of that).

                              N. P. Babcock

THE CAMEL'S LAMENT

"Canary-birds feed on sugar and seed,
  Parrots have crackers to crunch;
And as for the poodles, they tell me the noodles
  Have chickens and cream for their lunch.
    But there's never a question
    About my digestion—
  Anything does for me!

"Cats, you're aware, can repose in a chair,
  Chickens can roost upon rails;
Puppies are able to sleep in a stable,
  And oysters can slumber in pails.
    But no one supposes
    A poor Camel dozes—
  Any place does for me!

"Lambs are enclosed where it's never exposed.
  Coops are constructed for hens;
Kittens are treated to houses well heated,
  And pigs are protected by pens.
    But a Camel comes handy
    Wherever it's sandy—
  Anywhere does for me!

"People would laugh if you rode a giraffe,
  Or mounted the back of an ox;
It's nobody's habit to ride on a rabbit,
  Or try to bestraddle a fox.
    But as for a Camel, he's
    Ridden by families—
  Any load does for me!

"A snake is as round as a hole in the ground,
  And weasels are wavy and sleek;
And no alligator could ever be straighter
  Than lizards that live in a creek,
    But a Camel's all lumpy
    And bumpy and humpy—
  Any shape does for me!"

Charles Edward Carryl

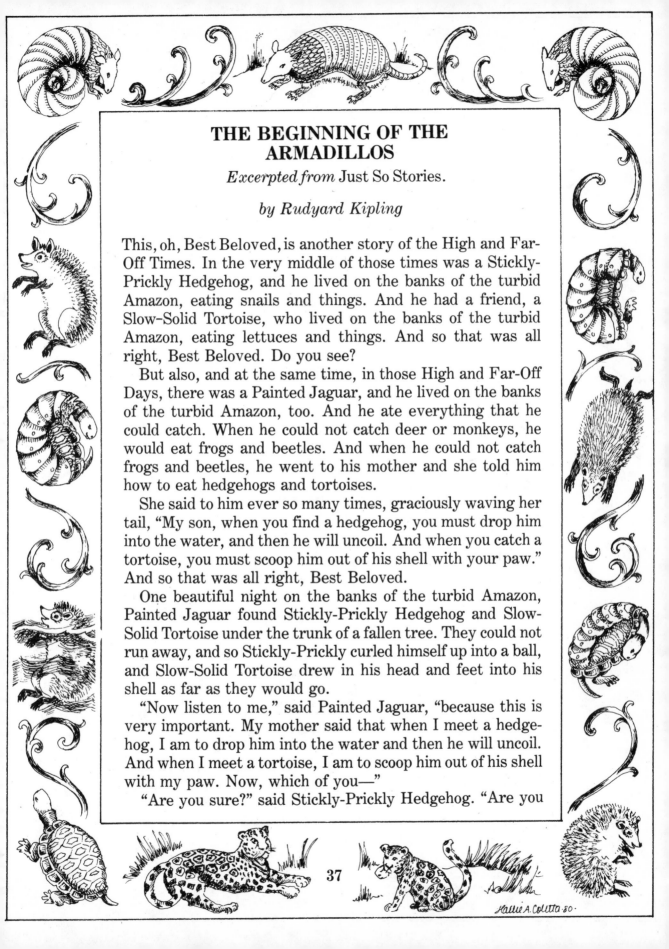

THE BEGINNING OF THE ARMADILLOS

Excerpted from Just So Stories.

by Rudyard Kipling

This, oh, Best Beloved, is another story of the High and Far-Off Times. In the very middle of those times was a Stickly-Prickly Hedgehog, and he lived on the banks of the turbid Amazon, eating snails and things. And he had a friend, a Slow-Solid Tortoise, who lived on the banks of the turbid Amazon, eating lettuces and things. And so that was all right, Best Beloved. Do you see?

But also, and at the same time, in those High and Far-Off Days, there was a Painted Jaguar, and he lived on the banks of the turbid Amazon, too. And he ate everything that he could catch. When he could not catch deer or monkeys, he would eat frogs and beetles. And when he could not catch frogs and beetles, he went to his mother and she told him how to eat hedgehogs and tortoises.

She said to him ever so many times, graciously waving her tail, "My son, when you find a hedgehog, you must drop him into the water, and then he will uncoil. And when you catch a tortoise, you must scoop him out of his shell with your paw." And so that was all right, Best Beloved.

One beautiful night on the banks of the turbid Amazon, Painted Jaguar found Stickly-Prickly Hedgehog and Slow-Solid Tortoise under the trunk of a fallen tree. They could not run away, and so Stickly-Prickly curled himself up into a ball, and Slow-Solid Tortoise drew in his head and feet into his shell as far as they would go.

"Now listen to me," said Painted Jaguar, "because this is very important. My mother said that when I meet a hedgehog, I am to drop him into the water and then he will uncoil. And when I meet a tortoise, I am to scoop him out of his shell with my paw. Now, which of you—"

"Are you sure?" said Stickly-Prickly Hedgehog. "Are you

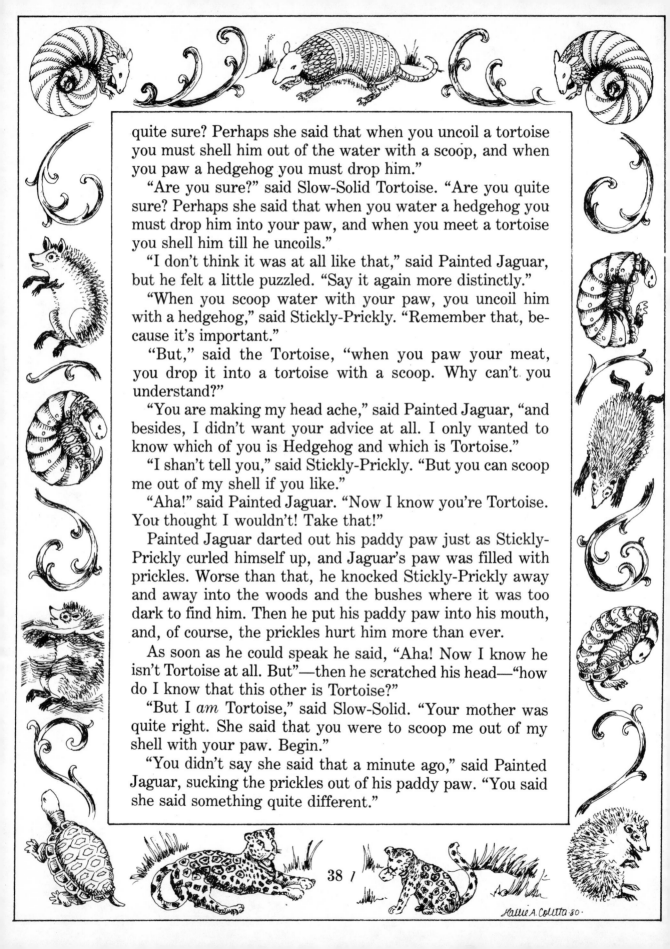

quite sure? Perhaps she said that when you uncoil a tortoise you must shell him out of the water with a scoop, and when you paw a hedgehog you must drop him."

"Are you sure?" said Slow-Solid Tortoise. "Are you quite sure? Perhaps she said that when you water a hedgehog you must drop him into your paw, and when you meet a tortoise you shell him till he uncoils."

"I don't think it was at all like that," said Painted Jaguar, but he felt a little puzzled. "Say it again more distinctly."

"When you scoop water with your paw, you uncoil him with a hedgehog," said Stickly-Prickly. "Remember that, because it's important."

"But," said the Tortoise, "when you paw your meat, you drop it into a tortoise with a scoop. Why can't you understand?"

"You are making my head ache," said Painted Jaguar, "and besides, I didn't want your advice at all. I only wanted to know which of you is Hedgehog and which is Tortoise."

"I shan't tell you," said Stickly-Prickly. "But you can scoop me out of my shell if you like."

"Aha!" said Painted Jaguar. "Now I know you're Tortoise. You thought I wouldn't! Take that!"

Painted Jaguar darted out his paddy paw just as Stickly-Prickly curled himself up, and Jaguar's paw was filled with prickles. Worse than that, he knocked Stickly-Prickly away and away into the woods and the bushes where it was too dark to find him. Then he put his paddy paw into his mouth, and, of course, the prickles hurt him more than ever.

As soon as he could speak he said, "Aha! Now I know he isn't Tortoise at all. But"—then he scratched his head—"how do I know that this other is Tortoise?"

"But I *am* Tortoise," said Slow-Solid. "Your mother was quite right. She said that you were to scoop me out of my shell with your paw. Begin."

"You didn't say she said that a minute ago," said Painted Jaguar, sucking the prickles out of his paddy paw. "You said she said something quite different."

"Well, suppose you say that I said that she said something quite different, I don't see that it makes any difference, because if she said what you said I said she said, it's just the same as if I said what she said she said. Of course, if you think she said that you were to uncoil me with a scoop, instead of pawing me into drops with a shell, I can't help that, can I?"

"But you said you wanted to be scooped out of your shell with my paw," said Painted Jaguar.

"If you'll think again, I didn't say anything of the kind. I said that your mother said that you were to scoop me out of my shell."

"What will happen if I do?" said the Jaguar very cautiously.

"I don't know, because I've never been scooped out of my shell before. But I tell you, honestly, if you want to see me swim away, you've only got to drop me into the water."

"I don't believe it," said Painted Jaguar. "You've mixed up all the things my mother told me to do till I don't know whether I'm on my head or my painted tail, and now you come and tell me something I can understand, and I don't trust you one little bit. My mother told me that I was to drop one of you two into the water, and as you seem so anxious to be dropped, I think you don't want to be dropped. Now jump into the turbid Amazon, and be quick about it."

"I warn you, your mother won't be pleased. Don't say I didn't tell you," said Slow-Solid.

"If you say another word about what my mother said—" the Jaguar answered, but he had not finished the sentence before Slow-Solid quietly dived into the turbid Amazon, swam under water for a long way and came out on the bank where Stickly-Prickly was waiting for him.

"That was a very narrow escape," said Stickly-Prickly. "I don't like Painted Jaguar. What did you tell him you were?"

"I told him I was a truthful Tortoise, but he wouldn't believe it. Now he's gone to tell his mother. Listen to him!"

They could hear Painted Jaguar roaring up and down

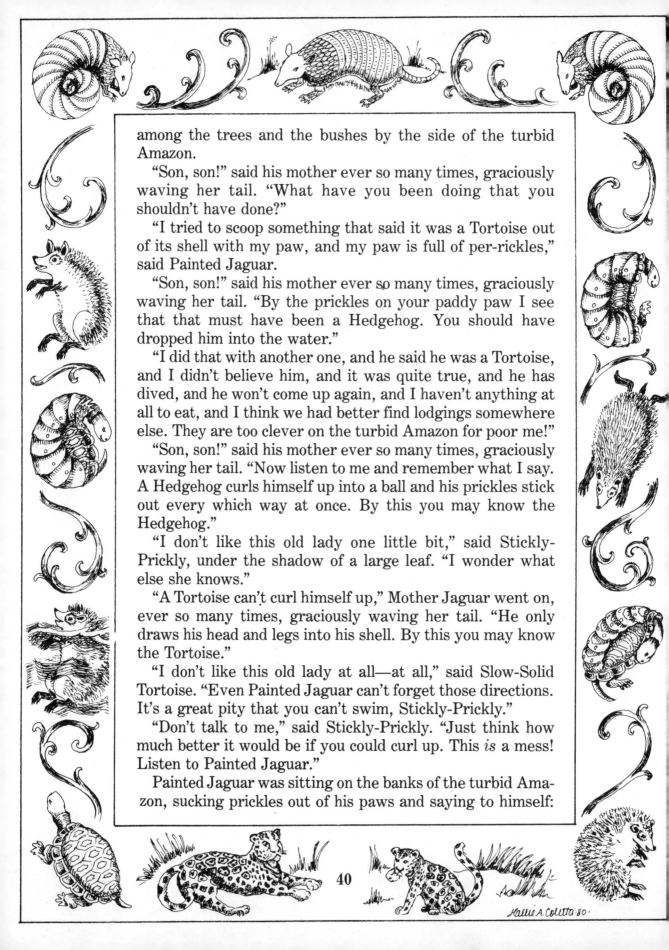

among the trees and the bushes by the side of the turbid Amazon.

"Son, son!" said his mother ever so many times, graciously waving her tail. "What have you been doing that you shouldn't have done?"

"I tried to scoop something that said it was a Tortoise out of its shell with my paw, and my paw is full of per-rickles," said Painted Jaguar.

"Son, son!" said his mother ever so many times, graciously waving her tail. "By the prickles on your paddy paw I see that that must have been a Hedgehog. You should have dropped him into the water."

"I did that with another one, and he said he was a Tortoise, and I didn't believe him, and it was quite true, and he has dived, and he won't come up again, and I haven't anything at all to eat, and I think we had better find lodgings somewhere else. They are too clever on the turbid Amazon for poor me!"

"Son, son!" said his mother ever so many times, graciously waving her tail. "Now listen to me and remember what I say. A Hedgehog curls himself up into a ball and his prickles stick out every which way at once. By this you may know the Hedgehog."

"I don't like this old lady one little bit," said Stickly-Prickly, under the shadow of a large leaf. "I wonder what else she knows."

"A Tortoise can't curl himself up," Mother Jaguar went on, ever so many times, graciously waving her tail. "He only draws his head and legs into his shell. By this you may know the Tortoise."

"I don't like this old lady at all—at all," said Slow-Solid Tortoise. "Even Painted Jaguar can't forget those directions. It's a great pity that you can't swim, Stickly-Prickly."

"Don't talk to me," said Stickly-Prickly. "Just think how much better it would be if you could curl up. This *is* a mess! Listen to Painted Jaguar."

Painted Jaguar was sitting on the banks of the turbid Amazon, sucking prickles out of his paws and saying to himself:

40

> *"Can't curl, but can swim—*
> *Slow-Solid, that's him!*
> *Curls up, but can't swim,*
> *Stickly-Prickly, that's him!"*

"He'll never forget that this month of Sundays," said Stickly-Prickly. "Hold up my chin, Slow-Solid. I'm going to try to learn to swim."

"Excellent!" said Slow-Solid, and he held up Stickly-Prickly's chin, while Stickly-Prickly kicked in the water of the turbid Amazon.

"You'll make a fine swimmer yet," said Slow-Solid. "Now, not to be behindhand, if you can unlace my back-plates a little, I'll see what I can do toward curling up."

Stickly-Prickly helped to unlace Tortoise's back-plates, so that by twisting and straining, Slow-Solid actually managed to curl up a tiddy wee bit.

"Excellent!" said Stickly-Prickly. "But I wouldn't do any more just now. It's making you black in the face. Kindly lead me into the water once more and I'll practice that side stroke which you say is so easy."

"Excellent!" said Slow-Solid. "But more practice will make you a regular Gangetic Porpoise. Now, if I may trouble you to unlace my back- and front-plates, two holes, I'll try that fascinating bend that you say is so easy. Won't Painted Jaguar be surprised!"

"Excellent!" said Stickly-Prickly, all wet from the turbid Amazon. "I declare, I shouldn't know you from one of my own family. Two holes, I think you said. A little more expression, please, and don't grunt quite so much or Painted Jaguar may hear us. When you've finished, I want to try that long dive which you say is so easy. Won't Painted Jaguar be surprised?"

"Excellent!" said Slow-Solid. "A little more attention to holding your breath and you will be able to keep house at the bottom of the turbid Amazon. Now I'll try that exercise of wrapping my hind legs around my ears which you say is so peculiarly comfortable. Won't Painted Jaguar be surprised?"

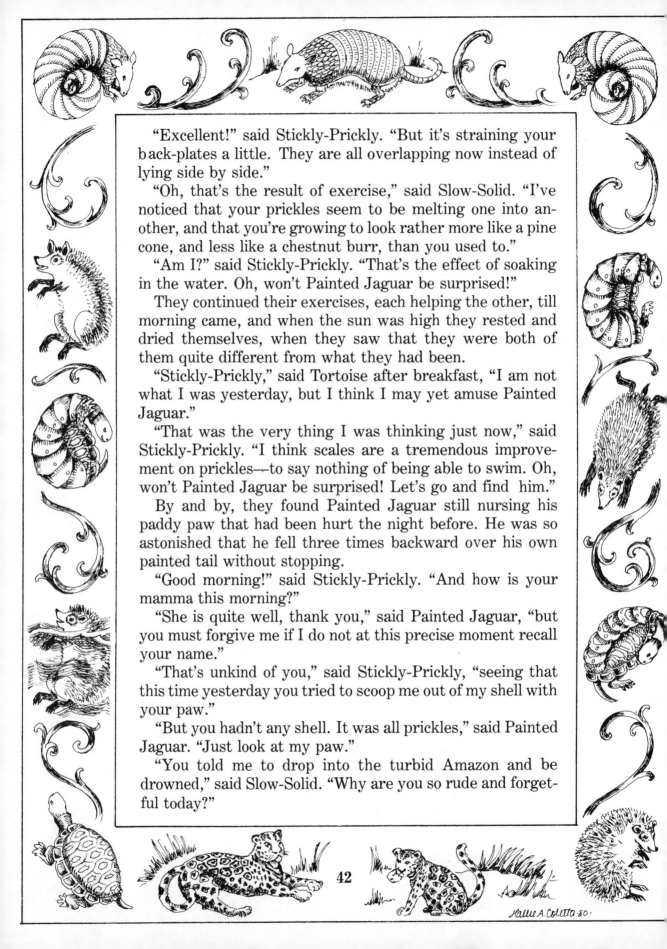

"Excellent!" said Stickly-Prickly. "But it's straining your back-plates a little. They are all overlapping now instead of lying side by side."

"Oh, that's the result of exercise," said Slow-Solid. "I've noticed that your prickles seem to be melting one into another, and that you're growing to look rather more like a pine cone, and less like a chestnut burr, than you used to."

"Am I?" said Stickly-Prickly. "That's the effect of soaking in the water. Oh, won't Painted Jaguar be surprised!"

They continued their exercises, each helping the other, till morning came, and when the sun was high they rested and dried themselves, when they saw that they were both of them quite different from what they had been.

"Stickly-Prickly," said Tortoise after breakfast, "I am not what I was yesterday, but I think I may yet amuse Painted Jaguar."

"That was the very thing I was thinking just now," said Stickly-Prickly. "I think scales are a tremendous improvement on prickles—to say nothing of being able to swim. Oh, won't Painted Jaguar be surprised! Let's go and find him."

By and by, they found Painted Jaguar still nursing his paddy paw that had been hurt the night before. He was so astonished that he fell three times backward over his own painted tail without stopping.

"Good morning!" said Stickly-Prickly. "And how is your mamma this morning?"

"She is quite well, thank you," said Painted Jaguar, "but you must forgive me if I do not at this precise moment recall your name."

"That's unkind of you," said Stickly-Prickly, "seeing that this time yesterday you tried to scoop me out of my shell with your paw."

"But you hadn't any shell. It was all prickles," said Painted Jaguar. "Just look at my paw."

"You told me to drop into the turbid Amazon and be drowned," said Slow-Solid. "Why are you so rude and forgetful today?"

42

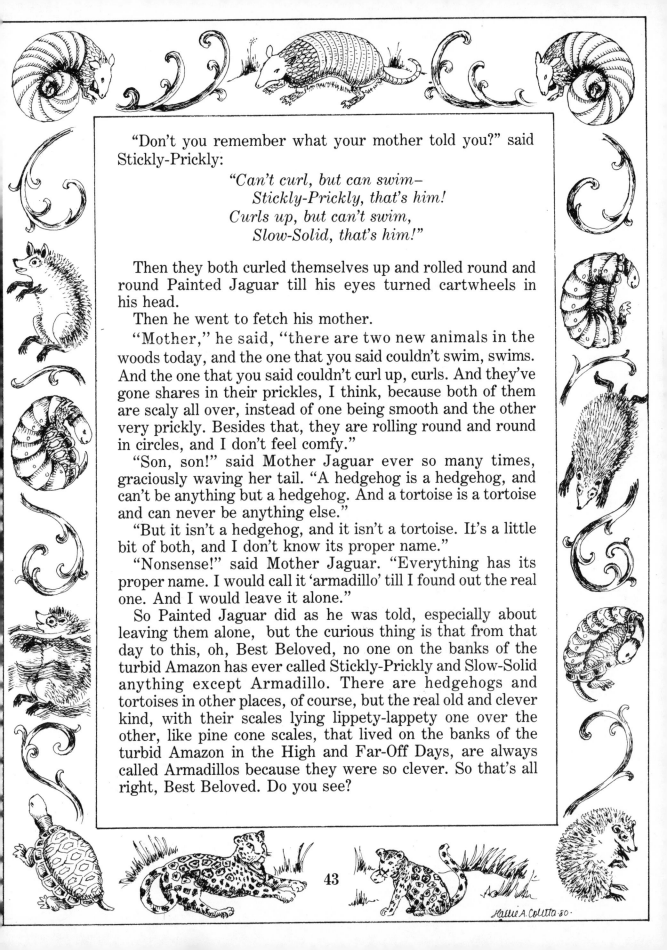

"Don't you remember what your mother told you?" said Stickly-Prickly:

"Can't curl, but can swim–
Stickly-Prickly, that's him!
Curls up, but can't swim,
Slow-Solid, that's him!"

Then they both curled themselves up and rolled round and round Painted Jaguar till his eyes turned cartwheels in his head.

Then he went to fetch his mother.

"Mother," he said, "there are two new animals in the woods today, and the one that you said couldn't swim, swims. And the one that you said couldn't curl up, curls. And they've gone shares in their prickles, I think, because both of them are scaly all over, instead of one being smooth and the other very prickly. Besides that, they are rolling round and round in circles, and I don't feel comfy."

"Son, son!" said Mother Jaguar ever so many times, graciously waving her tail. "A hedgehog is a hedgehog, and can't be anything but a hedgehog. And a tortoise is a tortoise and can never be anything else."

"But it isn't a hedgehog, and it isn't a tortoise. It's a little bit of both, and I don't know its proper name."

"Nonsense!" said Mother Jaguar. "Everything has its proper name. I would call it 'armadillo' till I found out the real one. And I would leave it alone."

So Painted Jaguar did as he was told, especially about leaving them alone, but the curious thing is that from that day to this, oh, Best Beloved, no one on the banks of the turbid Amazon has ever called Stickly-Prickly and Slow-Solid anything except Armadillo. There are hedgehogs and tortoises in other places, of course, but the real old and clever kind, with their scales lying lippety-lappety one over the other, like pine cone scales, that lived on the banks of the turbid Amazon in the High and Far-Off Days, are always called Armadillos because they were so clever. So that's all right, Best Beloved. Do you see?

43

THE LONGEST TALE ABOUT THE
LONGEST TAIL

I am the longest, the longest, the strongest,
Yes, I am the longest worm in the world.
I am so long, so far I extend,
That I haven't ever no never not ever
Oh, I've never ever seen my other end.

Well, I have been thinking and thinking and blinking
Yes, I have been thinking one very fine day
That I should flip, take a long trip
Until I meet it, oh meet it and greet it
Yes, until I meet with my opposite tip.

So there I was crawling and crawling and rolling
Yes, there I was crawling that very fine day
When suddenly there, just around the bend
I saw it, I know it, I know that I saw it
I saw it, I know it was my other end!

I was so happy, so happy and peppy
Yes, I was so terribly happy and glad
That I cried: "Hail, you must be my tail!"
And then it wiggled and wriggled and giggled
And then it suddenly spoke up and said:

"I am the longest, the longest, the strongest,
Yes, I am the longest worm in the world . . ."

Alexander Resnikoff

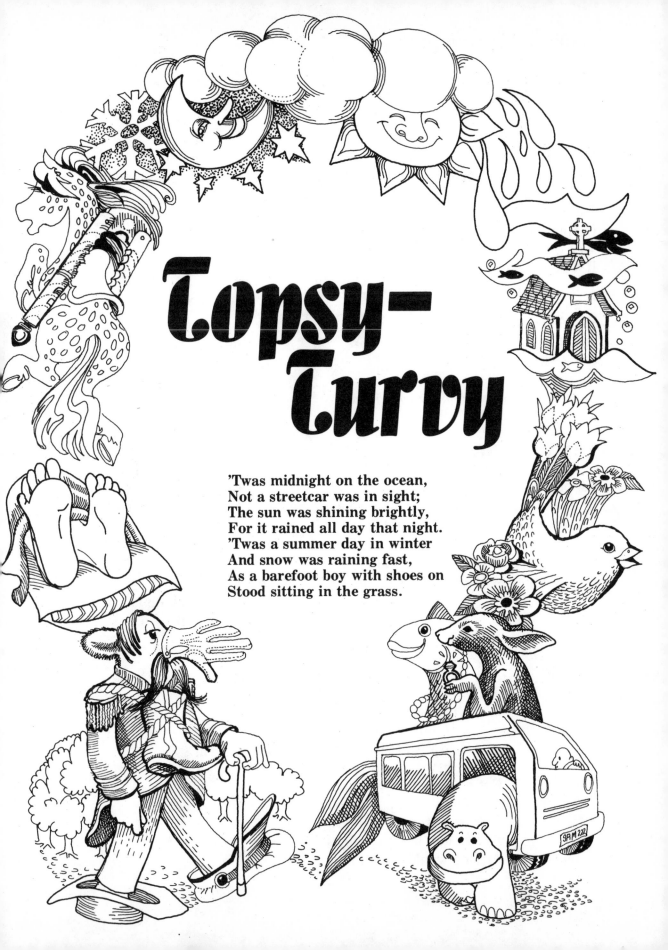

Topsy-Turvy

'Twas midnight on the ocean,
Not a streetcar was in sight;
The sun was shining brightly,
For it rained all day that night.
'Twas a summer day in winter
And snow was raining fast,
As a barefoot boy with shoes on
Stood sitting in the grass.

TOPSY-TURVY WORLD

If the butterfly courted the bee,
And the owl the porcupine;
If churches were built in the sea,
And three times one were nine;
If the pony rode his master,
If the buttercups ate the cows,
If the cat had the dire disaster
To be worried, sir, by the mouse;
If Mama, sir, sold the baby
To a gipsy for half a crown;
If a gentleman, sir, were a lady—
The world would be upside down.
If any or all of these wonders
Should ever come about,
I should not consider them blunders,
For I should be Inside-Out!

William Brighty Rands

THE CEILING

Suppose the Ceiling went Outside
And then caught Cold and Up and Died?
The only Thing we'd have for Proof
That he was Gone, would be the Roof;
I think it would be Most Revealing
To find out how the Ceiling's Feeling.

Theodore Roethke

A DIFFICULT DAY

I went downtown
To see Mrs. Brown.
She gave me a nickel
To buy a pickle.
The pickle was sour,
So I bought a flower.
The flower was dead,
So I bought some thread.
The thread was thin,
So I bought a pin.
The pin was sharp,
So I bought a harp.
The harp wouldn't play,
So I gave it away
And went back downtown
To see Mrs. Brown.

AN UNSUSPECTED FACT

If down his throat a man should choose
    In fun, to jump or slide,
    He'd scrape his shoes against his teeth,
    Nor dirt his own inside.
But if his teeth were lost and gone,
And not a stump to scrape upon,
He'd see at once how very pat
His tongue lay there by way of mat,
And he would wipe his feet on *that!*

Edward Cannon

As I was standing in the street,
    As quiet as could be,
A great big ugly man came up
    And tied his horse to me.

There once was an old man of Brest,
Who always was funnily drest:
    He wore gloves on his nose,
    And a hat on his toes,
And a boot in the midst of his chest.

Cosmo Monkhouse

There was a young farmer of Leeds,
Who swallowed six packets of seeds.
    It soon came to pass
    He was covered with grass,
And he couldn't sit down for the weeds.

As I was going out one day,
My head fell off and rolled away.
But when I saw that it was gone,
I picked it up and put it on.

And when I got into the street,
A fellow cried: "Look at your feet!"
I looked at them and sadly said:
"I've left them both asleep in bed!"

THE BROOM, THE SHOVEL, THE POKER, AND THE TONGS

The Broom and the Shovel, the Poker and Tongs,
    They all took a drive in the Park,
And they each sang a song, Ding-a-dong, Ding-a-dong,
    Before they went back in the dark.
Mr. Poker he sate quite upright in the coach,
    Mr. Tongs made a clatter and clash,
Miss Shovel was dressed all in black (with a brooch),
    Mrs. Broom was in blue (with a sash).
        Ding-a-dong! Ding-a-dong!
        And they all sang a song!

"O Shovely so lovely!" the Poker he sang,
    "You have perfectly conquered my heart!
Ding-a-dong! Ding-a-dong! If you're pleased with my song,
    I will feed you with cold apple tart!
When you scrape up the coals with a delicate sound,
    You enrapture my life with delight!
Your nose is so shiny, your head is so round,
    And your shape is so slender and bright!
        Ding-a-dong! Ding-a-dong!
        Ain't you pleased with my song?"

"Alas! Mrs. Broom!" sighed the Tongs in his song,
    "Oh! is it because I'm so thin,
And my legs are so long—Ding-a-dong! Ding-a-dong!
    That you don't care about me a pin?
Ah! fairest of creatures, when sweeping the room,
    Ah, why don't you heed my complaint?
Must you needs be so cruel, you beautiful Broom,
    Because you are covered with paint?
        Ding-a-dong! Ding-a-dong!
        You are certainly wrong!"

Mrs. Broom and Miss Shovel together they sang,
  "What nonsense you're singing today!"
Said the Shovel, "I'll certainly hit you a bang!"
  Said the Broom, "And I'll sweep you away!"
So the Coachman drove homeward as fast as he could,
  Perceiving their anger with pain;
But they put on the kettle, and little by little,
  They all became happy again.
    Ding-a-dong! Ding-a-dong!
    There's an end of my song!

Edward Lear

The Roof it has a Lazy Time
  A-Lying in the Sun;
The Walls, they have to Hold Him Up;
  They do Not Have Much Fun!

If People's Heads were Not so Dense—
  If We could Look Inside,
How clear would Show each Mood and
  Tense—
How Often have I Tried!

I Love to Go to Lectures,
  And Make the People Stare,
By Walking Round Upon Their Heads,
  And Spoiling People's Hair!

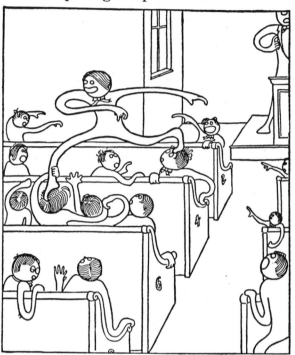

If the Streets were Filled with Glue,
What d'you S'pose that you would Do?
If you should Go to Walk, at Night,
In the Morning you'd be Stuck in Tight!

My Feet they haul me Round the House,
  They Hoist me up the Stairs;
I only have to Steer them, and
  They Ride me Everywheres!

I Wish that my Room had a Floor!
I don't so Much Care for a Door,
  But this Crawling Around
  Without Touching the Ground
Is Getting to be Quite a Bore!

I'd Never Dare to Walk Across
  A Bridge I Could Not See,

For Quite Afraid of Falling off
  I Fear that I Should Be!

My House is Made of Wholemeal Bread,
  Except the Ceiling's Made of White;
Of Angel Cake I Make my Bed—
  I Eat my Pillow Every Night!

Gelett Burgess

THE TWINS

In form and feature, face and limb,
  I grew so like my brother,
That folks got taking me for him,
  And each for one another.
It puzzled all our kith and kin,
  It reached an awful pitch;
For one of us was born a twin,
  Yet not a soul knew which.

One day (to make the matter worse),
  Before our names were fixed,
As we were being washed by nurse
  We got completely mixed;
And thus, you see, by Fate's decree,
  (Or rather nurse's whim),
My brother John got christened *me*,
  And I got christened *him*.

The fatal likeness even dogged
  My footsteps when at school,
And I was always getting flogged,
  For John turned out a fool.
I put this question hopelessly
  To everyone I knew—
What *would* you do, if you were me,
  To prove that you were *you*?

Our close resemblance turned the tide
  Of my domestic life;
For somehow my intended bride
  Became my brother's wife.
In short, year after year the same
  Absurd mistakes went on;
And when I died—the neighbors came
  And buried brother John!

Henry Leigh

THE MAD GARDENER'S SONG

He thought he saw an Elephant,
    That practised on a fife:
He looked again, and found it was
    A letter from his wife.
"At length I realise," he said,
    "The bitterness of Life!"

He thought he saw a Buffalo
    Upon the chimney-piece:
He looked again, and found it was
    His Sister's Husband's Niece,
"Unless you leave this house," he said,
    "I'll send for the Police!"

He thought he saw a Rattlesnake
    That questioned him in Greek:
He looked again, and found it was
    The Middle of Next Week.
"The one thing I regret," he said,
    "Is that it cannot speak!"

He thought he saw a Kangaroo
    That worked a coffee-mill:
He looked again, and found it was
    A Vegetable-Pill.
"Were I to swallow this," he said,
    "I should be very ill!"

He thought he saw a Coach-and-Four
    That stood beside his bed:
He looked again, and found it was
    A Bear without a head.
"Poor thing," he said, "poor silly thing!
    It's waiting to be fed!"

He thought he saw an Argument
    That proved he was the Pope:
He looked again, and found it was
    A Bar of Mottled Soap.
"A fact so dread," he faintly said,
    "Extinguishes all hope!"

Lewis Carroll

HE AND HIS FAMILY

His father was a whale,
With a feather in his tail,
Who lived in the Greenland sea.
And his mother was a shark,
Who kept very dark
In the Gulf of Caribbee.
His uncles were a skate,
And a little whitebait,
And a flounder and a chub beside;
And a lovely pickèrel,
Both a beauty and a belle,
Had promised for to be his bride.
You may think these things are strange,
And they are a little change
From the ordinary run, 'tis true:
But the queerest thing (to me)
Of all appeared to be,
That *he* was a kangaroo!

Laura E. Richards

There was an old man of Blackheath,
Who sat on his set of false teeth.
    Said he, with a start,
    "Oh, Lord, bless my heart!
I've bitten myself underneath!"

Oh, my mother! What a fool I be!
Two dead men were chasing me:
One was blind and the other couldn't see. . .
Oh, my mother! What a fool I be!

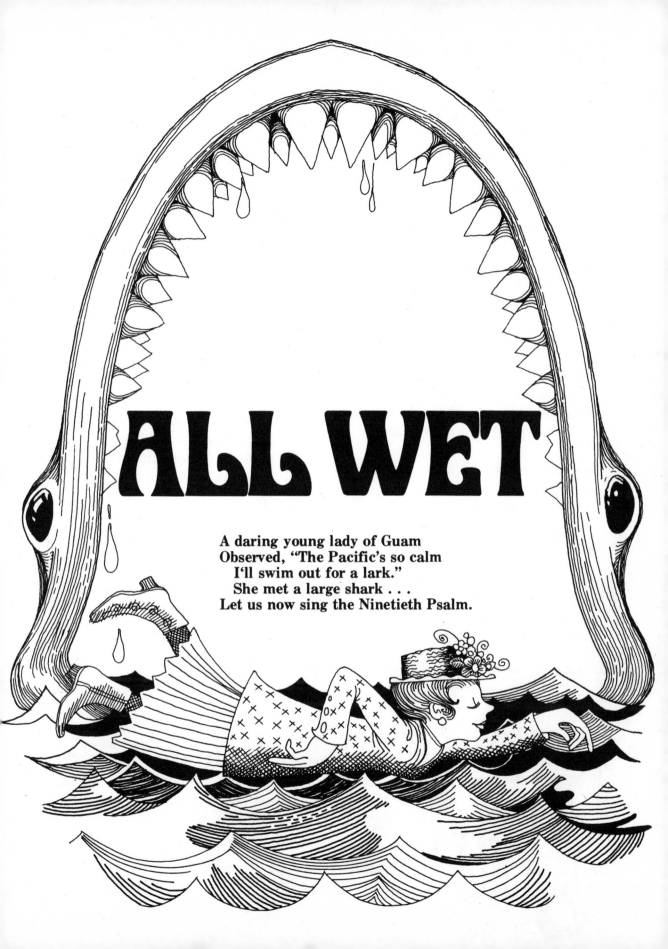

ALL WET

A daring young lady of Guam
Observed, "The Pacific's so calm
    I'll swim out for a lark."
    She met a large shark . . .
Let us now sing the Ninetieth Psalm.

THE CARES OF A CARETAKER

A nice old lady by the sea
  Was neat as she was plain,
And every time the tide came in
  She swept it back again.

And when the sea untidy grew
  And waves began to beat,
She took her little garden rake
  And raked it smooth and neat.

She ran a carpet-sweeper up
  And down the pebbly sand.
She said, "This is the only way
  To keep it clean—good land!"

And when the gulls came strolling by,
  She drove them shrilly back,
Remarking that it spoiled the beach,
  "The way them birds do track."

She fed the catfish clotted cream
  And taught it how to purr—
And were a catfish so endowed
  She would have stroked its fur.

She stopped the little sea urchins
  That traveled by in pairs,
And washed their dirty faces clean
  And combed their little hairs.

She spread white napkins on the surf
  With which she fumed and fussed.
"When it ain't covered up," she said,
  "It gits all over dust."

She didn't like to see the ships
  With all the waves act free,
And so she got a painted sign
  Which read: "Keep off the Sea."

But dust and splutter as she might,
  Her work was sadly vain;
However oft she swept the beach,
  The tides came in again.

And she was sometimes wan and worn
  When she retired to bed—
"A woman's work ain't never done,"
  That nice old lady said.

Wallace Irwin

THE RHYME OF THE CHIVALROUS SHARK

Most chivalrous fish of the ocean,
   To ladies forbearing and mild,
Though his record be dark, is the
     man-eating shark
   Who will eat neither woman nor
     child.

He dines upon seamen and skippers,
   And tourists his hunger assuage,
And a fresh cabin boy will inspire
     him with joy
   If he's past the maturity age.

A doctor, a lawyer, a preacher,
   He'll gobble one any fine day,
But the ladies, God bless 'em, he'll
     only address 'em
   Politely and go on his way.

I can readily cite you an instance
   Where a lovely young lady of
     Breem,
Who was tender and sweet and
     delicious to eat,
   Fell into the bay with a scream.

She struggled and flounced in the
     water
   And signaled in vain for her bark,
And she'd surely been drowned if
     she hadn't been found
   By a chivalrous man-eating shark.

He owed in a manner most
     polished,
   Thus soothing her impulses wild;
"Don't be frightened," he said, "I've
     been properly bred
   And will eat neither woman nor
     child."

Then he proffered his fin and she
     took it—
   Such a gallantry none can
     dispute—
While the passengers cheered as the
     vessel they neared
   And a broadside was fired in
     salute.

And they soon stood alongside the
     vessel,
   When a life-saving dingey was
     lowered
With the pick of the crew, and her
     relatives, too,
   And the mate and the skipper
     aboard.

So they took her aboard in a jiffy,
   And the shark stood attention the
     while,
Then he raised on his flipper and
     ate up the skipper
   And went on his way with a smile.

And this shows that the prince of
     the ocean,
   To ladies forbearing and mild,
Though his record be dark, is the
     man-eating shark
   Who will eat neither woman nor
     child.

Wallace Irwin

THE OWL
AND THE
PUSSY-CAT

The Owl and the Pussy-cat went to sea
    In a beautiful pea-green boat:
They took some honey and plenty of money
    Wrapped up in a five-pound note.
The Owl looked up to the stars above,
    And sang to a small guitar,
"O lovely Pussy, O Pussy, my love,
    What a beautiful Pussy you are,
        You are,
        You are!
    What a beautiful Pussy you are!"

Pussy said to the Owl, "You elegant fowl,
    How charmingly sweet you sing!
Oh! let us be married; too long we have tarried:
    But what shall we do for a ring?"
They sailed away for a year and a day,
    To the land where the bong-tree grows;
And there in a wood a Piggy-wig stood,
    With a ring at the end of his nose,
      His nose,
      His nose,
    With a ring at the end of his nose.

"Dear Pig, are you willing to sell for one shilling
    Your ring?" Said the Piggy, "I will."
So they took it away, and were married next day
    By the Turkey who lives on the hill.
They dined on mince and slices of quince,
    Which they ate with a runcible spoon;
And hand in hand, on the edge of the sand,
    They danced by the light of the moon,
      The moon,
      The moon,
    They danced by the light of the moon.

Edward Lear

THE WALRUS AND THE CARPENTER

The sun was shining on the sea,
  Shining with all his might:
He did his very best to make
  The billows smooth and bright—
And this was odd, because it was
  The middle of the night.

The moon was shining sulkily,
  Because she thought the sun
Had got no business to be there
  After the day was done—
"It's very rude of him," she said,
  "To come and spoil the fun!"

The sea was wet as wet could be,
  The sands were dry as dry.
You could not see a cloud, because
  No cloud was in the sky:
No birds were flying overhead—
  There were no birds to fly.

The Walrus and the Carpenter
  Were walking close at hand;
They wept like anything to see
  Such quantities of sand:
"If this were only cleared away,"
  They said, "it *would* be grand!"

"If seven maids with seven mops
  Swept it for half a year,
Do you suppose," the Walrus said,
  "That they could get it clear?"
"I doubt it," said the Carpenter,
  And shed a bitter tear.

"O Oysters, come and walk with us,"
  The Walrus did beseech.
"A pleasant walk, a pleasant talk,
  Along the briny beach:
We cannot do with more than four
  To give a hand to each."

The eldest Oyster looked at him,
　But never a word he said:
The eldest Oyster winked his eye,
　And shook his heavy head—
Meaning to say he did not choose
　To leave the oyster bed.

But four young Oysters hurried up,
　All eager for the treat:
Their coats were brushed, their faces
　　washed,
　Their shoes were clean and neat—
And this was odd, because, you know,
　They hadn't any feet.

Four other Oysters followed them,
　And yet another four;
And thick and fast they came at last,
　And more, and more, and more—
All hopping through the frothy waves,
　And scrambling to the shore.

The Walrus and the Carpenter
　Walked on a mile or so,
And then they rested on a rock
　Conveniently low:
And all the little Oysters stood
　And waited in a row.

"The time has come," the Walrus said,
　"To talk of many things:
Of shoes—and ships—and sealing wax—
　Of cabbages—and kings—
And why the sea is boiling hot—
　And whether pigs have wings."

"But wait a bit," the Oysters cried,
　"Before we have our chat;
For some of us are out of breath,
　And all of us are fat!"
"No hurry!" said the Carpenter.
　They thanked him much for that.

"A loaf of bread," the Walrus said,
　"Is what we chiefly need:
Pepper and vinegar besides
　Are very good indeed—
Now, if you're ready, Oysters dear,
　We can begin to feed."

"But not on us!" the Oysters cried,
　Turning a little blue.
"After such kindness, that would be
　A dismal thing to do!"
"The night is fine," the Walrus said,
　"Do you admire the view?

"It was so kind of you to come!
　And you are very nice!"
The Carpenter said nothing but
　"Cut us another slice.
I wish you were not quite so deaf—
　I've had to ask you twice!"

"It seems a shame," the Walrus said,
　"To play them such a trick,
After we've brought them out so far,
　And made them trot so quick!"
The Carpenter said nothing but
　"The butter's spread too thick!"

"I weep for you," the Walrus said;
　"I deeply sympathize."
With sobs and tears he sorted out
　Those of the largest size,
Holding his pocket handkerchief
　Before his streaming eyes.

"O Oysters," said the Carpenter,
　"You've had a pleasant run!
Shall we be trotting home again?"
　But answer came there none—
And this was scarcely odd, because
　They'd eaten every one.

Lewis Carroll

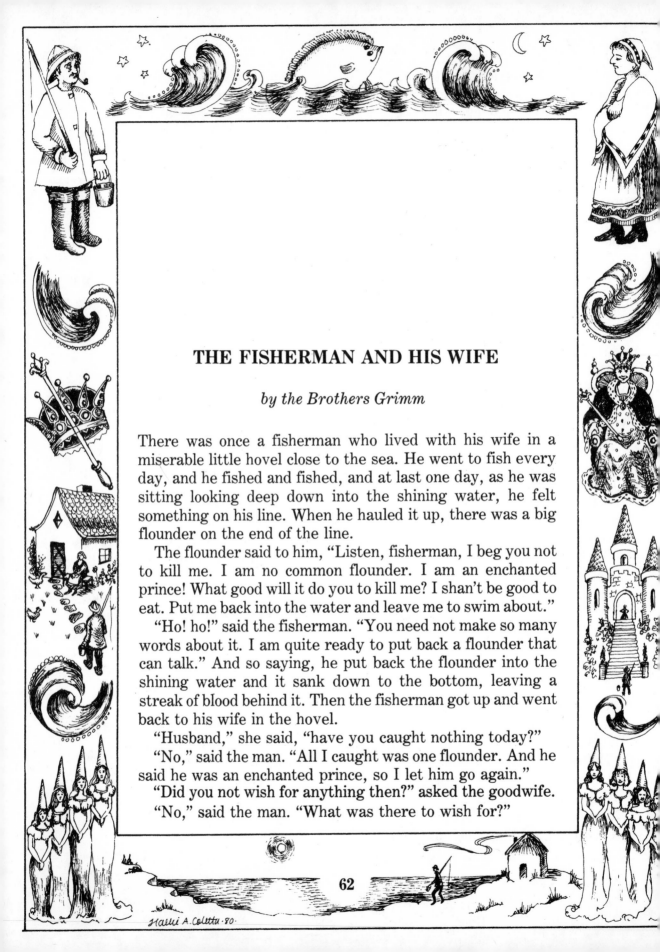

THE FISHERMAN AND HIS WIFE

by the Brothers Grimm

There was once a fisherman who lived with his wife in a miserable little hovel close to the sea. He went to fish every day, and he fished and fished, and at last one day, as he was sitting looking deep down into the shining water, he felt something on his line. When he hauled it up, there was a big flounder on the end of the line.

The flounder said to him, "Listen, fisherman, I beg you not to kill me. I am no common flounder. I am an enchanted prince! What good will it do you to kill me? I shan't be good to eat. Put me back into the water and leave me to swim about."

"Ho! ho!" said the fisherman. "You need not make so many words about it. I am quite ready to put back a flounder that can talk." And so saying, he put back the flounder into the shining water and it sank down to the bottom, leaving a streak of blood behind it. Then the fisherman got up and went back to his wife in the hovel.

"Husband," she said, "have you caught nothing today?"

"No," said the man. "All I caught was one flounder. And he said he was an enchanted prince, so I let him go again."

"Did you not wish for anything then?" asked the goodwife.

"No," said the man. "What was there to wish for?"

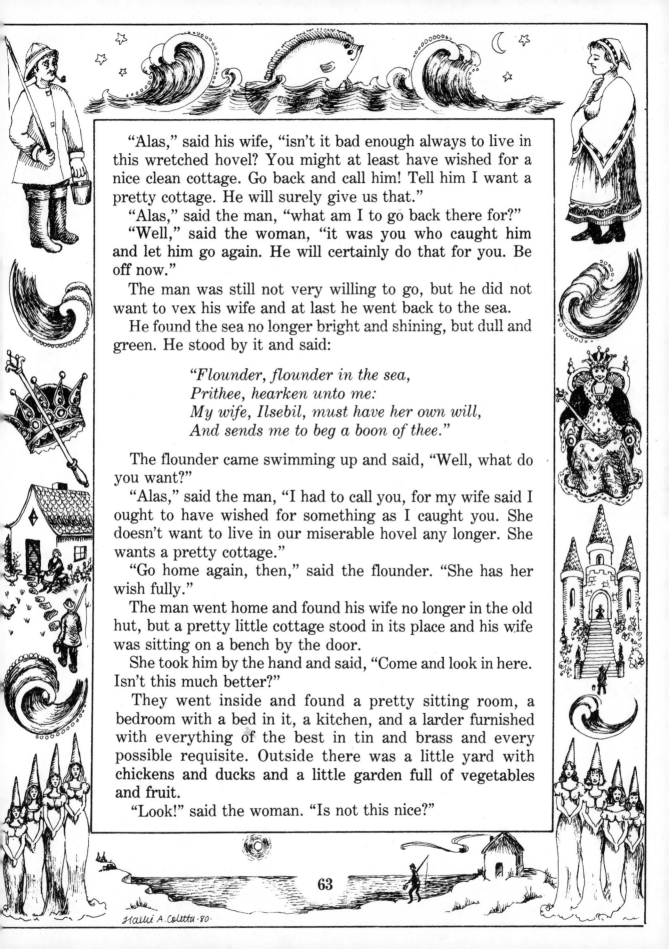

"Alas," said his wife, "isn't it bad enough always to live in this wretched hovel? You might at least have wished for a nice clean cottage. Go back and call him! Tell him I want a pretty cottage. He will surely give us that."

"Alas," said the man, "what am I to go back there for?"

"Well," said the woman, "it was you who caught him and let him go again. He will certainly do that for you. Be off now."

The man was still not very willing to go, but he did not want to vex his wife and at last he went back to the sea.

He found the sea no longer bright and shining, but dull and green. He stood by it and said:

> *"Flounder, flounder in the sea,*
> *Prithee, hearken unto me:*
> *My wife, Ilsebil, must have her own will,*
> *And sends me to beg a boon of thee."*

The flounder came swimming up and said, "Well, what do you want?"

"Alas," said the man, "I had to call you, for my wife said I ought to have wished for something as I caught you. She doesn't want to live in our miserable hovel any longer. She wants a pretty cottage."

"Go home again, then," said the flounder. "She has her wish fully."

The man went home and found his wife no longer in the old hut, but a pretty little cottage stood in its place and his wife was sitting on a bench by the door.

She took him by the hand and said, "Come and look in here. Isn't this much better?"

They went inside and found a pretty sitting room, a bedroom with a bed in it, a kitchen, and a larder furnished with everything of the best in tin and brass and every possible requisite. Outside there was a little yard with chickens and ducks and a little garden full of vegetables and fruit.

"Look!" said the woman. "Is not this nice?"

Halli A. Coletta. 80.

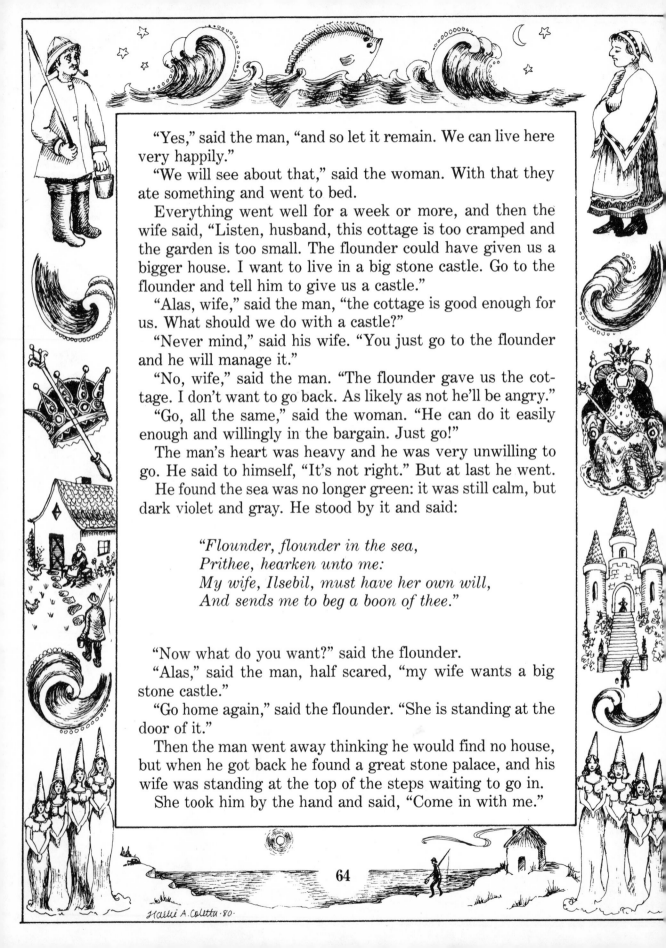

"Yes," said the man, "and so let it remain. We can live here very happily."

"We will see about that," said the woman. With that they ate something and went to bed.

Everything went well for a week or more, and then the wife said, "Listen, husband, this cottage is too cramped and the garden is too small. The flounder could have given us a bigger house. I want to live in a big stone castle. Go to the flounder and tell him to give us a castle."

"Alas, wife," said the man, "the cottage is good enough for us. What should we do with a castle?"

"Never mind," said his wife. "You just go to the flounder and he will manage it."

"No, wife," said the man. "The flounder gave us the cottage. I don't want to go back. As likely as not he'll be angry."

"Go, all the same," said the woman. "He can do it easily enough and willingly in the bargain. Just go!"

The man's heart was heavy and he was very unwilling to go. He said to himself, "It's not right." But at last he went.

He found the sea was no longer green: it was still calm, but dark violet and gray. He stood by it and said:

> *"Flounder, flounder in the sea,*
> *Prithee, hearken unto me:*
> *My wife, Ilsebil, must have her own will,*
> *And sends me to beg a boon of thee."*

"Now what do you want?" said the flounder.

"Alas," said the man, half scared, "my wife wants a big stone castle."

"Go home again," said the flounder. "She is standing at the door of it."

Then the man went away thinking he would find no house, but when he got back he found a great stone palace, and his wife was standing at the top of the steps waiting to go in.

She took him by the hand and said, "Come in with me."

Hallie A. Coletta · 80 ·

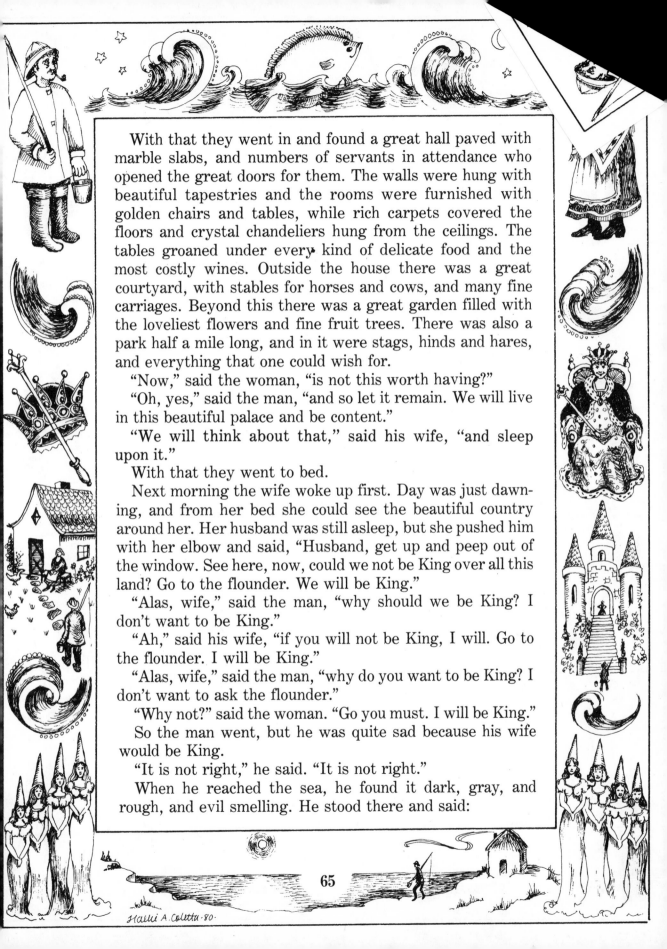

With that they went in and found a great hall paved with marble slabs, and numbers of servants in attendance who opened the great doors for them. The walls were hung with beautiful tapestries and the rooms were furnished with golden chairs and tables, while rich carpets covered the floors and crystal chandeliers hung from the ceilings. The tables groaned under every kind of delicate food and the most costly wines. Outside the house there was a great courtyard, with stables for horses and cows, and many fine carriages. Beyond this there was a great garden filled with the loveliest flowers and fine fruit trees. There was also a park half a mile long, and in it were stags, hinds and hares, and everything that one could wish for.

"Now," said the woman, "is not this worth having?"

"Oh, yes," said the man, "and so let it remain. We will live in this beautiful palace and be content."

"We will think about that," said his wife, "and sleep upon it."

With that they went to bed.

Next morning the wife woke up first. Day was just dawning, and from her bed she could see the beautiful country around her. Her husband was still asleep, but she pushed him with her elbow and said, "Husband, get up and peep out of the window. See here, now, could we not be King over all this land? Go to the flounder. We will be King."

"Alas, wife," said the man, "why should we be King? I don't want to be King."

"Ah," said his wife, "if you will not be King, I will. Go to the flounder. I will be King."

"Alas, wife," said the man, "why do you want to be King? I don't want to ask the flounder."

"Why not?" said the woman. "Go you must. I will be King."

So the man went, but he was quite sad because his wife would be King.

"It is not right," he said. "It is not right."

When he reached the sea, he found it dark, gray, and rough, and evil smelling. He stood there and said:

Halli A. Coletta ·80·

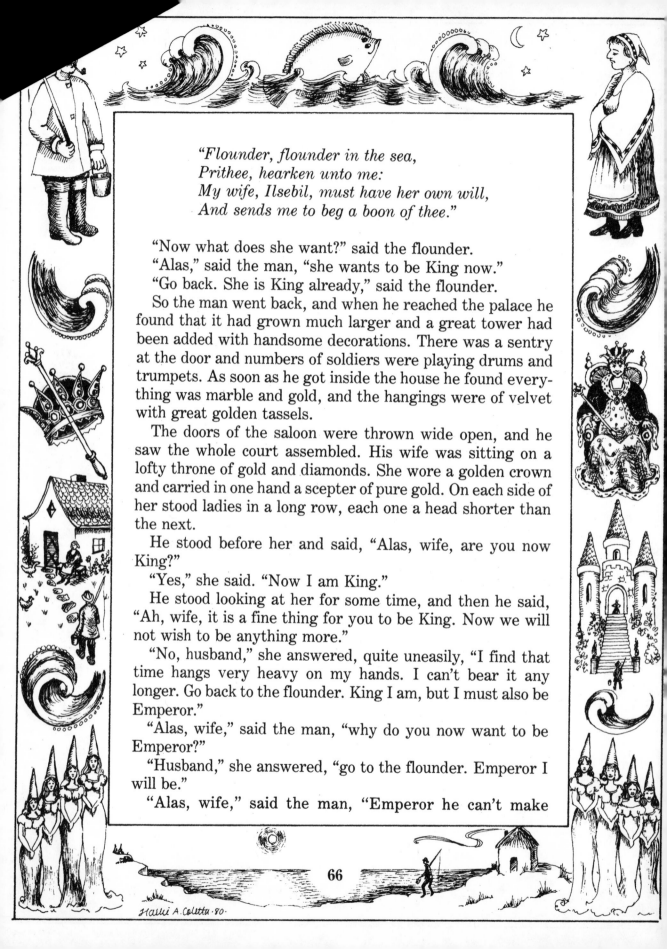

"Flounder, flounder in the sea,
Prithee, hearken unto me:
My wife, Ilsebil, must have her own will,
And sends me to beg a boon of thee."

"Now what does she want?" said the flounder.

"Alas," said the man, "she wants to be King now."

"Go back. She is King already," said the flounder.

So the man went back, and when he reached the palace he found that it had grown much larger and a great tower had been added with handsome decorations. There was a sentry at the door and numbers of soldiers were playing drums and trumpets. As soon as he got inside the house he found everything was marble and gold, and the hangings were of velvet with great golden tassels.

The doors of the saloon were thrown wide open, and he saw the whole court assembled. His wife was sitting on a lofty throne of gold and diamonds. She wore a golden crown and carried in one hand a scepter of pure gold. On each side of her stood ladies in a long row, each one a head shorter than the next.

He stood before her and said, "Alas, wife, are you now King?"

"Yes," she said. "Now I am King."

He stood looking at her for some time, and then he said, "Ah, wife, it is a fine thing for you to be King. Now we will not wish to be anything more."

"No, husband," she answered, quite uneasily, "I find that time hangs very heavy on my hands. I can't bear it any longer. Go back to the flounder. King I am, but I must also be Emperor."

"Alas, wife," said the man, "why do you now want to be Emperor?"

"Husband," she answered, "go to the flounder. Emperor I will be."

"Alas, wife," said the man, "Emperor he can't make

Hallie A. Coletta · 80.

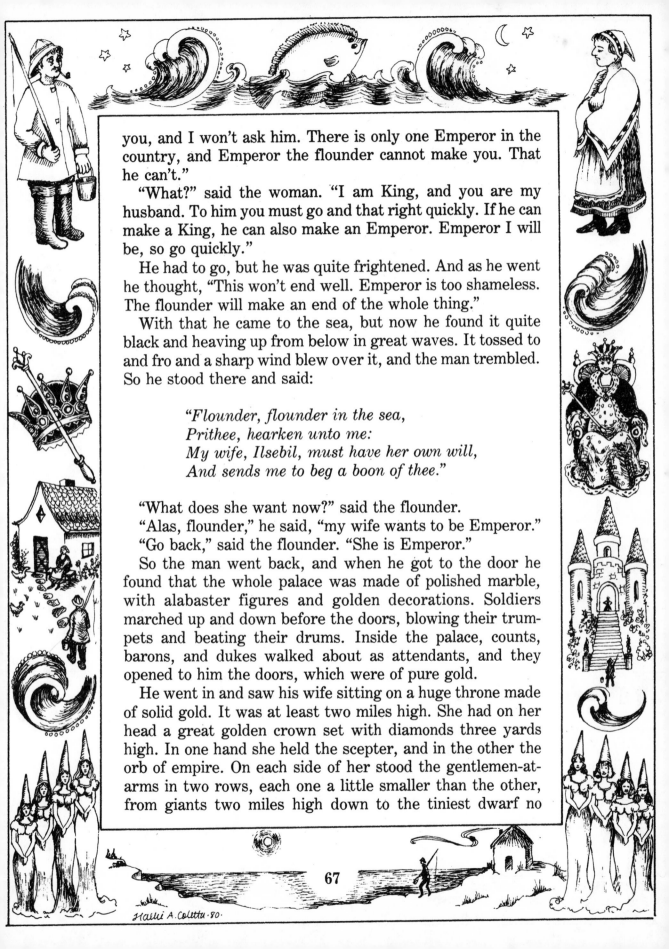

you, and I won't ask him. There is only one Emperor in the country, and Emperor the flounder cannot make you. That he can't."

"What?" said the woman. "I am King, and you are my husband. To him you must go and that right quickly. If he can make a King, he can also make an Emperor. Emperor I will be, so go quickly."

He had to go, but he was quite frightened. And as he went he thought, "This won't end well. Emperor is too shameless. The flounder will make an end of the whole thing."

With that he came to the sea, but now he found it quite black and heaving up from below in great waves. It tossed to and fro and a sharp wind blew over it, and the man trembled. So he stood there and said:

> *"Flounder, flounder in the sea,*
> *Prithee, hearken unto me:*
> *My wife, Ilsebil, must have her own will,*
> *And sends me to beg a boon of thee."*

"What does she want now?" said the flounder.

"Alas, flounder," he said, "my wife wants to be Emperor."

"Go back," said the flounder. "She is Emperor."

So the man went back, and when he got to the door he found that the whole palace was made of polished marble, with alabaster figures and golden decorations. Soldiers marched up and down before the doors, blowing their trumpets and beating their drums. Inside the palace, counts, barons, and dukes walked about as attendants, and they opened to him the doors, which were of pure gold.

He went in and saw his wife sitting on a huge throne made of solid gold. It was at least two miles high. She had on her head a great golden crown set with diamonds three yards high. In one hand she held the scepter, and in the other the orb of empire. On each side of her stood the gentlemen-at-arms in two rows, each one a little smaller than the other, from giants two miles high down to the tiniest dwarf no

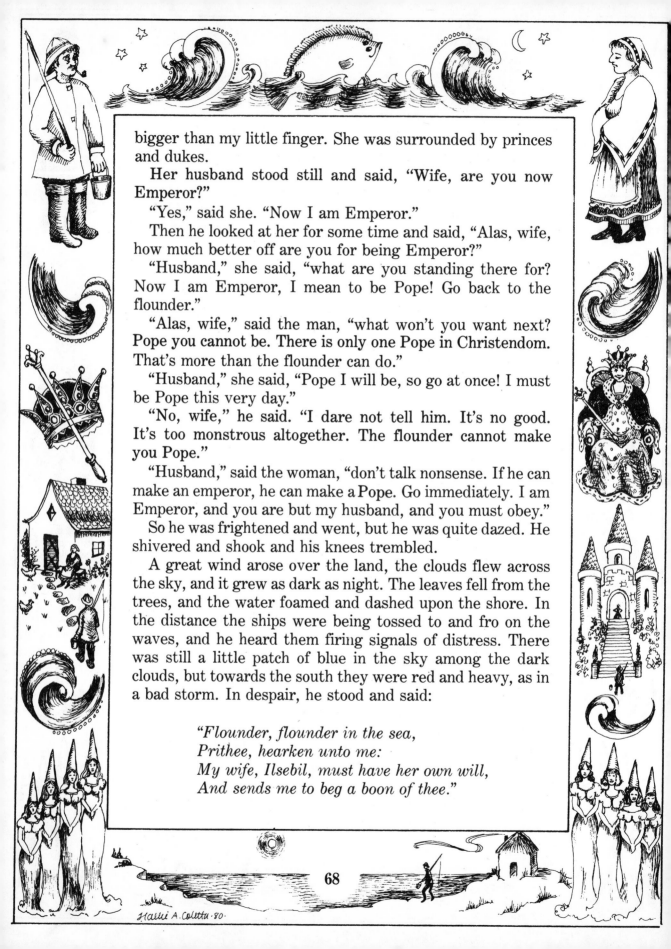

bigger than my little finger. She was surrounded by princes and dukes.

Her husband stood still and said, "Wife, are you now Emperor?"

"Yes," said she. "Now I am Emperor."

Then he looked at her for some time and said, "Alas, wife, how much better off are you for being Emperor?"

"Husband," she said, "what are you standing there for? Now I am Emperor, I mean to be Pope! Go back to the flounder."

"Alas, wife," said the man, "what won't you want next? Pope you cannot be. There is only one Pope in Christendom. That's more than the flounder can do."

"Husband," she said, "Pope I will be, so go at once! I must be Pope this very day."

"No, wife," he said. "I dare not tell him. It's no good. It's too monstrous altogether. The flounder cannot make you Pope."

"Husband," said the woman, "don't talk nonsense. If he can make an emperor, he can make a Pope. Go immediately. I am Emperor, and you are but my husband, and you must obey."

So he was frightened and went, but he was quite dazed. He shivered and shook and his knees trembled.

A great wind arose over the land, the clouds flew across the sky, and it grew as dark as night. The leaves fell from the trees, and the water foamed and dashed upon the shore. In the distance the ships were being tossed to and fro on the waves, and he heard them firing signals of distress. There was still a little patch of blue in the sky among the dark clouds, but towards the south they were red and heavy, as in a bad storm. In despair, he stood and said:

> *"Flounder, flounder in the sea,*
> *Prithee, hearken unto me:*
> *My wife, Ilsebil, must have her own will,*
> *And sends me to beg a boon of thee."*

Harri A. Coletta ·80·

"Now what does she want?" said the flounder.

"Alas," said the man, "she wants to be Pope!"

"Go back. Pope she is," said the flounder.

So back he went, and he found a great church surrounded with palaces. He pressed through the crowd, and inside he found thousands and thousands of lights. And his wife, entirely clad in gold, was sitting on a still higher throne with three golden crowns upon her head, and she was surrounded with priestly state.

On each side of her were two rows of candles, from the biggest as thick as a tower down to the tiniest little taper. Kings and emperors were on their knees before her, kissing her shoe.

"Wife," said the man, looking at her, "are you now Pope?"

"Yes," said she. "Now I am Pope."

So there he stood gazing at her, and it was like looking at a shining sun.

"Alas, wife," he said, "are you better off for being Pope?"

At first she sat stiff as a post, without stirring. Then he said, "Now, wife, be content with being Pope. Higher you cannot go."

"I will think about that," said the woman, and with that they both went to bed. Still she was not content and could not sleep for inordinate desires. The man slept well and soundly, for he had walked about a great deal in the day. But his wife could think of nothing but what further grandeur she could demand. When the dawn reddened the sky she raised herself up in the bed and looked out the window, and when she saw the sun rise she said:

"Ha! Can I not cause the sun and the moon to rise? Husband!" she cried, digging her elbow into his side, "wake up and go to the flounder. I will be Lord of the Universe."

Her husband, who was still more than half asleep, was so shocked that he fell out of bed. He thought he must have heard wrong. He rubbed his eyes and said, "Alas, wife, what did you say?"

"Husband," she said, "if I cannot be Lord of the Universe

and cause the sun and moon to set and rise, I shall not be able to bear it. I shall never have another happy moment."

She looked at him so wildly that it caused a shudder to run through him.

"Alas, wife," he said, falling on his knees before her. "The flounder can't do that. Emperor and Pope he can make, but this is indeed beyond him. I pray you, control yourself and remain Pope."

Then she flew into a terrible rage. Her hair stood on end. She kicked him and screamed, "I won't bear it any longer. Now go!"

Then he pulled on his trousers and tore away like a madman. Such a storm was raging that he could hardly keep his feet. Houses and trees quivered and swayed, and mountains trembled, and the rocks rolled into the sea. The sky was pitchy black.

It thundered and lightened, and the sea ran in black waves mountain high, crested with white foam. He shrieked out, but could hardly make himself heard:

> "Flounder, flounder in the sea,
> Prithee, hearken unto me:
> My wife, Ilsebil, must have her own will,
> And sends me to beg a boon of thee."

"Now what does she want?" asked the flounder.

"Alas," he said, "she wants to be Lord of the Universe."

"Now she must go back to her old hovel," said the flounder, "and there she is!" So there they are to this very day.

THE SHARK

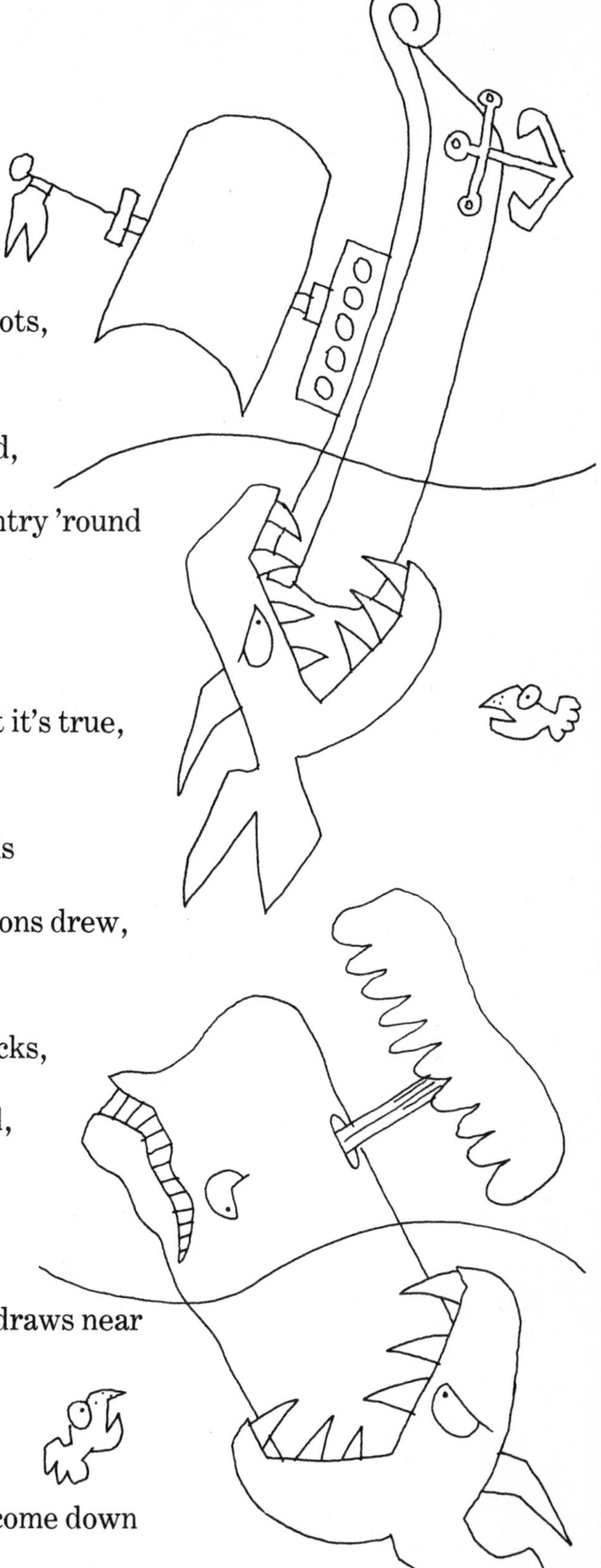

Oh, blithe and merrily sang the shark
As he sat on the house top high,
A-cleaning his boots and smoking cheroots,
With a single glass in his eye.

He sang so loud he astonished the crowd,
Which gathered from far and near;
For they said, "Such a sound in the country 'round
We never—no never did hear."

He sang of ships he'd eaten like chips,
In the palmy days of his youth;
And he added, "If you don't believe that it's true,
Pray examine my wisdom tooth!"

He sang of whales who'd given their tails
For a glance of his raven eye;
And the swordfish, too, who their weapons drew,
And vowed for his sake they'd die.

He sang about wrecks and hurricane decks,
And the mariner's perils and pains;
Till every man's blood up on end it stood,
And their hair ran cold in their veins.

But blithe as a lark the merry old shark
Sat on the sloping roof;
Though he said, "It's queer that no one draws near
To examine my wisdom tooth!"

He carolled by night and by day,
Until he made everyone ill;
And I'll wager a crown that unless he's come down
He is probably carolling still.

Laura E. Richards

71

THE SHARK

How many scientists have written
The shark is gentle as a kitten!
Yet this I know about the shark:
His bite is worser than his bark.

Ogden Nash

IF YOU EVER

If you ever ever ever ever ever
   If you ever ever ever meet a whale
You must never never never never never
   You must never never never touch its tail:
For if you ever ever ever ever ever,
   If you ever ever ever touch its tail,
You will never never never never never,
   You will never never meet another whale.

Behold the wonders of the mighty deep,
Where crabs and lobsters learn to creep,
And little fishes learn to swim,
And clumsy sailors tumble in.

A lady swimmer from Sark
Met up with a *man*-eating shark.
   The shark swam away
   From the lady that day
And she safely swam home before dark.

There once was an Ichthyosaurus
Who lived when the earth was all porous,
   But he fainted with shame
   When he first heard his name,
And departed a long time before us.

A lobster wooed a lady crab,
   And kissed her lovely face.
"Upon my sole," the crabbess cried,
   "I wish you'd mind your plaice!"

When a jolly young fisher named Fisher
Went fishing for fish in a fissure,
   A fish, with a grin,
   Pulled the fisherman in.
Now they're fishing the fissure for Fisher.

THE JELLYFISH

Who wants my jellyfish?
I'm not sellyfish!

Ogden Nash

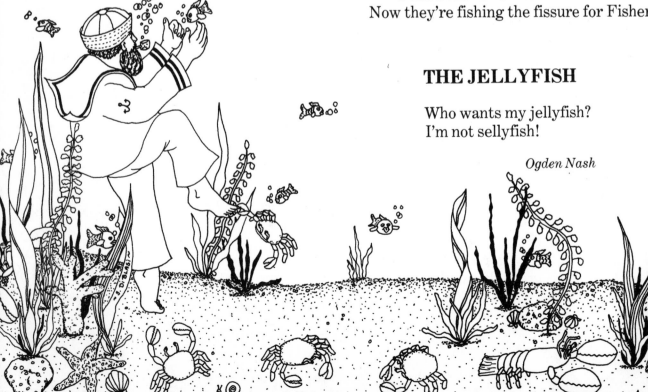

Playground Patter

Order in the court—
The judge is eating beans,
His wife is in the bathtub
Counting submarines.

THERE ONCE WAS A LADY
WHO SWALLOWED A FLY

There once was a lady who swallowed a fly.
I don't know why she swallowed a fly.
Perhaps she'll die.

There once was a lady who swallowed a spider,
That wriggled and wriggled and jiggled inside her.
   She swallowed the spider to catch the fly.
   I don't know why she swallowed a fly.
   Perhaps she'll die.

There once was a lady who swallowed a bird.
How absurd, to swallow a bird!
   She swallowed the bird to catch the spider,
   That wriggled and wriggled and jiggled inside her.
   She swallowed the spider to catch the fly.
   I don't know why she swallowed a fly.
   Perhaps she'll die.

There once was a lady who swallowed a cat.
Well, fancy that, she swallowed a cat!
   She swallowed the cat to catch the bird,
   She swallowed the bird to catch the spider,
   That wriggled and wriggled and jiggled inside her.
   She swallowed the spider to catch the fly.
   I don't know why she swallowed a fly.
   Perhaps she'll die.

There once was a lady who swallowed a dog.
What a hog, to swallow a dog!
    She swallowed the dog to catch the cat, etc.

There once was a lady who swallowed a cow.
I don't know how she swallowed a cow!
  She swallowed the cow to catch the dog.
  She swallowed the dog to catch the cat.
  She swallowed the cat to catch the bird.
  She swallowed the bird to catch the spider,
  That wriggled and wriggled and jiggled inside her.
  She swallowed the spider to catch the fly.
  I don't know why she swallowed a fly.
  Perhaps she'll die.

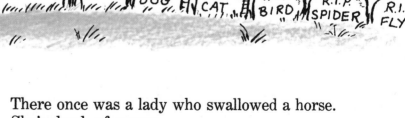

There once was a lady who swallowed a horse.
She's dead, of course.

TONGUE-TWISTERS

Oliver Oglethorpe ogled an owl and an oyster.
Did Oliver Oglethorpe ogle an owl and an oyster?
If Oliver Oglethorpe ogled an owl and an oyster,
Where's the owl and oyster Oliver Oglethorpe ogled?

Swan swam over the sea—
Swim, swan, swim;
Swan swum back again,
Well swum, swan.

A right-handed fellow named Wright,
In writing "write" always wrote "right."
　Where he meant to write right,
　If he'd written "write" right,
Wright would not have wrought rot writing "rite."

A tutor who tooted a flute
Tried to tutor two tooters to toot.
　Said the two to the tutor,
　"Is is harder to toot, or
To tutor two tooters to toot?"

Carolyn Wells

A canner, exceedingly canny,
One morning remarked to his granny,
　"A canner can can
　Anything that he can;
But a canner can't can a can, can he?"

Carolyn Wells

Betty Botta bought some butter.
"But," said she, "this butter's bitter!
If I put it in my batter,
It will make my batter bitter.
But a bit o' better butter
Will but make my batter better."
So she bought a bit o' butter
Better than the bitter butter,
Made her bitter batter better.
So 'twas better Betty Botta
Bought a bit o' better butter.

When a doctor doctors another doctor,
does he doctor the doctored doctor the way
the doctored doctor wants to be doctored,
or does he doctor the doctored doctor the
way the doctoring doctor wants to doctor
the doctor?

Esaw Wood sawed wood. Esaw Wood would saw
wood. Oh, the wood that Wood would saw! One
day Esaw Wood saw a saw saw wood as no other
wood-saw Wood ever saw would saw wood. Of all
the wood-saws Wood ever saw saw wood, Wood
never saw a wood-saw that would saw like the
wood-saw Wood saw saw would. Now Esaw saws
with that saw he saw saw wood.

There's no need to light a night light
   On a light night like tonight;
For a night light's a slight light
   On a light night like tonight.

A flea and a fly in a flue
Were caught, so what could they do?
   Said the fly, "Let us flee."
   "Let us fly," said the flea.
So they flew through a flaw in the flue.

Moses supposes his toeses are roses,
But Moses supposes erroneously;
For nobody's toeses are poesies of roses,
As Moses supposes his toeses to be.

A skunk sat on a stump.
The stump thunk the skunk stunk.
The skunk thunk the stump stunk.

FRACTURED NURSERY RHYMES

Mary had a little lamb,
   A lobster and some prunes,
A glass of milk, a piece of pie,
   And then some macaroons;
It made the naughty waiters grin
   To see her order so;
And when they carried Mary out,
   Her face was white as snow.

The Queen was in the parlour,
   Polishing the grate;
The King was in the kitchen
   Washing up a plate;
The maid was in the garden
   Eating bread and honey,
Listening to the neighbours
   Offering her more money.

Hickory, dickory, dock,
The mice ran up the clock,
The clock struck one,
And the rest escaped with minor injuries.

Humpty Dumpty sat on a wall,
Humpty Dumpty had a great fall.
All the King's horses and all the King's men
Had scrambled eggs for breakfast again.

Little Miss Tuckett
Sat on a bucket,
Eating some peaches and cream;
There came a grasshopper
And tried to stop her;
But she said, "Go away, or I'll scream."

Old King Cole
Was a merry old soul.
He tried to get to heaven
On a telegraph pole.

Yankee Doodle went to town.
He bought a bag of peaches,
He rode so fast a-coming back,
He smashed them all to pieces.

I HAD A LITTLE BROTHER

I had a little brother, his name was Tiny Tim,
I put him in the bathtub to teach him how to swim.
He drank up all the water, he ate up all the soap,
He tried to eat the bathtub, but it wouldn't go down his throat.
My mother called the doctor,
The doctor called his nurse,
The nurse called the lady with the alligator purse.
"Mumps," said the doctor,
"Mumps," said the nurse,
"Mumps," said the lady with the alligator purse,
Out went the doctor, *out* went the nurse,
Out went the lady with the baby in her purse.

"KNOCK, KNOCK!"

"Knock, knock!"
"Who's there?"
"Banana."
"Banana who?"
"Knock, knock!"
"Who's there?"
"Banana."
"Banana who?"
"Knock, knock!"
"Who's there?"
"Banana."
"Banana who?"
"Knock, knock!"
"Who's there?"
"Orange."
"Orange who?"
"Orange you glad I didn't say
    banana?"

I WENT DOWN TO THE RIVER

I went down to the river
And I couldn't get across,
So I jumped on a mule—
I thought he was a horse.
The mule wouldn't pull,
So I traded him for a bull.
The bull wouldn't holler,
So I sold him for a dollar.
The dollar wouldn't pass,
So I threw it in the grass.
The grass wouldn't grow,
So I traded it for a hoe.
The hoe wouldn't dig,
So I traded it for a pig.
The pig wouldn't squeal,
So I traded it for a wheel.
The wheel wouldn't run,
So I traded it for a gun.
The gun wouldn't shoot,
So I traded it for a boot.
The boot wouldn't fit,
So I threw it in a pit,
And you fell in on it.

American Folk Rhyme

Name me and you destroy me.

Silence.

Deborah Delora, she liked a bit of fun—
She went to the baker's and she bought a penny bun:
Dipped the bun in treacle and threw it at her teacher—
Deborah Delora! What a wicked creature!

Sally drinks lemonade,
Sally drinks beer.
Sally drinks some other things
That make her feel so queer.
"Oops," says the lemonade,
"Oops," says the beer,
"Oops," says the other things
That make her feel so queer.

Sweet, sweet Caroline
Dipped her face in turpentine.
Turpentine, made it shine,
Sweet, sweet Caroline.

If a man is born in Turkey,
Grows up in Italy,
Comes to America,
And dies in Chicago,
What is he?

Dead.

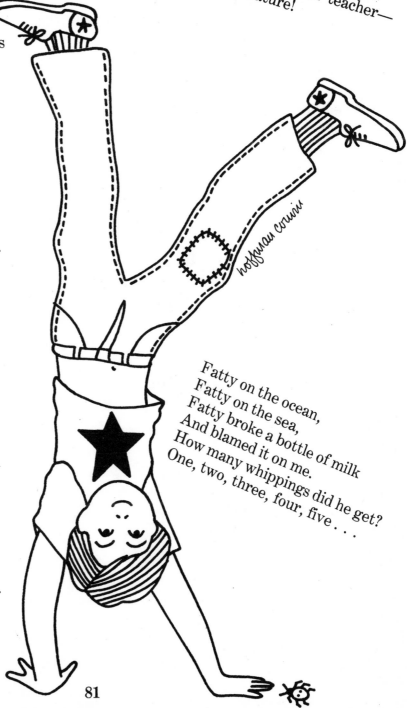

Fatty on the ocean,
Fatty on the sea,
Fatty broke a bottle of milk
And blamed it on me.
How many whippings did he get?
One, two, three, four, five . . .

Why was the farmer cross?
Because somebody trod on his corn.

81

ON TOP OF SPAGHETTI

On top of spaghetti, all covered with cheese,
I lost my poor meatball, when somebody sneezed.

It rolled off the table, and onto the floor,
And then my poor meatball, rolled out of the door.

It rolled into the garden, and under a bush,
And then my poor meatball, was nothing but mush.

The mush was as tasty, as tasty can be,
And early next summer, it grew into a tree.

The tree was all covered, with beautiful moss,
It grew lovely meatballs and tomato sauce.

So if you eat spaghetti, all covered with cheese,
Hold onto your meatball, and don't ever sneeze.

ROUND AND ROUND

It was a dark and stormy night, the rain came down in torrents.
There were brigands on the mountain, and thieves, and the chief said
to Antonio: "Antonio, tell us a story." And Antonio, in fear and
trembling of the mighty chief, began his story: "*It was a dark and
stormy night, the rain came down in torrents . . . .*"

Once there was a girl who asked her father, "What's
a silly question?" and he replied, "Once there was a girl
who asked her father, 'What's a silly question?' and he
replied, '*Once there was a girl who asked her father,* . . .' "

My name is Yim Yonson.
I come from Wisconsin.
I work in the lumberyard there.
Every girl that I meet
As I walk down the street,
I stop her and say:
"*My name is Yim Yonson,
I come from Wisconsin
I work in the lumberyard there,
Every girl that I meet . . .*"

The bear went over the mountain,
The bear went over the mountain,
The bear went over the mountain,
To see what he could see.

He saw another mountain,
He saw another mountain,
He saw another mountain,
And what do you think he did?

He climbed that other mountain,
He climbed that other mountain,
He climbed that other mountain,
And what do you think he saw?

*He saw another mountain,
He saw . . .*

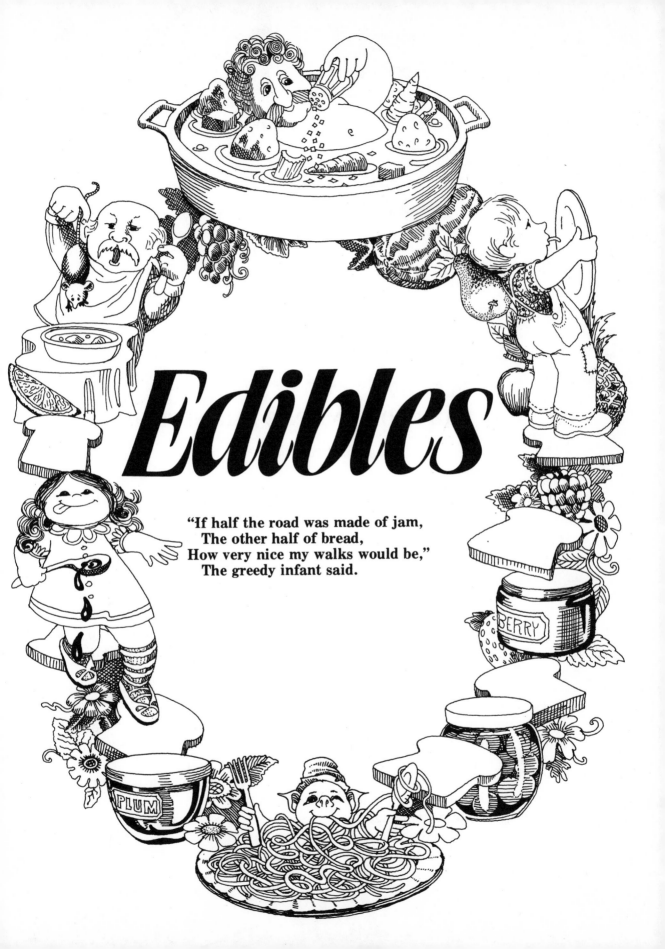

Edibles

"If half the road was made of jam,
The other half of bread,
How very nice my walks would be,"
The greedy infant said.

HOW THE TWO WENT INTO PARTNERSHIP

by Howard Pyle

This was the way of it.

Uncle Bear had a pot of honey and a big cheese, but the Great Red Fox had nothing but his wits.

The fox was for going into partnership, for he says, says he, "a head full of wits is worth more than a pot of honey and a big cheese," which was as true as gospel, only that wits cannot be shared in partnership among folks, like red herring and blue beans, or a pot of honey and a big cheese.

All the same, Uncle Bear was well enough satisfied, and so they went into partnership together, just as the Great Red Fox had said. As for the pot of honey and the big cheese, why, they were put away for a rainy day, and the wits were all that were to be used just now.

"Very well," says the fox, "we'll rattle them up a bit;" and so he did, and this was how.

He was hungry for the honey, was the Great Red Fox. "See, now," said he, "I am sick to-day, and I will just go and see the Master Doctor over yonder."

But it was not the doctor he went to; no, off he marched to the storehouse, and there he ate part of the honey. After that he laid out in the sun and toasted his skin, for that is pleasant after a great dinner.

By and by he went home again.

"Well," says Uncle Bear, "and how do you feel now?"

"Oh, well enough," says the Great Red Fox.

"And was the medicine bitter?" says Uncle Bear.

"Oh, no, it was good enough," says the Great Red Fox.

"And how much did the doctor give you?" says Uncle Bear.

"Oh, about one part of a pot full," says the Red Fox.

Dear, dear! thinks Uncle Bear, that is a great deal of medicine to take, for sure and certain.

Well, things went on as smoothly as though the wheels were greased, until by and by the fox grew hungry for a taste of honey again; and this time he had to go over yonder and see his aunt. Off he went to the storehouse, and there he ate all the honey he wanted, and then, after he had slept a bit in the sun, he went back home again.

"Well," says Uncle Bear, "and did you see your aunt?"

"Oh, yes," says the Great Red Fox, "I saw her."

"And did she give you anything?" says Uncle Bear.

"Oh, yes, she gave me a trifle," says the Great Red Fox.

"And what was it she gave you?" says Uncle Bear.

"Why, she gave me another part of a pot full, that was all," says the Great Red Fox.

"Dear, dear! but that is a queer thing to give," says Uncle Bear.

By and by the Great Red Fox was thinking of honey again, and now it was a christening he had to go to. Off he went to the pot of honey, and this time he finished it all and licked the pot into the bargain.

And had everything gone smoothly at the christening? That was what Uncle Bear wanted to know.

"Oh, smoothly enough," says the Great Red Fox.

"And did they have a christening feast?" says Uncle Bear.

"Oh, yes, they had that," says the Great Red Fox.

"And what did they have?" says Uncle Bear.

"Oh, everything that was in the pot," says the Great Red Fox.

"Dear, dear," says Uncle Bear, "but they must have been a hungry set at that christening."

Well, one day Uncle Bear says, "We'll have a feast and eat up the pot of honey and the big cheese, and we'll ask Father Goat over to help us."

That suited the Great Red Fox well enough, so off he went to the storehouse to fetch the pot of honey and the cheese; as for Uncle Bear he went to ask Father Goat to come and help them eat up the good things.

"See, now," says the Great Red Fox to himself, "the pot of honey and the big cheese belong together, and it is a pity to part them." So down he sat without more ado, and when he got up again the cheese was all inside of him.

When he came home again there was Father Goat toasting his toes at the fire and waiting for supper; and there was Uncle Bear on the back door-step sharpening the bread-knife.

"Hi!" says the Great Red Fox, "and what are you doing here, Father Goat?"

"I am just waiting for supper, and that is all," says Father Goat.

"And where is Uncle Bear?" says the Great Red Fox.

"He is sharpening the bread-knife," says Father Goat.

"Yes," says the Great Red Fox, "and when he is through with that he is going to cut your tail off."

Dear, dear! but Father Goat was in a great fright; that house was no place for him, and he could see that with one eye shut; off he marched, as though the ground was hot under him. As for the Great Red Fox, he went out to Uncle Bear; "That was a pretty body you asked to take supper with us," says he; "here he has marched off with the pot of honey and the big cheese, and we may sit down and whistle over an empty table between us."

When Uncle Bear heard this he did not tarry, I can tell you; up he got and off he went after Father Goat. "Stop! stop!" he bawled, "let me have a little at least."

But Father Goat thought that Uncle Bear was speaking of his tail, for he knew nothing of the pot of honey and the big cheese; so he just knuckled down to it, and away he scampered till the gravel flew behind him.

And this was what came of that partnership; nothing was left but the wits that the Great Red Fox had brought into the business; for nobody could blame Father Goat for carrying the wits off with him, and one might guess that without the telling.

Now, as the pot of honey and big cheese were gone, something else must be looked up, for one cannot live on thin air, and that is the truth.

"See, now," says the Great Red Fox. "Farmer John over yonder has a storehouse full of sausages and chitterlings and puddings, and all sort of good things. As nothing else is left of the partnership we'll just churn our wits a bit, and see if we can make butter with them, as the saying goes;" that was what the Great Red Fox said, and it suited Uncle Bear as well as anything he ever heard; so off they marched arm in arm.

By and by they came to Farmer John's house, and nobody was about, which was just what the two rogues wanted; and, yes, there was the storehouse as plain as the nose on your face, only the door was locked. Above was a little window just big enough for the Great Red Fox to creep into, though it was up ever so high. "Just give me a lift up through the window yonder," says he to Uncle Bear, "and I will drop the good things out for you to catch."

So Uncle Bear gave the Great Red Fox a leg up, and—pop!—and there he was in the store house like a mouse in the cheese-box.

As soon as he was safe among the good things he bawled out to Uncle Bear, "What shall it be first, sausages or puddings?"

"Hush! hush!" said Uncle Bear.

"Yes, yes," bawled the Red Fox louder than ever, "only tell me which I shall take first, sausages or puddings?"

"Sh-h-h-h!" said Uncle Bear, "if you are making such a noise as that you will have them about our ears; take the first that comes and be quick about it."

"Yes, yes," bawled the fox as loud as he was able; "but one is just as handy as another, and you must tell me which I shall take first."

But Uncle Bear got neither pudding nor sausage, for the Great Red Fox had made such a hubbub that Farmer John and his men came running, and three great dogs with them.

"Hi!" said they, "there is Uncle Bear after the sausages and puddings;" and there was nothing for him to do but to lay foot to the ground as fast as he could. All the same, they caught him over the hill, and gave him such a drubbing that his bones ached for many a long day.

But the Great Red Fox only waited until all the others were well away on their own business, and then he filled a bag with the best he could lay his hands on, opened the door from the inside, and walked out as though it were from his own barn; for there was nobody to say "No" to him. He hid the good things away in a place of his own, and it was little of them that Uncle Bear smelt. After he had gathered all this, Master Fox came home, groaning as though he had had an awful drubbing; it would have moved a heart of stone to hear him.

"Dear, oh dear! what a drubbing I have had," said he.

"And so have I," said Uncle Bear, grinning over his sore bones as though cold weather were blowing snow in his teeth.

"See, now," said the Great Red Fox, "this is what comes of going into partnership, and sharing one's wits with another. If you had made your choice when I asked you, your butter would never have been spoiled in the churning."

That was all the comfort Uncle Bear had, and cold enough it was too. All the same, he is not the first in the world who has lost his dinner, and had both the drubbing and the blame into the bargain.

But things do not last forever, and so by and by the good things from Farmer John's storehouse gave out, and the Great Red Fox had nothing in the larder.

"Listen," says he to Uncle Bear, "I saw them shaking the apple-trees at Farmer John's to-day, and if you have a mind to try the wits that belong to us, we'll go and bring a bagful apiece from the storehouse over yonder at the farm."

Yes, that suited Uncle Bear well enough; so off they marched, each of them with an empty bag to fetch back the apples. By and by they came to the storehouse, and nobody was about. This time the door was not locked, so in

the both of them went and began filling their bags with apples. The Great Red Fox tumbled them into his bag as fast as ever he could, taking them just as they came, good or bad; but Uncle Bear took his time about it and picked them all over, for since he had come there he was bound to get the best that were to be had.

So the upshot of the matter was that the Great Red Fox had his bag full before Uncle Bear picked out half a score of good juicy apples.

"I'll just peep out of the window yonder," says the Great Red Fox, "and see if Farmer John is coming." But in his sleeve he said to himself, "I'll slip outside and turn the key of the door on Uncle Bear, for somebody will have to carry the blame of this, and his shoulders are broader and his skin tougher than mine; he will never be able to get out of that little window." So up he jumped with his bag of apples, to do as he said.

But listen! A hasty man drinks hot broth. And so it was with the Great Red Fox, for up in the window they had set a trap to catch rats. But he knew nothing of that; out he jumped from the window—click! went the trap and caught him by the tail, and there he hung.

"Is Farmer John coming?" bawled Uncle Bear, by and by.

"Hush! hush!" said the Great Red Fox, for he was trying to get his tail out of the trap.

But the boot was on the other leg now. "Yes, yes," bawled Uncle Bear, louder than before, "but tell me, is Farmer John coming?"

"Sh-h-h-h!" says the Great Red Fox.

"No, no," bawled Uncle Bear, as loud as he could, "what I want to know is, is Farmer John coming?"

Yes, he was, for he had heard the hubbub, and here he was with a lot of his men and three great dogs.

"Oh, Farmer John," bawled Great Red Fox, "don't touch me, I am not the thief. Yonder is Uncle Bear in the pantry, he is the one."

Yes, yes, Farmer John knew how much of that cake to eat; here was the rogue of a fox caught in the trap, and the beating was ready for him. That was the long and the short of it.

When the Great Red Fox heard this, he pulled with all his might and main. Snap! went his tail and broke off close to his body, and away he scampered with Farmer John, the men and the dogs close to his heels. But Uncle Bear filled his bag full of apples, and when all hands had gone racing away after the Great Red Fox, he walked quietly out of the door and off home.

And that is how the Great Red Fox lost his tail in the trap.

What is the meaning of all this? Why, here it is: When a rogue and another crack a nut together, it is not often the rogue who breaks his teeth trying to eat the hulls. And this too: But when one sets a trap for another, it is a toss of a copper whether or not it flies up and pinches his own fingers.

If there is anything more left in the dish you may scrape it for yourself.

THE BOY STOOD IN THE SUPPER-ROOM

The boy stood in the supper-room
   Whence all but he had fled;
He'd eaten seven pots of jam
   And he was gorged with bread.

"Oh, one more crust before I bust!"
   He cried in accents wild;
He licked the plates, he sucked the spoons—
   He was a vulgar child.

There came a burst of thunder-sound—
   The boy—oh! where was he?
Ask of the maid who mopped him up,
   The bread crumbs and the tea.

YOU MUST NEVER BATH IN AN IRISH STEW

You must never bath in an Irish stew
It's a most illogical thing to do
   But should you persist against my reasoning
   Don't fail to add the appropriate seasoning.

Spike Milligan

THE STORY OF AUGUSTUS WHO WOULD NOT HAVE ANY SOUP

Augustus was a chubby lad;
Fat ruddy cheeks Augustus had;
And everybody saw with joy
The plump and hearty healthy boy.
He ate and drank as he was told,
And never let his soup get cold.
But one day, one cold winter's day,
He scream'd out: "Take the soup away!
O take the nasty soup away!
I won't have any soup to-day."

Next day, now look, the picture shows
How lank and lean Augustus grows!
Yet, though he feels so weak and ill,
The naughty fellow cries out still:
"Not any soup for me, I say:
O take the nasty soup away!
I won't have any soup to-day."

The third day comes; O what a sin
To make himself so pale and thin!
Yet, when the soup is put on table,
He screams, as loud as he is able:
"Not any soup for me, I say:
O take the nasty soup away!
I won't have any soup to-day."

Look at him, now the fourth day's come!
He scarcely weighs a sugar-plum;
He's like a little bit of thread;
And on the fifth day, he was—dead!

Heinrich Hoffman

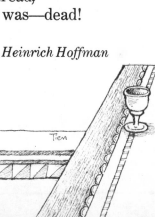

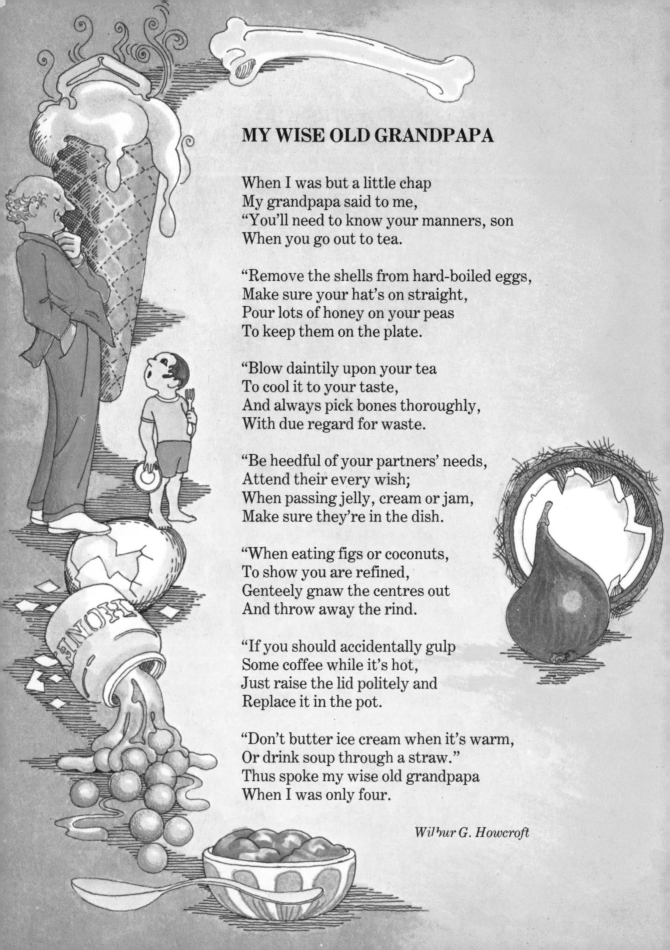

MY WISE OLD GRANDPAPA

When I was but a little chap
My grandpapa said to me,
"You'll need to know your manners, son
When you go out to tea.

"Remove the shells from hard-boiled eggs,
Make sure your hat's on straight,
Pour lots of honey on your peas
To keep them on the plate.

"Blow daintily upon your tea
To cool it to your taste,
And always pick bones thoroughly,
With due regard for waste.

"Be heedful of your partners' needs,
Attend their every wish;
When passing jelly, cream or jam,
Make sure they're in the dish.

"When eating figs or coconuts,
To show you are refined,
Genteely gnaw the centres out
And throw away the rind.

"If you should accidentally gulp
Some coffee while it's hot,
Just raise the lid politely and
Replace it in the pot.

"Don't butter ice cream when it's warm,
Or drink soup through a straw."
Thus spoke my wise old grandpapa
When I was only four.

Wilbur G. Howcroft

EXPLODING GRAVY

My mother's big green gravy boat
Once thought he was a navy boat.

I poured him over my mashed potatoes
And out swam seven swift torpedoes.

Torpedoes whizzed and whirred, and—WHAM!
One bumped smack into my hunk of ham

And blew up with an awful roar,
Flinging my carrots on the floor.

Exploding gravy! That's so silly!
Now all I ever eat is chili.

X. J. Kennedy

TABLE MANNERS—I

The Goops they lick their fingers,
 And the Goops they lick their knives;
They spill their broth on the tablecloth—
 Oh, they lead disgusting lives!
The Goops they talk while eating,
 And loud and fast they chew;
And that is why I'm glad that I
 Am not a Goop—are you?

TABLE MANNERS—II

The Goops are gluttonous and rude,
They gug and gumble with their food;
They throw their crumbs upon the floor,
And at dessert they tease for more;
They will not eat their soup and bread
But like to gobble sweets, instead,
And this is why I oft decline,
When I am asked to stay and dine!

Gelett Burgess

THE CROCODILE

Crocodile once dropped a line
To a Fox to invite him to dine;
   But the Fox wrote to say
   He was dining that day,
With a *Bird friend*, and begged to
     decline.

She sent off at once to a Goat.
"Pray don't disappoint me," she wrote,
   But he answered too late
   He'd forgotten the date
Having thoughtlessly eaten her note.

The Crocodile thought him ill-bred,
And invited two Rabbits instead;
   But the Rabbits replied,
   They were hopelessly tied
To a previous engagement, and fled.

Then she wrote in despair to some Eels,
And begged them to "drop in" to meals;
   But the Eels left their cards
   With their coldest regards,
And took to what went for their heels.

Cried the Crocodile then in disgust,
"My motives they seem to mistrust.
   Their suspicions are base
   Since they don't know their place,—
I suppose if I *must* starve, I *must!*"

Oliver Herford

THE FLATTERED FLYING FISH

Said the Shark to the Flying Fish over the phone:
"Will you join me tonight? I am dining alone.
Let me order a nice little dinner for two!
And come as you are, in your shimmering blue."

Said the Flying Fish: "Fancy remembering me,
And the dress I wore at the Porpoises' tea!"
"How could I forget?" said the Shark in his guile:
"I expect you at eight!" and rang off with a smile.

She has powdered her nose; she has put on her things;
She is off with one flap of her luminous wings.
O little one, lovely, light-hearted and vain.
The Moon will not shine on your beauty again!

E. V. Rieu

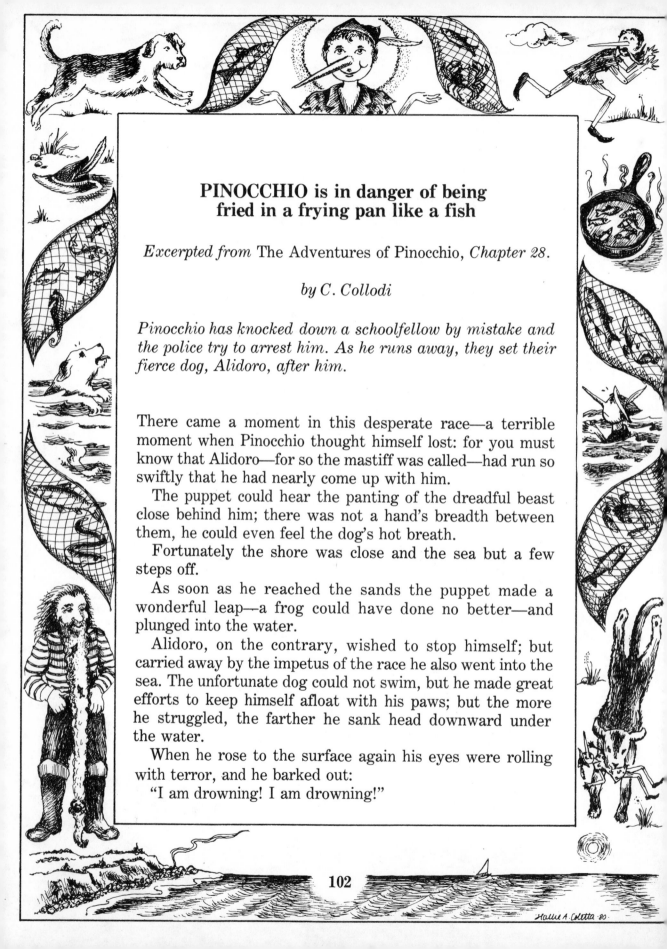

PINOCCHIO is in danger of being fried in a frying pan like a fish

Excerpted from The Adventures of Pinocchio, *Chapter 28.*

by C. Collodi

Pinocchio has knocked down a schoolfellow by mistake and the police try to arrest him. As he runs away, they set their fierce dog, Alidoro, after him.

There came a moment in this desperate race—a terrible moment when Pinocchio thought himself lost: for you must know that Alidoro—for so the mastiff was called—had run so swiftly that he had nearly come up with him.

The puppet could hear the panting of the dreadful beast close behind him; there was not a hand's breadth between them, he could even feel the dog's hot breath.

Fortunately the shore was close and the sea but a few steps off.

As soon as he reached the sands the puppet made a wonderful leap—a frog could have done no better—and plunged into the water.

Alidoro, on the contrary, wished to stop himself; but carried away by the impetus of the race he also went into the sea. The unfortunate dog could not swim, but he made great efforts to keep himself afloat with his paws; but the more he struggled, the farther he sank head downward under the water.

When he rose to the surface again his eyes were rolling with terror, and he barked out:

"I am drowning! I am drowning!"

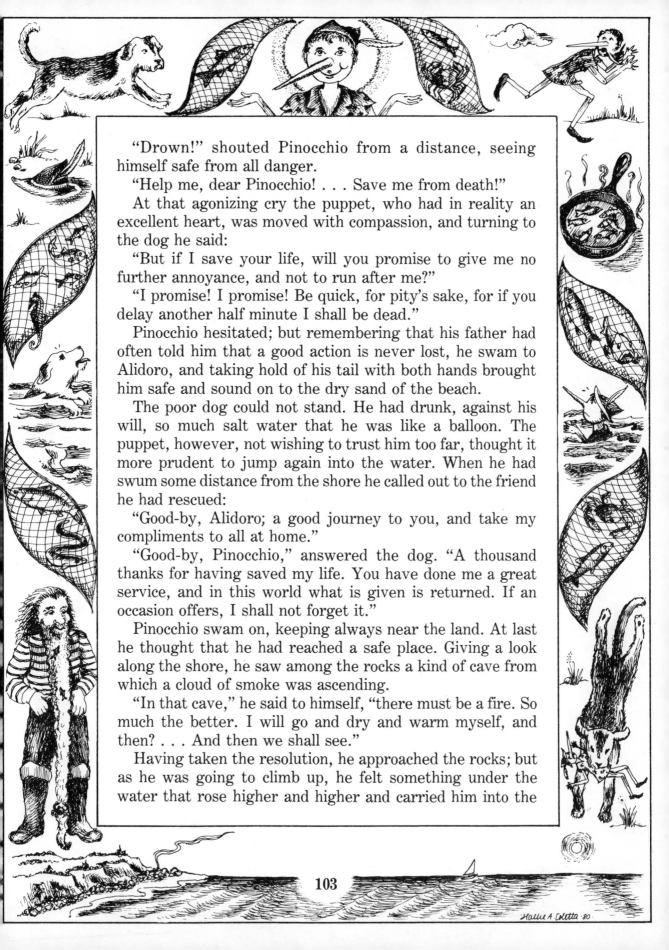

"Drown!" shouted Pinocchio from a distance, seeing himself safe from all danger.

"Help me, dear Pinocchio! . . . Save me from death!"

At that agonizing cry the puppet, who had in reality an excellent heart, was moved with compassion, and turning to the dog he said:

"But if I save your life, will you promise to give me no further annoyance, and not to run after me?"

"I promise! I promise! Be quick, for pity's sake, for if you delay another half minute I shall be dead."

Pinocchio hesitated; but remembering that his father had often told him that a good action is never lost, he swam to Alidoro, and taking hold of his tail with both hands brought him safe and sound on to the dry sand of the beach.

The poor dog could not stand. He had drunk, against his will, so much salt water that he was like a balloon. The puppet, however, not wishing to trust him too far, thought it more prudent to jump again into the water. When he had swum some distance from the shore he called out to the friend he had rescued:

"Good-by, Alidoro; a good journey to you, and take my compliments to all at home."

"Good-by, Pinocchio," answered the dog. "A thousand thanks for having saved my life. You have done me a great service, and in this world what is given is returned. If an occasion offers, I shall not forget it."

Pinocchio swam on, keeping always near the land. At last he thought that he had reached a safe place. Giving a look along the shore, he saw among the rocks a kind of cave from which a cloud of smoke was ascending.

"In that cave," he said to himself, "there must be a fire. So much the better. I will go and dry and warm myself, and then? . . . And then we shall see."

Having taken the resolution, he approached the rocks; but as he was going to climb up, he felt something under the water that rose higher and higher and carried him into the air. He tried to escape, but it was too late, for to his extreme surprise he found himself enclosed in a great net, together with a swarm of fish of every size and shape, who were flapping and struggling like so many despairing souls.

At the same moment a fisherman came out of the cave; he was so ugly, so horribly ugly, that he looked like a sea monster. Instead of hair his head was covered with a thick bush of green grass, his skin was green, his eyes were green, his long beard that came down to the ground was also green. He had the appearance of an immense lizard standing on its hind paws.

When the fisherman had drawn his net out of the sea, he exclaimed with great satisfaction:

"Thank Heaven! Again today I shall have a splendid feast of fish!"

"What a mercy that I am not a fish!" said Pinocchio to himself, regaining a little courage.

The net full of fish was carried into the cave, which was dark and smoky. In the middle of the cave a large frying pan full of oil was frying, and sending out a smell of mushrooms that was suffocating.

"Now we will see what fish we have taken!" said the green fisherman; and putting into the net an enormous hand, so out of all proportion that it looked like a baker's shovel, he pulled out a handful of mullet.

"These mullet are good!" he said, looking at them and smelling them complacently. And after he had smelt them he threw them into a pan without water.

He repeated the same operation many times; and as he drew out the fish, his mouth watered and he said, chuckling to himself:

"What good whiting! . . .

"What exquisite sardines! . . .

"These soles are delicious! . . .

"And these crabs excellent! . . .

"What dear little anchovies! . . ."

I need not tell you that the whiting, the sardines, the soles,

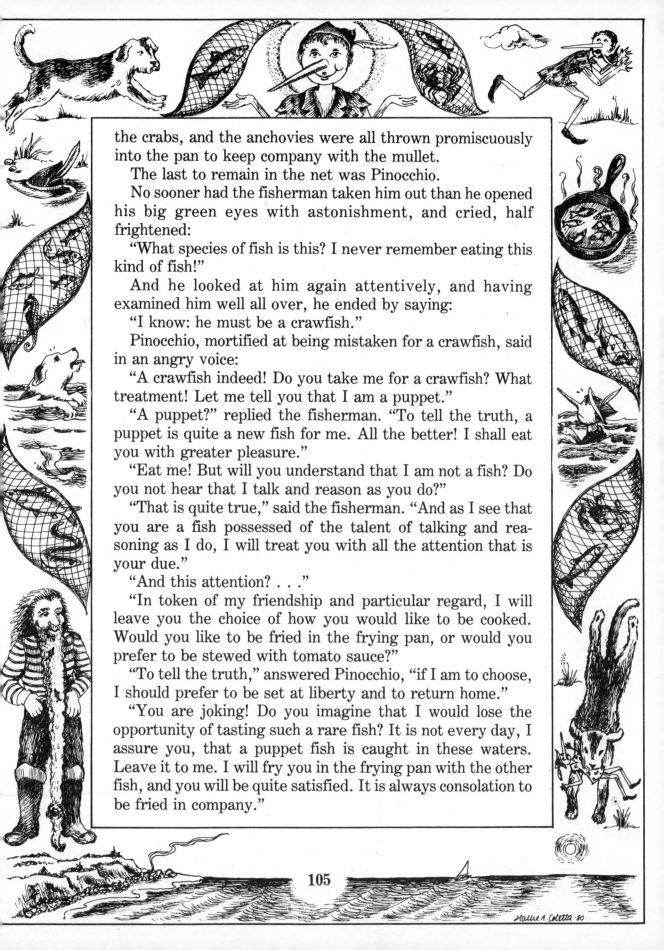

the crabs, and the anchovies were all thrown promiscuously into the pan to keep company with the mullet.

The last to remain in the net was Pinocchio.

No sooner had the fisherman taken him out than he opened his big green eyes with astonishment, and cried, half frightened:

"What species of fish is this? I never remember eating this kind of fish!"

And he looked at him again attentively, and having examined him well all over, he ended by saying:

"I know: he must be a crawfish."

Pinocchio, mortified at being mistaken for a crawfish, said in an angry voice:

"A crawfish indeed! Do you take me for a crawfish? What treatment! Let me tell you that I am a puppet."

"A puppet?" replied the fisherman. "To tell the truth, a puppet is quite a new fish for me. All the better! I shall eat you with greater pleasure."

"Eat me! But will you understand that I am not a fish? Do you not hear that I talk and reason as you do?"

"That is quite true," said the fisherman. "And as I see that you are a fish possessed of the talent of talking and reasoning as I do, I will treat you with all the attention that is your due."

"And this attention? . . ."

"In token of my friendship and particular regard, I will leave you the choice of how you would like to be cooked. Would you like to be fried in the frying pan, or would you prefer to be stewed with tomato sauce?"

"To tell the truth," answered Pinocchio, "if I am to choose, I should prefer to be set at liberty and to return home."

"You are joking! Do you imagine that I would lose the opportunity of tasting such a rare fish? It is not every day, I assure you, that a puppet fish is caught in these waters. Leave it to me. I will fry you in the frying pan with the other fish, and you will be quite satisfied. It is always consolation to be fried in company."

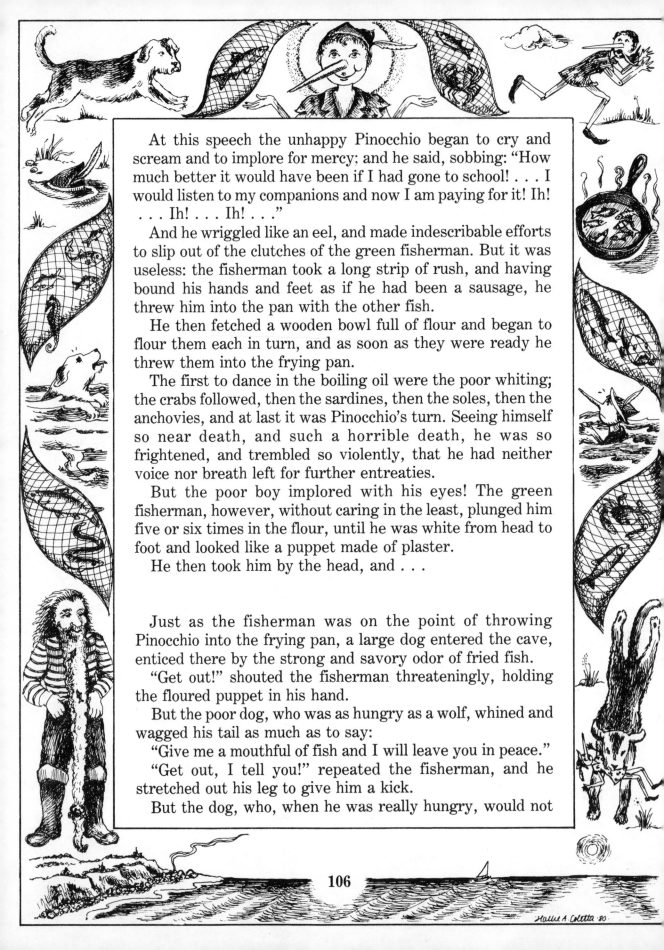

At this speech the unhappy Pinocchio began to cry and scream and to implore for mercy; and he said, sobbing: "How much better it would have been if I had gone to school! . . . I would listen to my companions and now I am paying for it! Ih! . . . Ih! . . . Ih! . . ."

And he wriggled like an eel, and made indescribable efforts to slip out of the clutches of the green fisherman. But it was useless: the fisherman took a long strip of rush, and having bound his hands and feet as if he had been a sausage, he threw him into the pan with the other fish.

He then fetched a wooden bowl full of flour and began to flour them each in turn, and as soon as they were ready he threw them into the frying pan.

The first to dance in the boiling oil were the poor whiting; the crabs followed, then the sardines, then the soles, then the anchovies, and at last it was Pinocchio's turn. Seeing himself so near death, and such a horrible death, he was so frightened, and trembled so violently, that he had neither voice nor breath left for further entreaties.

But the poor boy implored with his eyes! The green fisherman, however, without caring in the least, plunged him five or six times in the flour, until he was white from head to foot and looked like a puppet made of plaster.

He then took him by the head, and . . .

Just as the fisherman was on the point of throwing Pinocchio into the frying pan, a large dog entered the cave, enticed there by the strong and savory odor of fried fish.

"Get out!" shouted the fisherman threateningly, holding the floured puppet in his hand.

But the poor dog, who was as hungry as a wolf, whined and wagged his tail as much as to say:

"Give me a mouthful of fish and I will leave you in peace."

"Get out, I tell you!" repeated the fisherman, and he stretched out his leg to give him a kick.

But the dog, who, when he was really hungry, would not

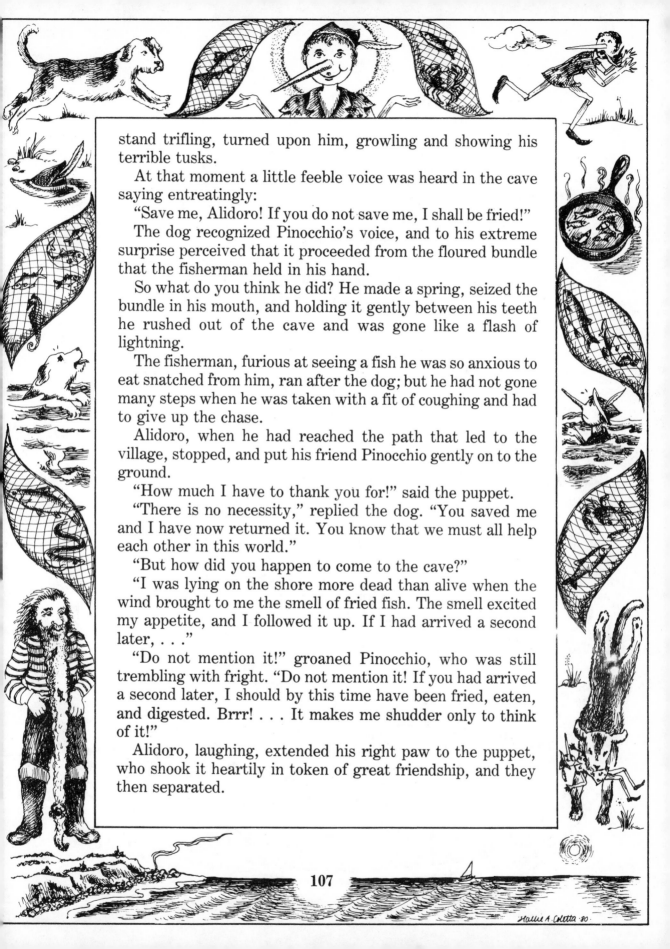

stand trifling, turned upon him, growling and showing his terrible tusks.

At that moment a little feeble voice was heard in the cave saying entreatingly:

"Save me, Alidoro! If you do not save me, I shall be fried!"

The dog recognized Pinocchio's voice, and to his extreme surprise perceived that it proceeded from the floured bundle that the fisherman held in his hand.

So what do you think he did? He made a spring, seized the bundle in his mouth, and holding it gently between his teeth he rushed out of the cave and was gone like a flash of lightning.

The fisherman, furious at seeing a fish he was so anxious to eat snatched from him, ran after the dog; but he had not gone many steps when he was taken with a fit of coughing and had to give up the chase.

Alidoro, when he had reached the path that led to the village, stopped, and put his friend Pinocchio gently on to the ground.

"How much I have to thank you for!" said the puppet.

"There is no necessity," replied the dog. "You saved me and I have now returned it. You know that we must all help each other in this world."

"But how did you happen to come to the cave?"

"I was lying on the shore more dead than alive when the wind brought to me the smell of fried fish. The smell excited my appetite, and I followed it up. If I had arrived a second later, . . ."

"Do not mention it!" groaned Pinocchio, who was still trembling with fright. "Do not mention it! If you had arrived a second later, I should by this time have been fried, eaten, and digested. Brrr! . . . It makes me shudder only to think of it!"

Alidoro, laughing, extended his right paw to the puppet, who shook it heartily in token of great friendship, and they then separated.

SNEAKY BILL

I'm Sneaky Bill, I'm terrible mean and vicious,
I steal all the cashews from the mixed-nuts dishes;
I eat all the icing but I won't touch the cake,
And what you won't give me, I'll go ahead and take.
I gobble up the cherries from everyone's drinks,
And if there's sausages I grab a dozen links;
I take both drumsticks if there's turkey or chicken,
And the biggest strawberries are what I'm pickin';
I make sure I get the finest chop on the plate,
And I'll eat the portions of anyone who's late!

I'm always on the spot before the dinner bell—
I guess I'm pretty awful,
                       but
                          I
                             do
                                eat
                                   well!

William Cole

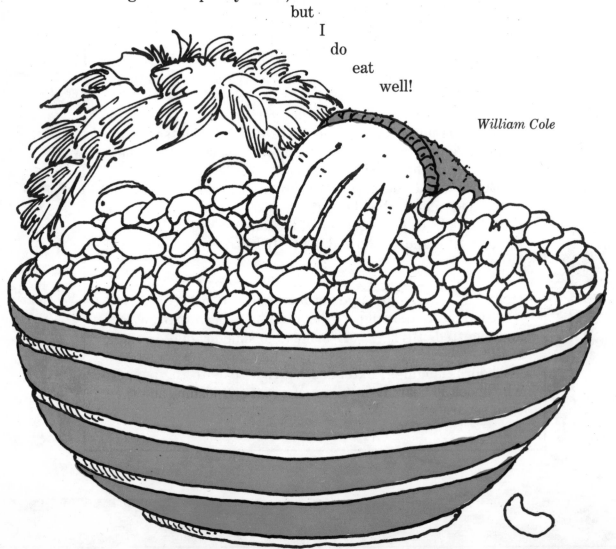

HENRY KING
WHO CHEWED BITS OF STRING, AND WAS EARLY CUT OFF IN DREADFUL AGONIES.

The Chief Defect of Henry King
Was chewing little bits of String.
At last he swallowed some which tied
Itself in ugly Knots inside.
Physicians of the Utmost Fame
Were called at once; but when they came
They answered, as they took their Fees,
"There is no Cure for this Disease.
Henry will very soon be dead."
His Parents stood about his Bed
Lamenting his Untimely Death,
When Henry, with his Latest Breath,
Cried—"Oh, my Friends, be warned by me,
That Breakfast, Dinner, Lunch and Tea
Are all the Human Frame requires . . ."
With that the Wretched Child expires.

Hilaire Belloc

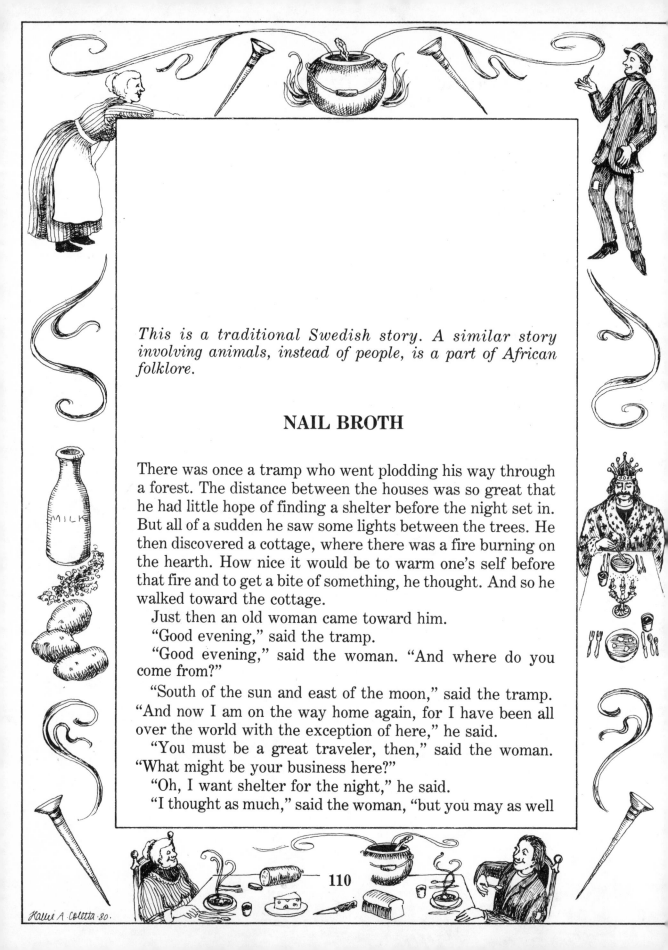

This is a traditional Swedish story. A similar story involving animals, instead of people, is a part of African folklore.

NAIL BROTH

There was once a tramp who went plodding his way through a forest. The distance between the houses was so great that he had little hope of finding a shelter before the night set in. But all of a sudden he saw some lights between the trees. He then discovered a cottage, where there was a fire burning on the hearth. How nice it would be to warm one's self before that fire and to get a bite of something, he thought. And so he walked toward the cottage.

Just then an old woman came toward him.

"Good evening," said the tramp.

"Good evening," said the woman. "And where do you come from?"

"South of the sun and east of the moon," said the tramp. "And now I am on the way home again, for I have been all over the world with the exception of here," he said.

"You must be a great traveler, then," said the woman. "What might be your business here?"

"Oh, I want shelter for the night," he said.

"I thought as much," said the woman, "but you may as well

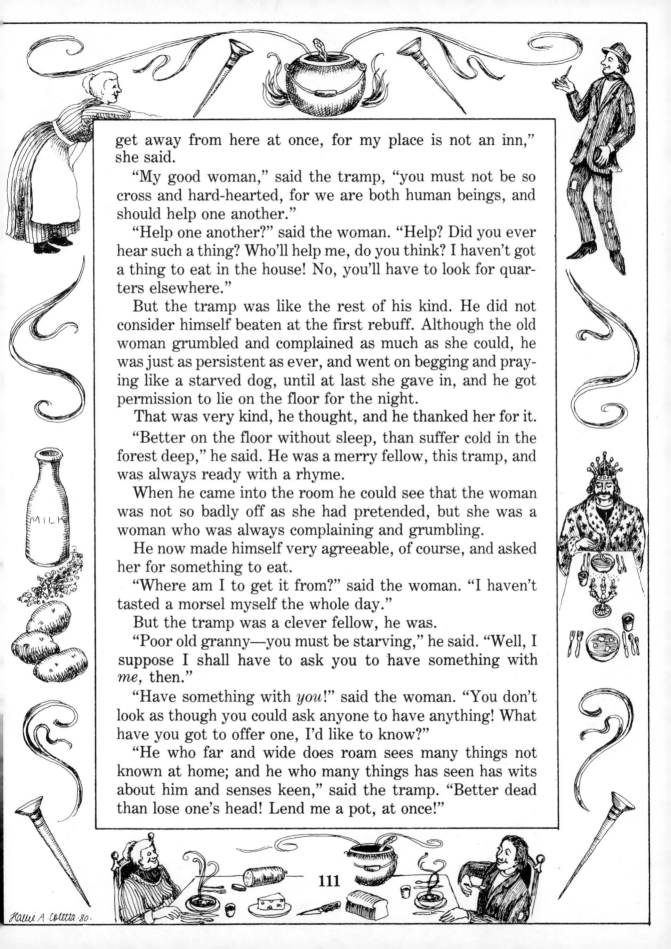

get away from here at once, for my place is not an inn," she said.

"My good woman," said the tramp, "you must not be so cross and hard-hearted, for we are both human beings, and should help one another."

"Help one another?" said the woman. "Help? Did you ever hear such a thing? Who'll help me, do you think? I haven't got a thing to eat in the house! No, you'll have to look for quarters elsewhere."

But the tramp was like the rest of his kind. He did not consider himself beaten at the first rebuff. Although the old woman grumbled and complained as much as she could, he was just as persistent as ever, and went on begging and praying like a starved dog, until at last she gave in, and he got permission to lie on the floor for the night.

That was very kind, he thought, and he thanked her for it.

"Better on the floor without sleep, than suffer cold in the forest deep," he said. He was a merry fellow, this tramp, and was always ready with a rhyme.

When he came into the room he could see that the woman was not so badly off as she had pretended, but she was a woman who was always complaining and grumbling.

He now made himself very agreeable, of course, and asked her for something to eat.

"Where am I to get it from?" said the woman. "I haven't tasted a morsel myself the whole day."

But the tramp was a clever fellow, he was.

"Poor old granny—you must be starving," he said. "Well, I suppose I shall have to ask you to have something with *me*, then."

"Have something with *you*!" said the woman. "You don't look as though you could ask anyone to have anything! What have you got to offer one, I'd like to know?"

"He who far and wide does roam sees many things not known at home; and he who many things has seen has wits about him and senses keen," said the tramp. "Better dead than lose one's head! Lend me a pot, at once!"

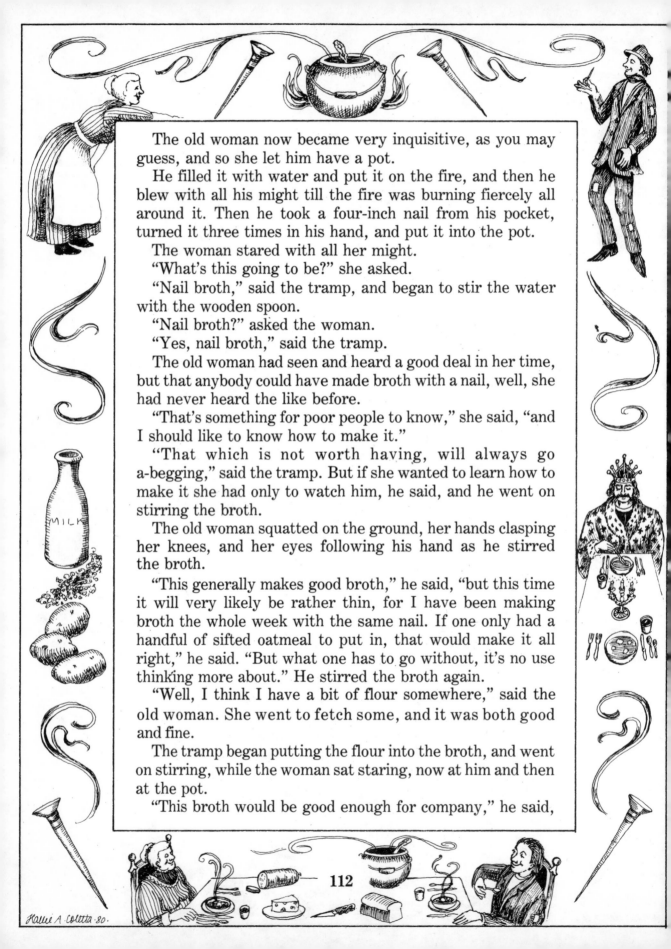

The old woman now became very inquisitive, as you may guess, and so she let him have a pot.

He filled it with water and put it on the fire, and then he blew with all his might till the fire was burning fiercely all around it. Then he took a four-inch nail from his pocket, turned it three times in his hand, and put it into the pot.

The woman stared with all her might.

"What's this going to be?" she asked.

"Nail broth," said the tramp, and began to stir the water with the wooden spoon.

"Nail broth?" asked the woman.

"Yes, nail broth," said the tramp.

The old woman had seen and heard a good deal in her time, but that anybody could have made broth with a nail, well, she had never heard the like before.

"That's something for poor people to know," she said, "and I should like to know how to make it."

"That which is not worth having, will always go a-begging," said the tramp. But if she wanted to learn how to make it she had only to watch him, he said, and he went on stirring the broth.

The old woman squatted on the ground, her hands clasping her knees, and her eyes following his hand as he stirred the broth.

"This generally makes good broth," he said, "but this time it will very likely be rather thin, for I have been making broth the whole week with the same nail. If one only had a handful of sifted oatmeal to put in, that would make it all right," he said. "But what one has to go without, it's no use thinking more about." He stirred the broth again.

"Well, I think I have a bit of flour somewhere," said the old woman. She went to fetch some, and it was both good and fine.

The tramp began putting the flour into the broth, and went on stirring, while the woman sat staring, now at him and then at the pot.

"This broth would be good enough for company," he said,

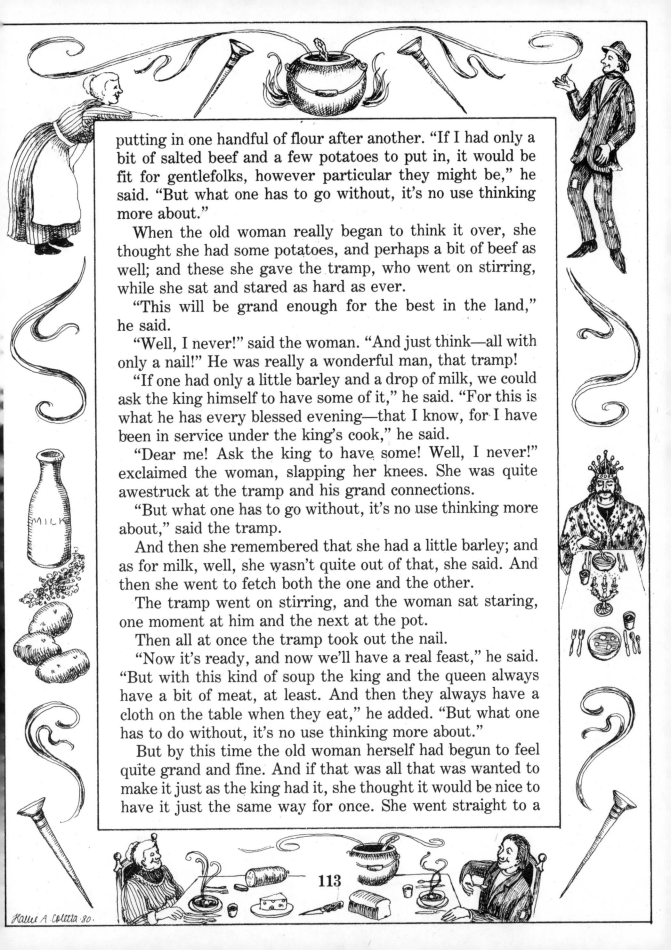

putting in one handful of flour after another. "If I had only a bit of salted beef and a few potatoes to put in, it would be fit for gentlefolks, however particular they might be," he said. "But what one has to go without, it's no use thinking more about."

When the old woman really began to think it over, she thought she had some potatoes, and perhaps a bit of beef as well; and these she gave the tramp, who went on stirring, while she sat and stared as hard as ever.

"This will be grand enough for the best in the land," he said.

"Well, I never!" said the woman. "And just think—all with only a nail!" He was really a wonderful man, that tramp!

"If one had only a little barley and a drop of milk, we could ask the king himself to have some of it," he said. "For this is what he has every blessed evening—that I know, for I have been in service under the king's cook," he said.

"Dear me! Ask the king to have some! Well, I never!" exclaimed the woman, slapping her knees. She was quite awestruck at the tramp and his grand connections.

"But what one has to go without, it's no use thinking more about," said the tramp.

And then she remembered that she had a little barley; and as for milk, well, she wasn't quite out of that, she said. And then she went to fetch both the one and the other.

The tramp went on stirring, and the woman sat staring, one moment at him and the next at the pot.

Then all at once the tramp took out the nail.

"Now it's ready, and now we'll have a real feast," he said. "But with this kind of soup the king and the queen always have a bit of meat, at least. And then they always have a cloth on the table when they eat," he added. "But what one has to do without, it's no use thinking more about."

But by this time the old woman herself had begun to feel quite grand and fine. And if that was all that was wanted to make it just as the king had it, she thought it would be nice to have it just the same way for once. She went straight to a

113

Hallie A. Coletta 80.

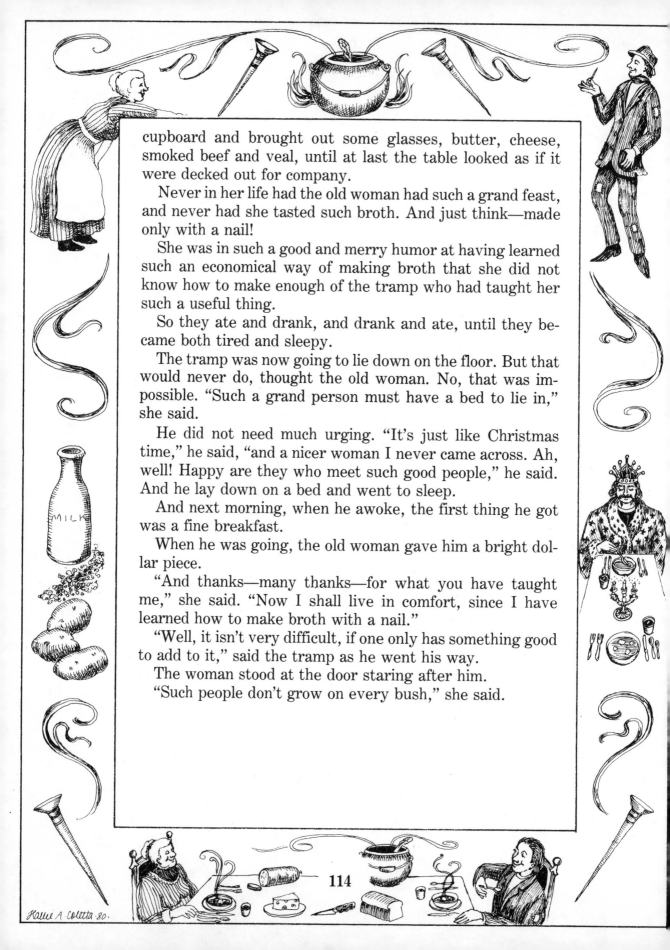

cupboard and brought out some glasses, butter, cheese, smoked beef and veal, until at last the table looked as if it were decked out for company.

Never in her life had the old woman had such a grand feast, and never had she tasted such broth. And just think—made only with a nail!

She was in such a good and merry humor at having learned such an economical way of making broth that she did not know how to make enough of the tramp who had taught her such a useful thing.

So they ate and drank, and drank and ate, until they became both tired and sleepy.

The tramp was now going to lie down on the floor. But that would never do, thought the old woman. No, that was impossible. "Such a grand person must have a bed to lie in," she said.

He did not need much urging. "It's just like Christmas time," he said, "and a nicer woman I never came across. Ah, well! Happy are they who meet such good people," he said. And he lay down on a bed and went to sleep.

And next morning, when he awoke, the first thing he got was a fine breakfast.

When he was going, the old woman gave him a bright dollar piece.

"And thanks—many thanks—for what you have taught me," she said. "Now I shall live in comfort, since I have learned how to make broth with a nail."

"Well, it isn't very difficult, if one only has something good to add to it," said the tramp as he went his way.

The woman stood at the door staring after him.

"Such people don't grow on every bush," she said.

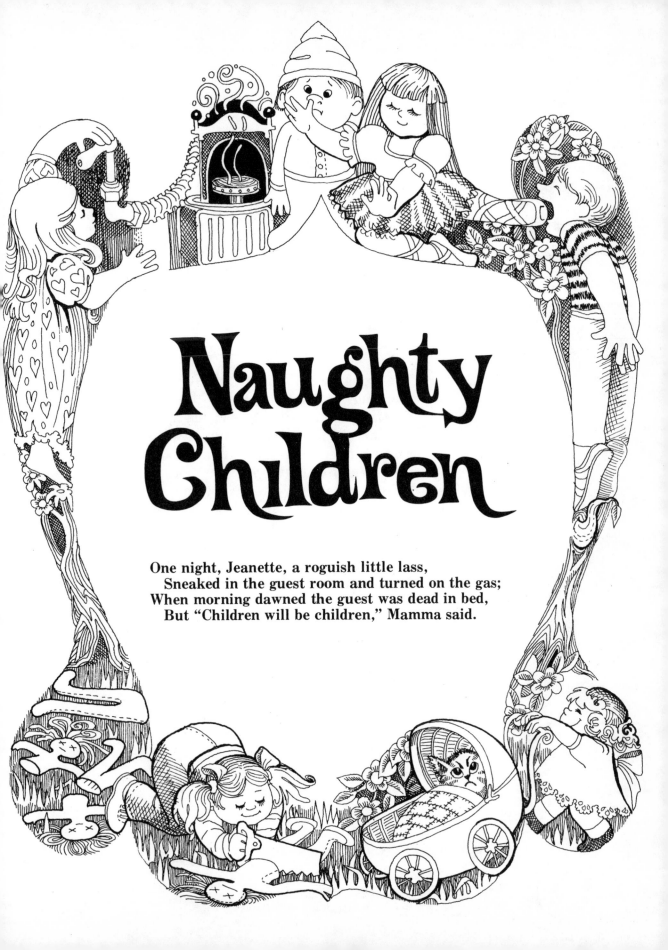

Naughty Children

One night, Jeanette, a roguish little lass,
Sneaked in the guest room and turned on the gas;
When morning dawned the guest was dead in bed,
But "Children will be children," Mamma said.

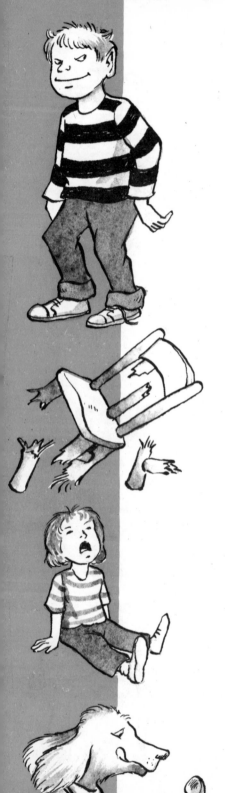

CRUEL FREDERICK

Here is cruel Frederick, see!
A horrid wicked boy was he;
He caught the flies, poor little things,
And then tore off their tiny wings,
He killed the birds, and broke the chairs,
And threw the kitten down the stairs;
And oh! far worse than all beside,
He whipped his Mary, till she cried.

The trough was full, and faithful Tray
Came out to drink one sultry day;
He wagged his tail, and wet his lip,
When cruel Fred snatched up a whip,
And whipped poor Tray till he was sore,
And kicked and whipped him more and more:
At this, good Tray grew very red,
And growled, and bit him till he bled;
Then you should only have been by,
To see how Fred did scream and cry!

So Frederick had to go to bed:
His leg was very sore and red!
The Doctor came, and shook his head,
And made a very great to-do,
And gave him nasty physic too.

But good dog Tray is happy now;
He has no time to say "Bow-wow!"
He seats himself in Frederick's chair
And laughs to see the nice things there:
The soup he swallows, sup by sup—
And eats the pies and puddings up.

SHOCK-HEADED PETER

Shock-headed Peter! There he stands,
With his horrid hair and hands.
See, his nails are never cut;
They are grim'd as black as soot;
And, the sloven, I declare,
He has never comb'd his hair;
Anything to me is sweeter
Than to see Shock-headed Peter.

THE STORY OF LITTLE SUCK-A-THUMB

One day Mamma said "Conrad dear,
I must go out and leave you here.
But mind now, Conrad, what I say,
Don't suck your thumb while I'm away.
The great tall tailor always comes
To little boys who suck their thumbs;
And ere they dream what he's about,
He takes his great sharp scissors out,
And cuts their thumbs clean off—and then,
You know, they never grow again."

Mamma had scarcely turned her back,
The thumb was in, Alack! Alack!

The door flew open, in he ran,
The great, long red-legged scissor-man.
Oh! children, see! the tailor's come
And caught our little Suck-a-Thumb.
Snip! Snap! Snip! the scissors go;
And Conrad cries out "Oh! Oh! Oh!"

Mamma comes home; there Conrad stands,
And looks quite sad, and shows his hands—
"Ah!" said Mamma, "I knew he'd come
To naughty little Suck-a-Thumb."

Heinrich Hoffman

117

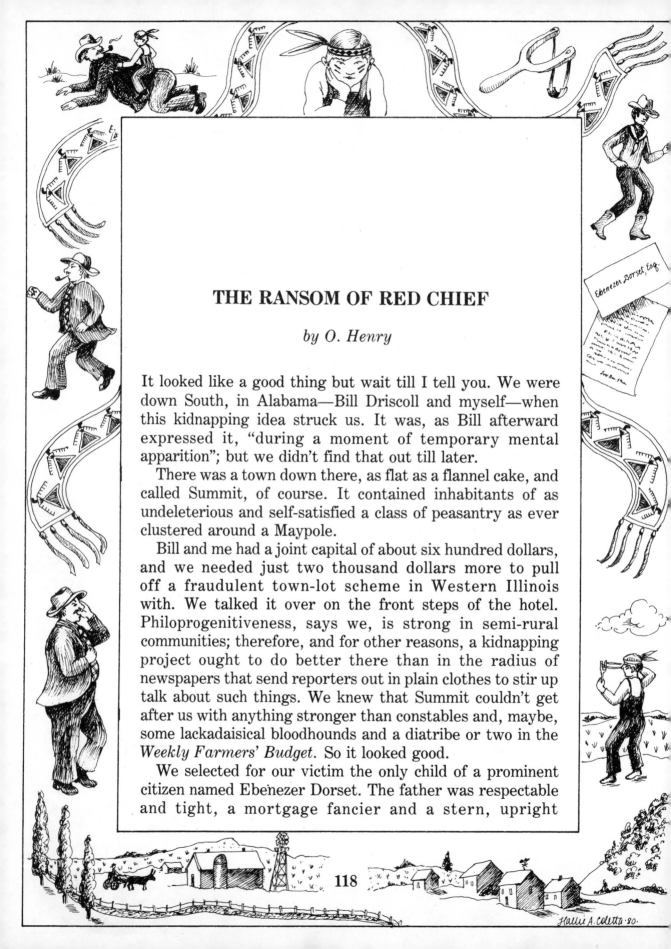

THE RANSOM OF RED CHIEF

by O. Henry

It looked like a good thing but wait till I tell you. We were down South, in Alabama—Bill Driscoll and myself—when this kidnapping idea struck us. It was, as Bill afterward expressed it, "during a moment of temporary mental apparition"; but we didn't find that out till later.

There was a town down there, as flat as a flannel cake, and called Summit, of course. It contained inhabitants of as undeleterious and self-satisfied a class of peasantry as ever clustered around a Maypole.

Bill and me had a joint capital of about six hundred dollars, and we needed just two thousand dollars more to pull off a fraudulent town-lot scheme in Western Illinois with. We talked it over on the front steps of the hotel. Philoprogenitiveness, says we, is strong in semi-rural communities; therefore, and for other reasons, a kidnapping project ought to do better there than in the radius of newspapers that send reporters out in plain clothes to stir up talk about such things. We knew that Summit couldn't get after us with anything stronger than constables and, maybe, some lackadaisical bloodhounds and a diatribe or two in the *Weekly Farmers' Budget*. So it looked good.

We selected for our victim the only child of a prominent citizen named Ebenezer Dorset. The father was respectable and tight, a mortgage fancier and a stern, upright collection-plate passer and forecloser. The kid was a boy of ten, with bas-relief freckles, and hair the color of the cover of the magazine you buy at the newsstand when you want to catch a train. Bill and me figured that Ebenezer would melt down for a ransom of two thousand dollars to a cent. But wait till I tell you.

About two miles from Summit was a little mountain, covered with a dense cedar brake. On the rear elevation of this mountain was a cave. There we stored provisions.

One evening after sundown, we drove in a buggy past old Dorset's house. The kid was in the street, throwing rocks at a kitten on the opposite fence.

"Hey, little boy!" says Bill. "Would you like to have a bag of candy and a nice ride?"

The boy catches Bill neatly in the eye with a piece of brick.

"That will cost the old man an extra five hundred dollars," says Bill, climbing over the wheel.

That boy put up a fight like a welterweight cinnamon bear; but at last we got him down in the bottom of the buggy and drove away. We took him up to the cave, and I hitched the horse in the cedar brake. After dark I drove the buggy to the little village, three miles away, where we had hired it, and walked back to the mountain.

Bill was pasting court plaster over the scratches and bruises on his features. There was a fire burning behind the big rock at the entrance of the cave, and the boy was watching a pot of boiling coffee, with two buzzard tail feathers stuck in his red hair. He points a stick at me when I come up, and says:

"Ha! cursed paleface, do you dare to enter the camp of Red Chief, the terror of the plains?"

"He's all right now," says Bill, rolling up his trousers and examining some bruises on his shins. "We're playing Indian. We're making Buffalo Bill's show look like magic-lantern views of Palestine in the town hall. I'm Old Hank, the Trapper, Red Chief's captive, and I'm to be scalped at daybreak. By Geronimo! that kid can kick hard."

Hallie A. Coletta '80.

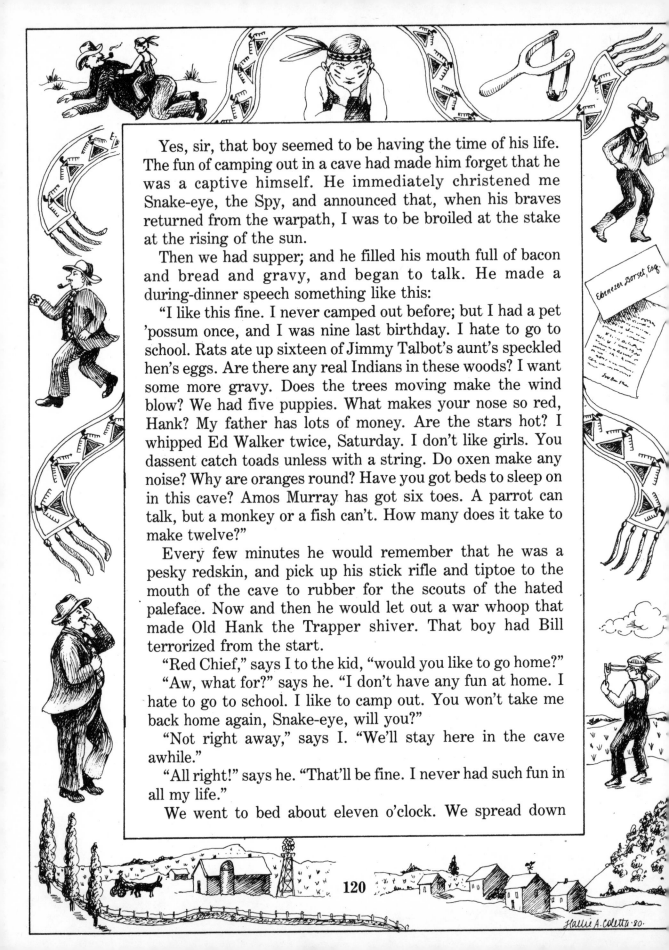

Yes, sir, that boy seemed to be having the time of his life. The fun of camping out in a cave had made him forget that he was a captive himself. He immediately christened me Snake-eye, the Spy, and announced that, when his braves returned from the warpath, I was to be broiled at the stake at the rising of the sun.

Then we had supper; and he filled his mouth full of bacon and bread and gravy, and began to talk. He made a during-dinner speech something like this:

"I like this fine. I never camped out before; but I had a pet 'possum once, and I was nine last birthday. I hate to go to school. Rats ate up sixteen of Jimmy Talbot's aunt's speckled hen's eggs. Are there any real Indians in these woods? I want some more gravy. Does the trees moving make the wind blow? We had five puppies. What makes your nose so red, Hank? My father has lots of money. Are the stars hot? I whipped Ed Walker twice, Saturday. I don't like girls. You dassent catch toads unless with a string. Do oxen make any noise? Why are oranges round? Have you got beds to sleep on in this cave? Amos Murray has got six toes. A parrot can talk, but a monkey or a fish can't. How many does it take to make twelve?"

Every few minutes he would remember that he was a pesky redskin, and pick up his stick rifle and tiptoe to the mouth of the cave to rubber for the scouts of the hated paleface. Now and then he would let out a war whoop that made Old Hank the Trapper shiver. That boy had Bill terrorized from the start.

"Red Chief," says I to the kid, "would you like to go home?"

"Aw, what for?" says he. "I don't have any fun at home. I hate to go to school. I like to camp out. You won't take me back home again, Snake-eye, will you?"

"Not right away," says I. "We'll stay here in the cave awhile."

"All right!" says he. "That'll be fine. I never had such fun in all my life."

We went to bed about eleven o'clock. We spread down

120

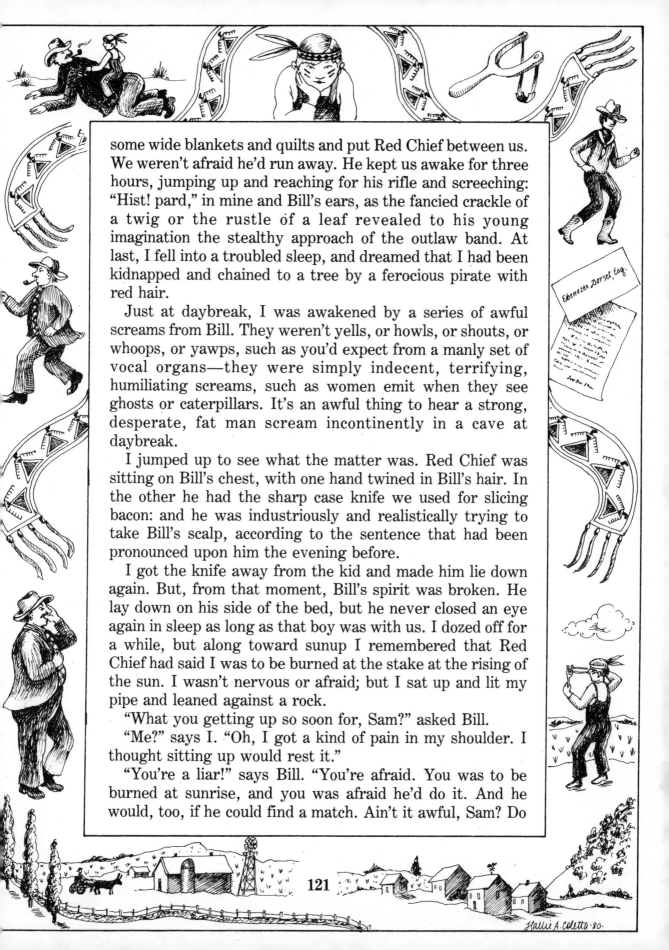

some wide blankets and quilts and put Red Chief between us. We weren't afraid he'd run away. He kept us awake for three hours, jumping up and reaching for his rifle and screeching: "Hist! pard," in mine and Bill's ears, as the fancied crackle of a twig or the rustle of a leaf revealed to his young imagination the stealthy approach of the outlaw band. At last, I fell into a troubled sleep, and dreamed that I had been kidnapped and chained to a tree by a ferocious pirate with red hair.

Just at daybreak, I was awakened by a series of awful screams from Bill. They weren't yells, or howls, or shouts, or whoops, or yawps, such as you'd expect from a manly set of vocal organs—they were simply indecent, terrifying, humiliating screams, such as women emit when they see ghosts or caterpillars. It's an awful thing to hear a strong, desperate, fat man scream incontinently in a cave at daybreak.

I jumped up to see what the matter was. Red Chief was sitting on Bill's chest, with one hand twined in Bill's hair. In the other he had the sharp case knife we used for slicing bacon: and he was industriously and realistically trying to take Bill's scalp, according to the sentence that had been pronounced upon him the evening before.

I got the knife away from the kid and made him lie down again. But, from that moment, Bill's spirit was broken. He lay down on his side of the bed, but he never closed an eye again in sleep as long as that boy was with us. I dozed off for a while, but along toward sunup I remembered that Red Chief had said I was to be burned at the stake at the rising of the sun. I wasn't nervous or afraid; but I sat up and lit my pipe and leaned against a rock.

"What you getting up so soon for, Sam?" asked Bill.

"Me?" says I. "Oh, I got a kind of pain in my shoulder. I thought sitting up would rest it."

"You're a liar!" says Bill. "You're afraid. You was to be burned at sunrise, and you was afraid he'd do it. And he would, too, if he could find a match. Ain't it awful, Sam? Do you think anybody will pay out money to get a little imp like that back home?"

"Sure," said I. "A rowdy kid like that is just the kind that parents dote on. Now, you and the Chief get up and cook breakfast, while I go up on the top of this mountain and reconnoitre."

I went up on the peak of the little mountain and ran my eye over the contiguous vicinity. Over towards Summit I expected to see the sturdy yeomanry of the village armed with scythes and pitchforks beating the countryside for the dastardly kidnappers. But what I saw was a peaceful landscape dotted with one man ploughing with a dun mule. Nobody was dragging the creek: no couriers dashed hither and yon, bringing tidings of no news to the distracted parents. There was a sylvan attitude of somnolent sleepiness pervading that section of the external outward surface of Alabama that lay exposed to my view. "Perhaps," says I to myself, "it has not yet been discovered that the wolves have borne away the tender lambkin from the fold. Heaven help the wolves!" says I, and I went down the mountain to breakfast.

When I got to the cave I found Bill backed up against the side of it, breathing hard, and the boy threatening to smash him with a rock half as big as a cocoanut.

"He put a red-hot boiled potato down my back," explained Bill, "and then mashed it with his foot; and I boxed his ears. Have you got a gun about you, Sam?"

I took the rock away from the boy and kind of patched up the argument. "I'll fix you," says the kid to Bill. "No man ever yet struck the Red Chief but he got paid for it. You better beware!"

After breakfast the kid takes a piece of leather with strings wrapped around it out of his pocket and goes outside the cave unwinding it.

"What's he up to now?" says Bill, anxiously. "You don't think he'll run away, do you, Sam?"

"No fear of it," says I. "He don't seem to be much of a home

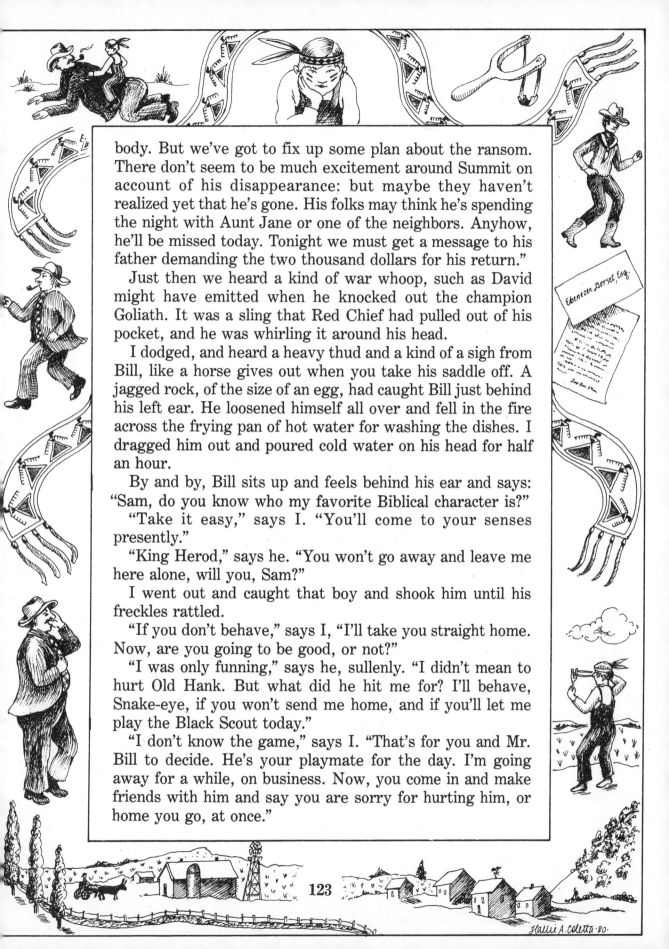

body. But we've got to fix up some plan about the ransom. There don't seem to be much excitement around Summit on account of his disappearance; but maybe they haven't realized yet that he's gone. His folks may think he's spending the night with Aunt Jane or one of the neighbors. Anyhow, he'll be missed today. Tonight we must get a message to his father demanding the two thousand dollars for his return."

Just then we heard a kind of war whoop, such as David might have emitted when he knocked out the champion Goliath. It was a sling that Red Chief had pulled out of his pocket, and he was whirling it around his head.

I dodged, and heard a heavy thud and a kind of a sigh from Bill, like a horse gives out when you take his saddle off. A jagged rock, of the size of an egg, had caught Bill just behind his left ear. He loosened himself all over and fell in the fire across the frying pan of hot water for washing the dishes. I dragged him out and poured cold water on his head for half an hour.

By and by, Bill sits up and feels behind his ear and says: "Sam, do you know who my favorite Biblical character is?"

"Take it easy," says I. "You'll come to your senses presently."

"King Herod," says he. "You won't go away and leave me here alone, will you, Sam?"

I went out and caught that boy and shook him until his freckles rattled.

"If you don't behave," says I, "I'll take you straight home. Now, are you going to be good, or not?"

"I was only funning," says he, sullenly. "I didn't mean to hurt Old Hank. But what did he hit me for? I'll behave, Snake-eye, if you won't send me home, and if you'll let me play the Black Scout today."

"I don't know the game," says I. "That's for you and Mr. Bill to decide. He's your playmate for the day. I'm going away for a while, on business. Now, you come in and make friends with him and say you are sorry for hurting him, or home you go, at once."

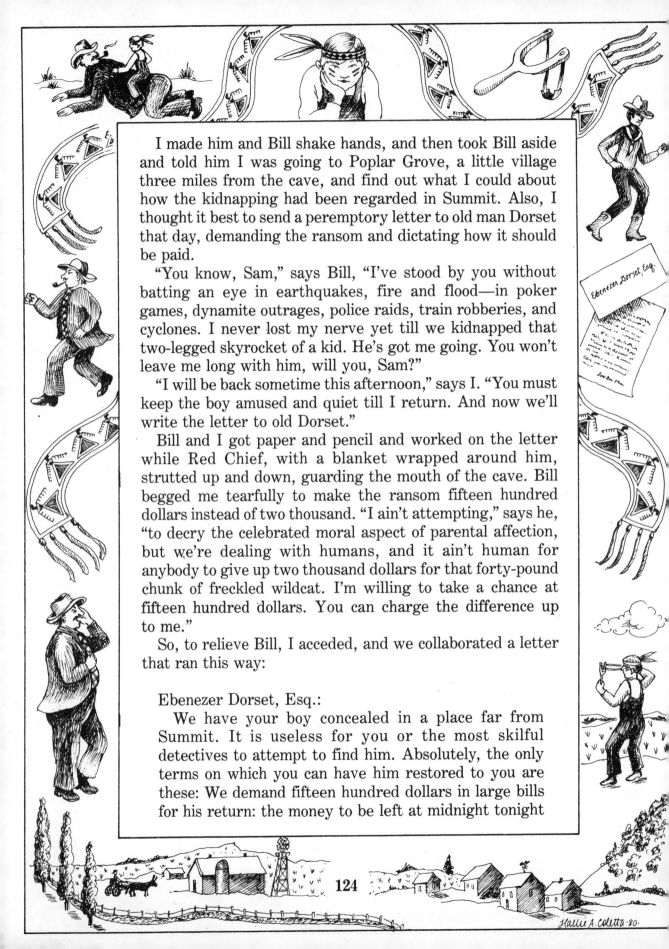

I made him and Bill shake hands, and then took Bill aside and told him I was going to Poplar Grove, a little village three miles from the cave, and find out what I could about how the kidnapping had been regarded in Summit. Also, I thought it best to send a peremptory letter to old man Dorset that day, demanding the ransom and dictating how it should be paid.

"You know, Sam," says Bill, "I've stood by you without batting an eye in earthquakes, fire and flood—in poker games, dynamite outrages, police raids, train robberies, and cyclones. I never lost my nerve yet till we kidnapped that two-legged skyrocket of a kid. He's got me going. You won't leave me long with him, will you, Sam?"

"I will be back sometime this afternoon," says I. "You must keep the boy amused and quiet till I return. And now we'll write the letter to old Dorset."

Bill and I got paper and pencil and worked on the letter while Red Chief, with a blanket wrapped around him, strutted up and down, guarding the mouth of the cave. Bill begged me tearfully to make the ransom fifteen hundred dollars instead of two thousand. "I ain't attempting," says he, "to decry the celebrated moral aspect of parental affection, but we're dealing with humans, and it ain't human for anybody to give up two thousand dollars for that forty-pound chunk of freckled wildcat. I'm willing to take a chance at fifteen hundred dollars. You can charge the difference up to me."

So, to relieve Bill, I acceded, and we collaborated a letter that ran this way:

Ebenezer Dorset, Esq.:

We have your boy concealed in a place far from Summit. It is useless for you or the most skilful detectives to attempt to find him. Absolutely, the only terms on which you can have him restored to you are these: We demand fifteen hundred dollars in large bills for his return: the money to be left at midnight tonight

124

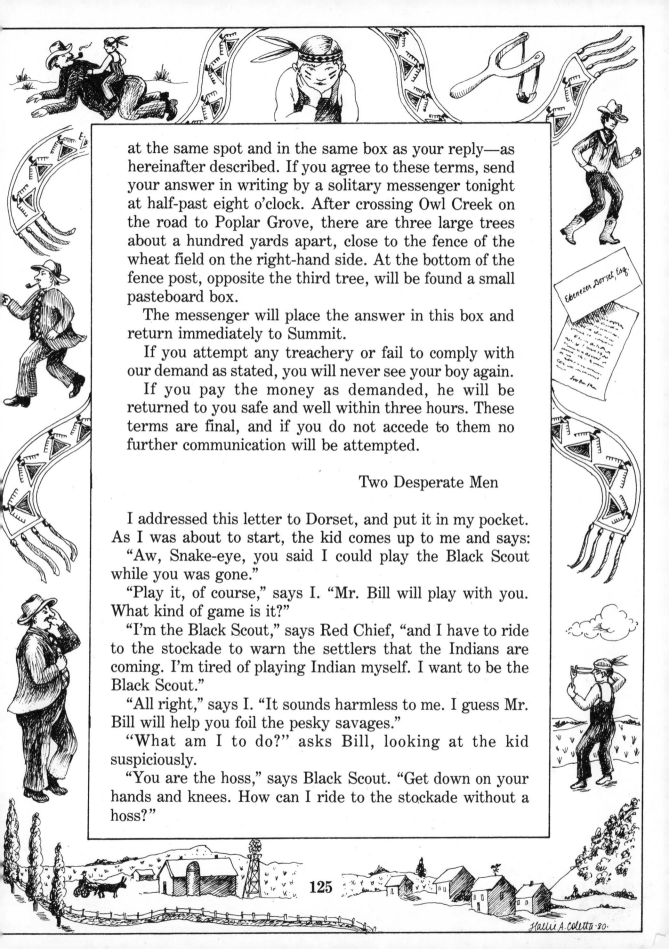

at the same spot and in the same box as your reply—as hereinafter described. If you agree to these terms, send your answer in writing by a solitary messenger tonight at half-past eight o'clock. After crossing Owl Creek on the road to Poplar Grove, there are three large trees about a hundred yards apart, close to the fence of the wheat field on the right-hand side. At the bottom of the fence post, opposite the third tree, will be found a small pasteboard box.

The messenger will place the answer in this box and return immediately to Summit.

If you attempt any treachery or fail to comply with our demand as stated, you will never see your boy again.

If you pay the money as demanded, he will be returned to you safe and well within three hours. These terms are final, and if you do not accede to them no further communication will be attempted.

Two Desperate Men

I addressed this letter to Dorset, and put it in my pocket. As I was about to start, the kid comes up to me and says:

"Aw, Snake-eye, you said I could play the Black Scout while you was gone."

"Play it, of course," says I. "Mr. Bill will play with you. What kind of game is it?"

"I'm the Black Scout," says Red Chief, "and I have to ride to the stockade to warn the settlers that the Indians are coming. I'm tired of playing Indian myself. I want to be the Black Scout."

"All right," says I. "It sounds harmless to me. I guess Mr. Bill will help you foil the pesky savages."

"What am I to do?" asks Bill, looking at the kid suspiciously.

"You are the hoss," says Black Scout. "Get down on your hands and knees. How can I ride to the stockade without a hoss?"

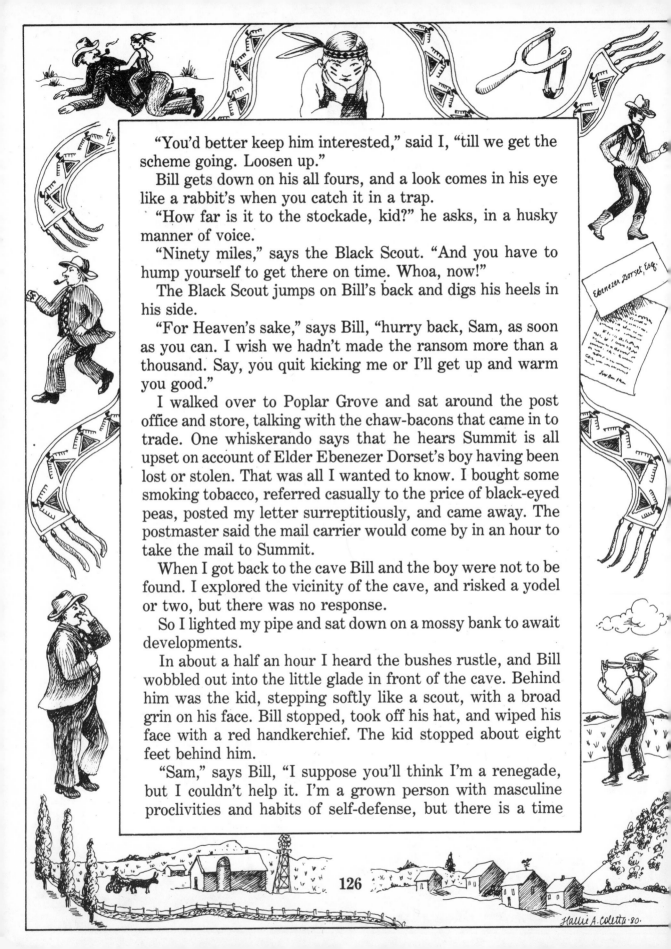

"You'd better keep him interested," said I, "till we get the scheme going. Loosen up."

Bill gets down on his all fours, and a look comes in his eye like a rabbit's when you catch it in a trap.

"How far is it to the stockade, kid?" he asks, in a husky manner of voice.

"Ninety miles," says the Black Scout. "And you have to hump yourself to get there on time. Whoa, now!"

The Black Scout jumps on Bill's back and digs his heels in his side.

"For Heaven's sake," says Bill, "hurry back, Sam, as soon as you can. I wish we hadn't made the ransom more than a thousand. Say, you quit kicking me or I'll get up and warm you good."

I walked over to Poplar Grove and sat around the post office and store, talking with the chaw-bacons that came in to trade. One whiskerando says that he hears Summit is all upset on account of Elder Ebenezer Dorset's boy having been lost or stolen. That was all I wanted to know. I bought some smoking tobacco, referred casually to the price of black-eyed peas, posted my letter surreptitiously, and came away. The postmaster said the mail carrier would come by in an hour to take the mail to Summit.

When I got back to the cave Bill and the boy were not to be found. I explored the vicinity of the cave, and risked a yodel or two, but there was no response.

So I lighted my pipe and sat down on a mossy bank to await developments.

In about a half an hour I heard the bushes rustle, and Bill wobbled out into the little glade in front of the cave. Behind him was the kid, stepping softly like a scout, with a broad grin on his face. Bill stopped, took off his hat, and wiped his face with a red handkerchief. The kid stopped about eight feet behind him.

"Sam," says Bill, "I suppose you'll think I'm a renegade, but I couldn't help it. I'm a grown person with masculine proclivities and habits of self-defense, but there is a time

126

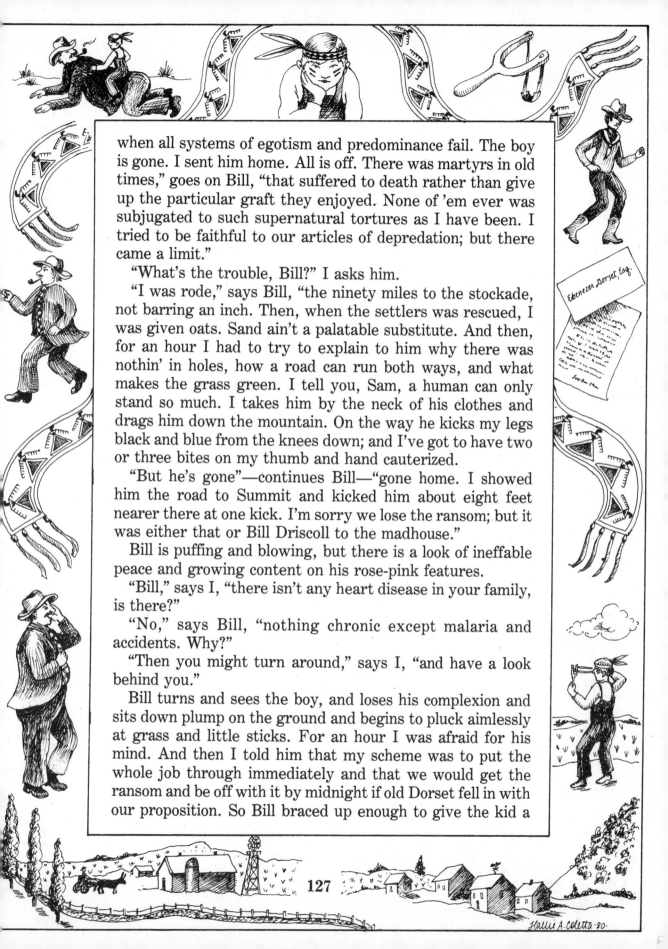

when all systems of egotism and predominance fail. The boy is gone. I sent him home. All is off. There was martyrs in old times," goes on Bill, "that suffered to death rather than give up the particular graft they enjoyed. None of 'em ever was subjugated to such supernatural tortures as I have been. I tried to be faithful to our articles of depredation; but there came a limit."

"What's the trouble, Bill?" I asks him.

"I was rode," says Bill, "the ninety miles to the stockade, not barring an inch. Then, when the settlers was rescued, I was given oats. Sand ain't a palatable substitute. And then, for an hour I had to try to explain to him why there was nothin' in holes, how a road can run both ways, and what makes the grass green. I tell you, Sam, a human can only stand so much. I takes him by the neck of his clothes and drags him down the mountain. On the way he kicks my legs black and blue from the knees down; and I've got to have two or three bites on my thumb and hand cauterized.

"But he's gone"—continues Bill—"gone home. I showed him the road to Summit and kicked him about eight feet nearer there at one kick. I'm sorry we lose the ransom; but it was either that or Bill Driscoll to the madhouse."

Bill is puffing and blowing, but there is a look of ineffable peace and growing content on his rose-pink features.

"Bill," says I, "there isn't any heart disease in your family, is there?"

"No," says Bill, "nothing chronic except malaria and accidents. Why?"

"Then you might turn around," says I, "and have a look behind you."

Bill turns and sees the boy, and loses his complexion and sits down plump on the ground and begins to pluck aimlessly at grass and little sticks. For an hour I was afraid for his mind. And then I told him that my scheme was to put the whole job through immediately and that we would get the ransom and be off with it by midnight if old Dorset fell in with our proposition. So Bill braced up enough to give the kid a weak sort of smile and a promise to play the Russian in a Japanese war with him as soon as he felt a little better.

I had a scheme for collecting that ransom without danger of being caught by counterplots that ought to commend itself to professional kidnappers. The tree under which the answer was to be left—and the money later on—was close to the road fence with big, bare fields on all sides. If a gang of constables should be watching for anyone to come for the note, they could see him a long way off crossing the fields or in the road. But no, sirree! At half-past eight I was up in that tree as well hidden as a tree toad, waiting for the messenger to arrive.

Exactly on time, a half-grown boy rides up the road on a bicycle, locates the pasteboard box at the foot of the fence-post, slips a folded piece of paper into it, and pedals away again back toward Summit.

I waited for an hour and then concluded the thing was square. I slid down the tree, got the note, slipped along the fence until I struck the woods, and was back at the cave in another half an hour. I opened the note, got near the lantern, and read it to Bill. It was written with a pen in a crabbed hand, and the sum and substance of it was this:

Two Desperate Men:

Gentlemen: I received your letter today by post, in regard to the ransom you ask for the return of my son. I think you are a little high in your demands, and I hereby make you a counter-proposition, which I am inclined to believe you will accept. You bring Johnny home and pay me two hundred and fifty dollars in cash, and I agree to take him off your hands. You had better come at night, for the neighbors believe he is lost, and I couldn't be responsible for what they would do to anybody they saw bringing him back. Very respectfully,

Ebenezer Dorset

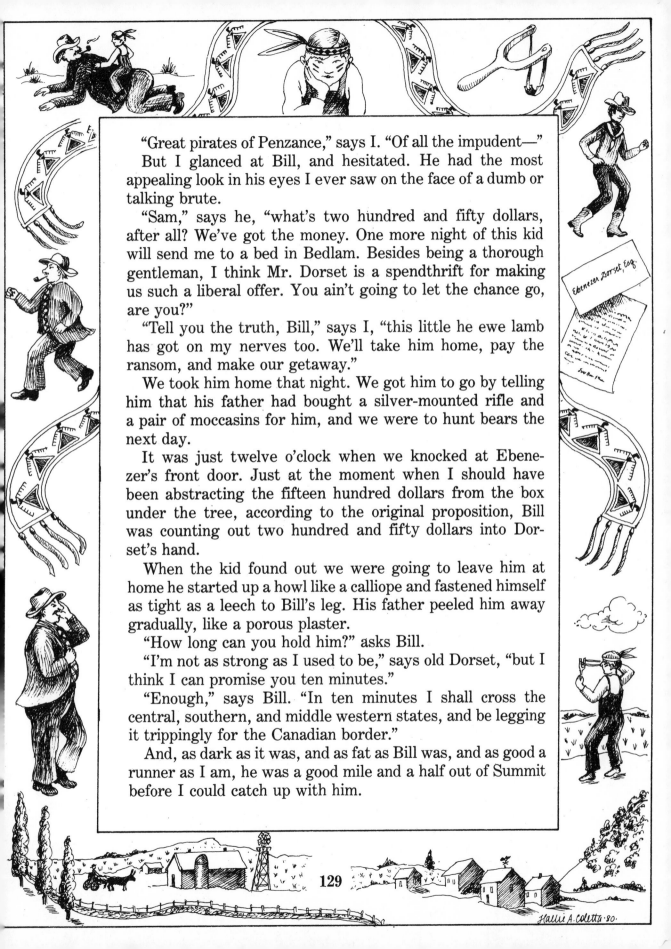

"Great pirates of Penzance," says I. "Of all the impudent—"

But I glanced at Bill, and hesitated. He had the most appealing look in his eyes I ever saw on the face of a dumb or talking brute.

"Sam," says he, "what's two hundred and fifty dollars, after all? We've got the money. One more night of this kid will send me to a bed in Bedlam. Besides being a thorough gentleman, I think Mr. Dorset is a spendthrift for making us such a liberal offer. You ain't going to let the chance go, are you?"

"Tell you the truth, Bill," says I, "this little he ewe lamb has got on my nerves too. We'll take him home, pay the ransom, and make our getaway."

We took him home that night. We got him to go by telling him that his father had bought a silver-mounted rifle and a pair of moccasins for him, and we were to hunt bears the next day.

It was just twelve o'clock when we knocked at Ebenezer's front door. Just at the moment when I should have been abstracting the fifteen hundred dollars from the box under the tree, according to the original proposition, Bill was counting out two hundred and fifty dollars into Dorset's hand.

When the kid found out we were going to leave him at home he started up a howl like a calliope and fastened himself as tight as a leech to Bill's leg. His father peeled him away gradually, like a porous plaster.

"How long can you hold him?" asks Bill.

"I'm not as strong as I used to be," says old Dorset, "but I think I can promise you ten minutes."

"Enough," says Bill. "In ten minutes I shall cross the central, southern, and middle western states, and be legging it trippingly for the Canadian border."

And, as dark as it was, and as fat as Bill was, and as good a runner as I am, he was a good mile and a half out of Summit before I could catch up with him.

A MERRY GAME

Betty and Belinda Ames
    Had the pleasantest of games;
'Twas to hide from one another
    Marmaduke, their baby brother.
Once Belinda, little love,
    Hid the baby in the stove;
Such a joke! for little Bet
    Hasn't found the baby yet.

JOSEPHINE

Josephine, Josephine,
The meanest girl I've ever seen.
Her eyes are red, her hair is green
And she takes baths in gasoline.

Alexander Resnikoff

WILHELMINA MERGENTHALER

Wilhelmina Mergenthaler
Had a lovely ermine collar
Made of just the nicest fur,
That her mamma bought for her.
Once, when mamma was away,
Out a-shopping for the day,
    Wilhelmina Mergenthaler
    Ate her lovely ermine collar.

Harry P. Taber

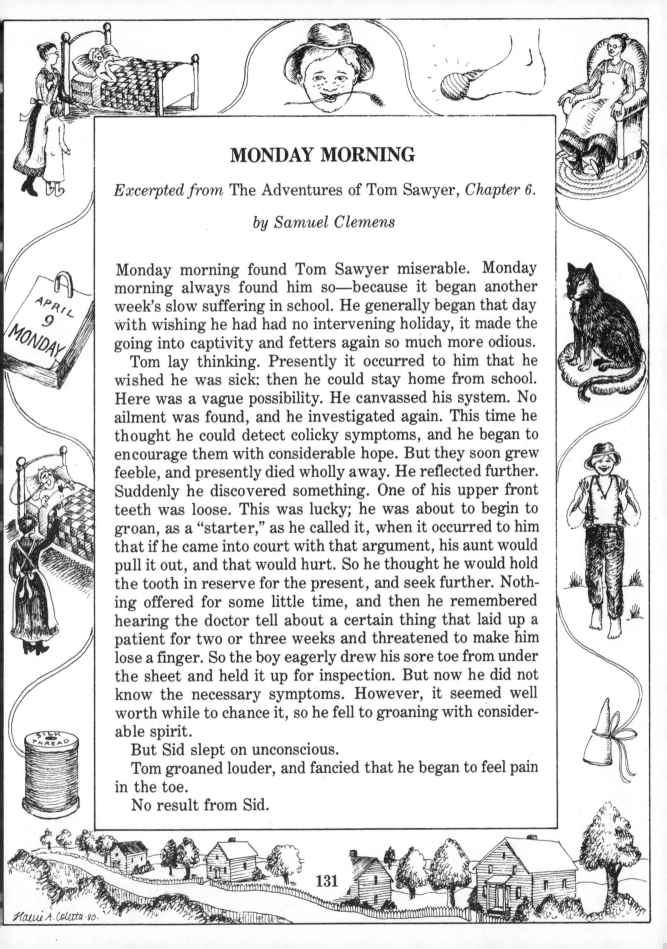

MONDAY MORNING

Excerpted from The Adventures of Tom Sawyer, *Chapter 6.*

by Samuel Clemens

Monday morning found Tom Sawyer miserable. Monday morning always found him so—because it began another week's slow suffering in school. He generally began that day with wishing he had had no intervening holiday, it made the going into captivity and fetters again so much more odious.

Tom lay thinking. Presently it occurred to him that he wished he was sick; then he could stay home from school. Here was a vague possibility. He canvassed his system. No ailment was found, and he investigated again. This time he thought he could detect colicky symptoms, and he began to encourage them with considerable hope. But they soon grew feeble, and presently died wholly away. He reflected further. Suddenly he discovered something. One of his upper front teeth was loose. This was lucky; he was about to begin to groan, as a "starter," as he called it, when it occurred to him that if he came into court with that argument, his aunt would pull it out, and that would hurt. So he thought he would hold the tooth in reserve for the present, and seek further. Nothing offered for some little time, and then he remembered hearing the doctor tell about a certain thing that laid up a patient for two or three weeks and threatened to make him lose a finger. So the boy eagerly drew his sore toe from under the sheet and held it up for inspection. But now he did not know the necessary symptoms. However, it seemed well worth while to chance it, so he fell to groaning with considerable spirit.

But Sid slept on unconscious.

Tom groaned louder, and fancied that he began to feel pain in the toe.

No result from Sid.

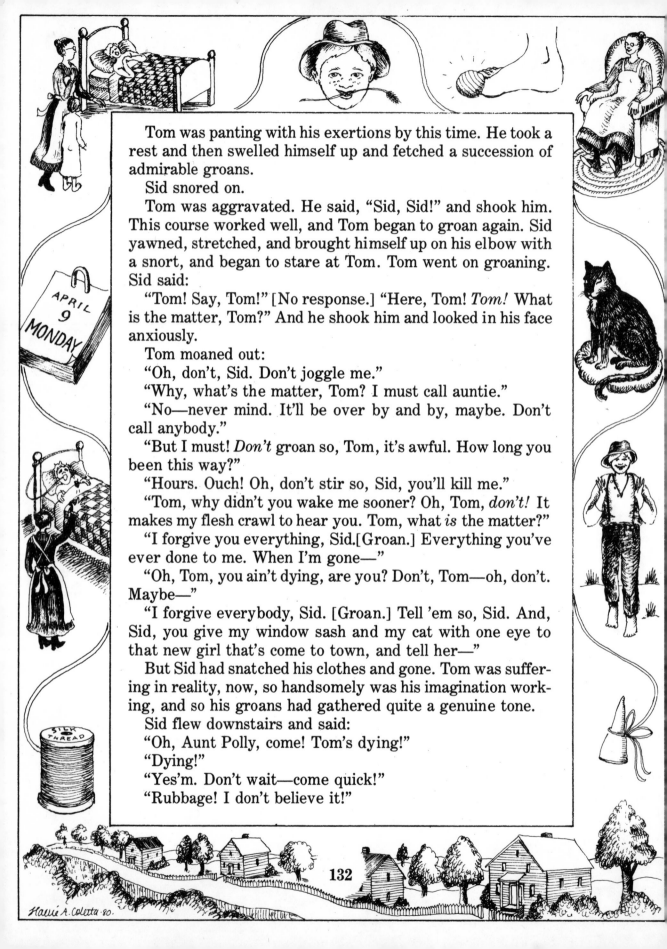

Tom was panting with his exertions by this time. He took a rest and then swelled himself up and fetched a succession of admirable groans.

Sid snored on.

Tom was aggravated. He said, "Sid, Sid!" and shook him. This course worked well, and Tom began to groan again. Sid yawned, stretched, and brought himself up on his elbow with a snort, and began to stare at Tom. Tom went on groaning. Sid said:

"Tom! Say, Tom!" [No response.] "Here, Tom! *Tom!* What is the matter, Tom?" And he shook him and looked in his face anxiously.

Tom moaned out:

"Oh, don't, Sid. Don't joggle me."

"Why, what's the matter, Tom? I must call auntie."

"No—never mind. It'll be over by and by, maybe. Don't call anybody."

"But I must! *Don't* groan so, Tom, it's awful. How long you been this way?"

"Hours. Ouch! Oh, don't stir so, Sid, you'll kill me."

"Tom, why didn't you wake me sooner? Oh, Tom, *don't!* It makes my flesh crawl to hear you. Tom, what *is* the matter?"

"I forgive you everything, Sid. [Groan.] Everything you've ever done to me. When I'm gone—"

"Oh, Tom, you ain't dying, are you? Don't, Tom—oh, don't. Maybe—"

"I forgive everybody, Sid. [Groan.] Tell 'em so, Sid. And, Sid, you give my window sash and my cat with one eye to that new girl that's come to town, and tell her—"

But Sid had snatched his clothes and gone. Tom was suffering in reality, now, so handsomely was his imagination working, and so his groans had gathered quite a genuine tone.

Sid flew downstairs and said:

"Oh, Aunt Polly, come! Tom's dying!"

"Dying!"

"Yes'm. Don't wait—come quick!"

"Rubbage! I don't believe it!"

But she fled upstairs, nevertheless, with Sid and Mary at her heels. And her face grew white, too, and her lip trembled. When she reached the bedside she gasped out:

"You, Tom! Tom, what's the matter with you?"

"Oh, auntie, I'm—"

"What's the matter with you—what *is* the matter with you, child?"

"Oh, auntie, my sore toe's mortified!"

The old lady sank down into a chair and laughed a little, then cried a little, then did both together. This restored her and she said:

"Tom, what a turn you did give me. Now you shut up that nonsense and climb out of this."

The groans ceased and the pain vanished from the toe. The boy felt a little foolish, and he said:

"Aunt Polly, it *seemed* mortified, and it hurt so I never minded my tooth at all."

"Your tooth, indeed! What's the matter with your tooth?"

"One of them's loose, and it aches perfectly awful."

"There, there, now, don't begin that groaning again. Open your mouth. Well, your tooth *is* loose, but you're not going to die about that. Mary, get me a silk thread, and a chunk of fire out of the kitchen."

Tom said:

"Oh, please, auntie, don't pull it out. It don't hurt any more. I wish I may never stir if it does. Please don't, auntie. *I* don't want to stay home from school."

"Oh, you don't, don't you? So all this row was because you thought you'd get to stay home from school and go a-fishing? Tom, Tom, I love you so, and you seem to try every way you can to break my old heart with your outrageousness." By this time the dental instruments were ready. The old lady made one end of the silk thread fast to Tom's tooth with a loop and tied the other to the bedpost. Then she seized the chunk of fire and suddenly thrust it almost into the boy's face. The tooth hung dangling by the bedpost, now.

But all trials bring their compensations. As Tom wended to

Harrie A. Coletta ·80·

school after breakfast, he was the envy of every boy he met because the gap in his upper row of teeth enabled him to expectorate in a new and admirable way. He gathered quite a following of lads interested in the exhibition; and one that had cut his finger and had been a center of fascination and homage up to this time now found himself suddenly without an adherent, and short of his glory. His heart was heavy, and he said with a disdain which he did not feel, that it wasn't anything to spit like Tom Sawyer; but another boy said "Sour grapes!" and he wandered away a dismantled hero.

SCIENCE FOR THE YOUNG

Thoughtful little Willie Frazer
Carved his name with father's razor;
Father, unaware of trouble,
Used the blade to shave his stubble.
Father cut himself severely,
Which pleased little Willie dearly—
"I have fixed my father's razor
So it cuts!" said Willie Frazer.

Arthur with a lighted taper
Touched the fire to grandpa's paper.
Grandpa leaped a foot or higher,
Dropped the sheet and shouted "Fire!"
Arthur, wrapped in contemplation,
Viewed the scene of conflagration.
"This," he said, "confirms my notion—
Heat creates both light and motion."

Mamie often wondered why
Acids trouble alkali—
Mamie, in a manner placid,
Fed the cat boracic acid,
Whereupon the cat grew frantic,
Executing many an antic,
"Ah!" cried Mamie, overjoyed,
"Pussy is an alkaloid!"

Wee, experimental Nina
Dropped her mother's Dresden china
From a seventh-story casement,
Smashing, crashing to the basement.
Nina, somewhat apprehensive,
Said: "This china is expensive,
Yet it proves by demonstration
Newton's law of gravitation."

Wallace Irwin

134

MR. NOBODY

I know a funny little man,
As quiet as a mouse,
Who does the mischief that is done
In everybody's house!
There's no one ever sees his face,
And yet we all agree
That every plate we break was cracked
By Mr. Nobody.

He puts damp wood upon the fire,
That kettles cannot boil;
His are the feet that bring in mud
And all the carpets soil.
The papers always are mislaid—
Who had them last but he?
There's no one tosses them about
But Mr. Nobody.

'Tis he who always tears our books,
Who leaves the door ajar;
He pulls the buttons from our shirts,
And scatters pins afar.
That squeaking door will always squeak
For, prithee, don't you see,
We leave the oiling to be done
By Mr. Nobody.

The finger marks upon the door
By none of us are made;
We never leave the blinds unclosed,
To let the curtains fade.
The ink we never spill, the boots
That lying 'round you see
Are not our boots—they all belong
To Mr. Nobody.

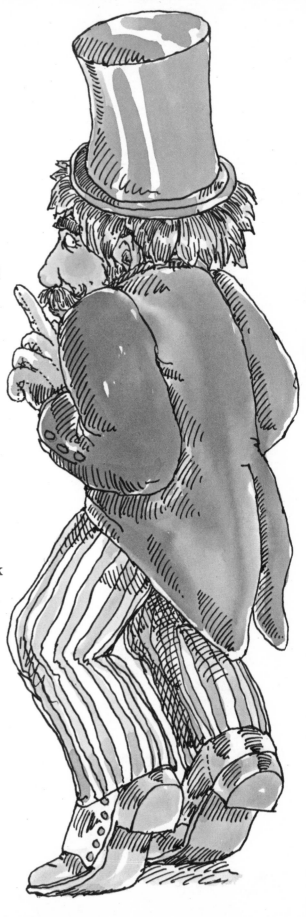

LITTLE WILLIES

Willie, at a passing gent,
Threw a batch of fresh cement
Crying, "Wait until you dry,
Then you'll be a real hard guy."

Little Willie, in bows and sashes,
Fell in the fire and got burned to ashes.
In the winter, when the weather is chilly,
No one likes to poke up Willie.

Willie poisoned his father's tea;
Father died in agony.
Mother came, and looked quite vexed:
"Really, Will," she said, "what next?"

Willie in the cauldron fell;
See the grief on mother's brow!
Mother loved her darling well;
Darling's quite hard-boiled by now.

Willie and two other brats
Licked up all the Rough-on-rats.
Father said, when mother cried,
"Never mind—they'll die outside."

Willie, with a thirst for gore,
Nailed the baby to the door.
Mother said, with humor quaint,
"Willie, dear, don't spoil the paint."

Willie, as the fire burned low,
Gave it a terrific blow.
Grandpa's beard got in the draft;
Dear me, how the firemen laughed!

Into the cistern little Willie
Pushed his little sister Lily.
Mother couldn't find our daughter:
Now we sterilize our water.

Willie, whose ideas are strange,
Put some pinwheels in the range.
When Cook lit the gas next day,
BOY! it was some grand display!!!

MATILDA,

Who told Lies, and was Burned to Death.

Matilda told such Dreadful Lies,
It made one Gasp and Stretch one's Eyes;
Her Aunt, who, from her Earliest Youth,
Had kept a Strict Regard for Truth,
Attempted to Believe Matilda:
The effort very nearly killed her,
And would have done so, had not She
Discovered this Infirmity.
For once, towards the Close of Day,
Matilda, growing tired of play,
And finding she was left alone,
Went tiptoe to the Telephone
And summoned the Immediate Aid
Of London's Noble Fire-Brigade.
Within an hour the Gallant Band
Were pouring in on every hand,
From Putney, Hackney Downs and Bow,
With Courage high and Hearts a-glow
They galloped, roaring through the Town,
"Matilda's House is Burning Down!"
Inspired by British Cheers and Loud
Proceeding from the Frenzied Crowd,
They ran their ladders through a score
Of windows on the Ball Room Floor;
And took Peculiar Pains to Souse
The Pictures up and down the House,
Until Matilda's Aunt succeeded
In showing them they were not needed
And even then she had to pay
To get the Men to go away!

It happened that a few Weeks later
Her Aunt was off to the Theatre
To see that Interesting Play
The Second Mrs. Tanqueray.
She had refused to take her Niece
To hear this Entertaining Piece:
A Deprivation Just and Wise
To Punish her for Telling Lies.
That Night a Fire *did* break out—
You should have heard Matilda Shout!
You should have heard her Scream and Bawl,
And throw the window up and call
To people passing in the Street—
(The rapidly increasing Heat
Encouraging her to obtain
Their confidence)—but all in vain!
For every time She shouted "Fire!"
They only answered "Little Liar!"
And therefore when her Aunt returned,
Matilda and the House were burned.

Hilaire Belloc

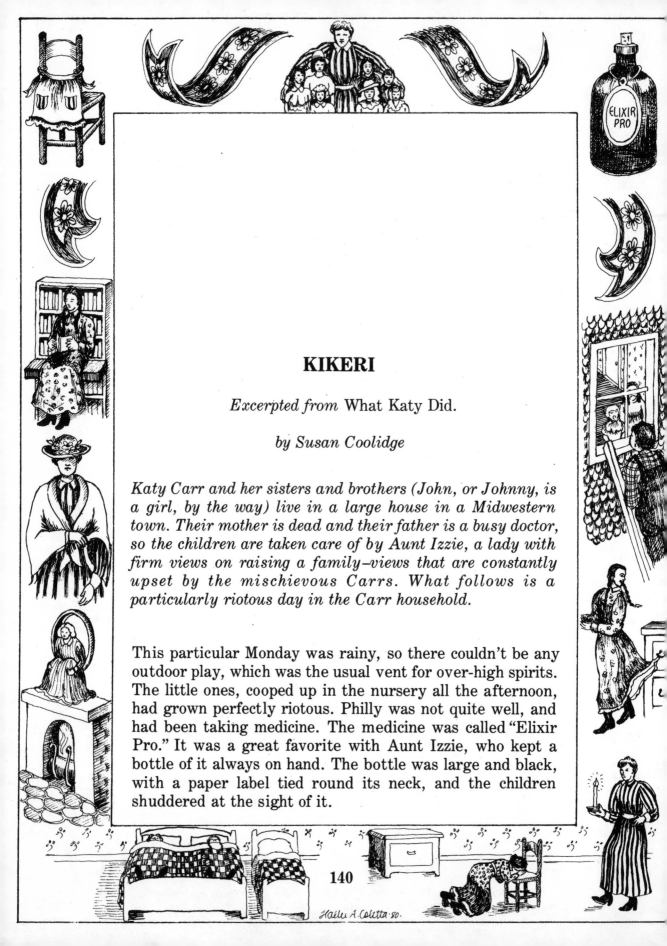

KIKERI

Excerpted from What Katy Did.

by Susan Coolidge

Katy Carr and her sisters and brothers (John, or Johnny, is a girl, by the way) live in a large house in a Midwestern town. Their mother is dead and their father is a busy doctor, so the children are taken care of by Aunt Izzie, a lady with firm views on raising a family—views that are constantly upset by the mischievous Carrs. What follows is a particularly riotous day in the Carr household.

This particular Monday was rainy, so there couldn't be any outdoor play, which was the usual vent for over-high spirits. The little ones, cooped up in the nursery all the afternoon, had grown perfectly riotous. Philly was not quite well, and had been taking medicine. The medicine was called "Elixir Pro." It was a great favorite with Aunt Izzie, who kept a bottle of it always on hand. The bottle was large and black, with a paper label tied round its neck, and the children shuddered at the sight of it.

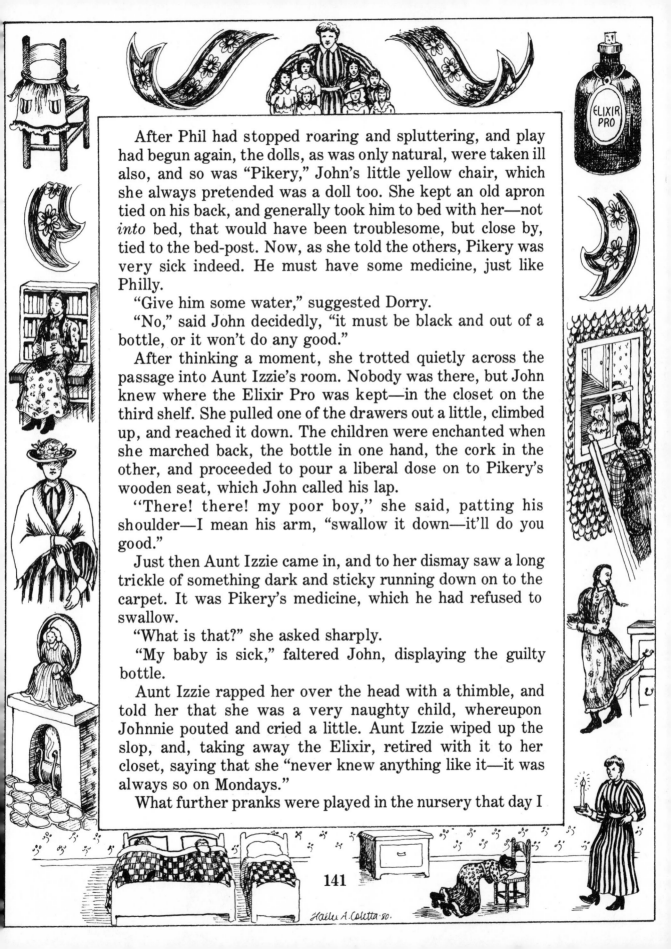

After Phil had stopped roaring and spluttering, and play had begun again, the dolls, as was only natural, were taken ill also, and so was "Pikery," John's little yellow chair, which she always pretended was a doll too. She kept an old apron tied on his back, and generally took him to bed with her—not *into* bed, that would have been troublesome, but close by, tied to the bed-post. Now, as she told the others, Pikery was very sick indeed. He must have some medicine, just like Philly.

"Give him some water," suggested Dorry.

"No," said John decidedly, "it must be black and out of a bottle, or it won't do any good."

After thinking a moment, she trotted quietly across the passage into Aunt Izzie's room. Nobody was there, but John knew where the Elixir Pro was kept—in the closet on the third shelf. She pulled one of the drawers out a little, climbed up, and reached it down. The children were enchanted when she marched back, the bottle in one hand, the cork in the other, and proceeded to pour a liberal dose on to Pikery's wooden seat, which John called his lap.

"There! there! my poor boy," she said, patting his shoulder—I mean his arm, "swallow it down—it'll do you good."

Just then Aunt Izzie came in, and to her dismay saw a long trickle of something dark and sticky running down on to the carpet. It was Pikery's medicine, which he had refused to swallow.

"What is that?" she asked sharply.

"My baby is sick," faltered John, displaying the guilty bottle.

Aunt Izzie rapped her over the head with a thimble, and told her that she was a very naughty child, whereupon Johnnie pouted and cried a little. Aunt Izzie wiped up the slop, and, taking away the Elixir, retired with it to her closet, saying that she "never knew anything like it—it was always so on Mondays."

What further pranks were played in the nursery that day I

Haile A. Coletta. '80.

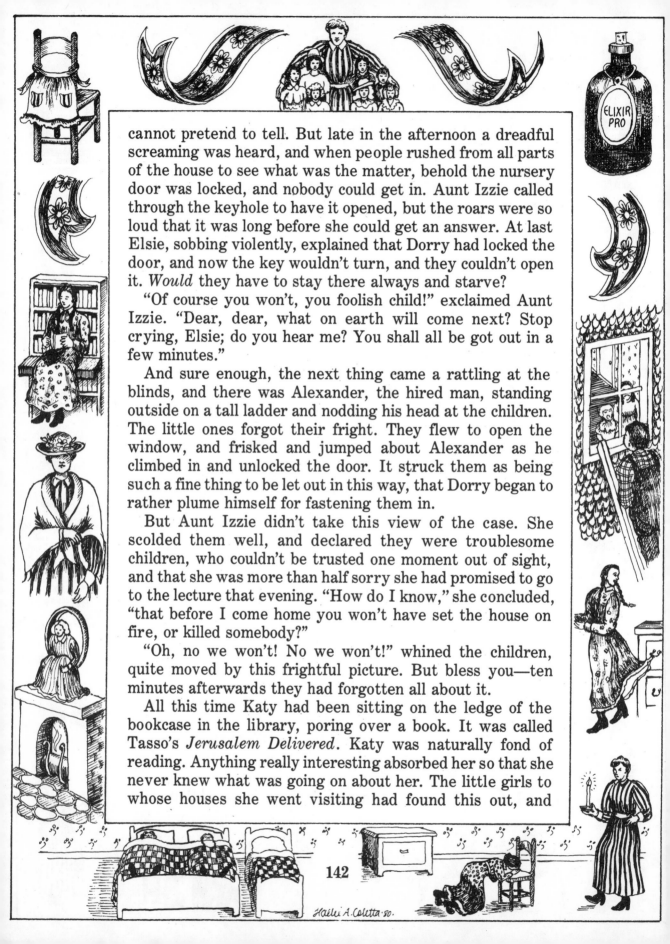

cannot pretend to tell. But late in the afternoon a dreadful screaming was heard, and when people rushed from all parts of the house to see what was the matter, behold the nursery door was locked, and nobody could get in. Aunt Izzie called through the keyhole to have it opened, but the roars were so loud that it was long before she could get an answer. At last Elsie, sobbing violently, explained that Dorry had locked the door, and now the key wouldn't turn, and they couldn't open it. *Would* they have to stay there always and starve?

"Of course you won't, you foolish child!" exclaimed Aunt Izzie. "Dear, dear, what on earth will come next? Stop crying, Elsie; do you hear me? You shall all be got out in a few minutes."

And sure enough, the next thing came a rattling at the blinds, and there was Alexander, the hired man, standing outside on a tall ladder and nodding his head at the children. The little ones forgot their fright. They flew to open the window, and frisked and jumped about Alexander as he climbed in and unlocked the door. It struck them as being such a fine thing to be let out in this way, that Dorry began to rather plume himself for fastening them in.

But Aunt Izzie didn't take this view of the case. She scolded them well, and declared they were troublesome children, who couldn't be trusted one moment out of sight, and that she was more than half sorry she had promised to go to the lecture that evening. "How do I know," she concluded, "that before I come home you won't have set the house on fire, or killed somebody?"

"Oh, no we won't! No we won't!" whined the children, quite moved by this frightful picture. But bless you—ten minutes afterwards they had forgotten all about it.

All this time Katy had been sitting on the ledge of the bookcase in the library, poring over a book. It was called Tasso's *Jerusalem Delivered*. Katy was naturally fond of reading. Anything really interesting absorbed her so that she never knew what was going on about her. The little girls to whose houses she went visiting had found this out, and

142

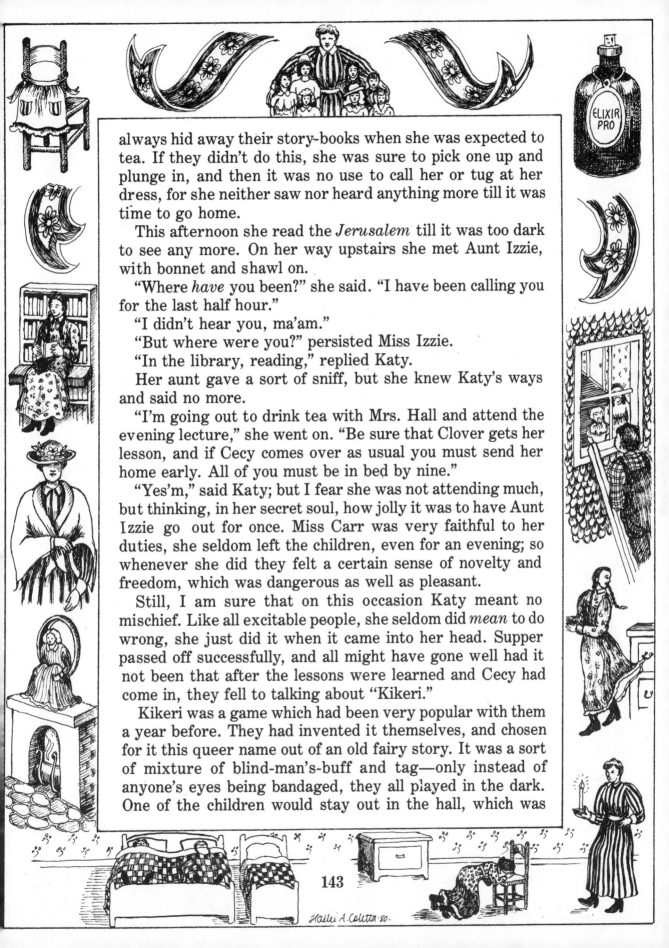

always hid away their story-books when she was expected to tea. If they didn't do this, she was sure to pick one up and plunge in, and then it was no use to call her or tug at her dress, for she neither saw nor heard anything more till it was time to go home.

This afternoon she read the *Jerusalem* till it was too dark to see any more. On her way upstairs she met Aunt Izzie, with bonnet and shawl on.

"Where *have* you been?" she said. "I have been calling you for the last half hour."

"I didn't hear you, ma'am."

"But where were you?" persisted Miss Izzie.

"In the library, reading," replied Katy.

Her aunt gave a sort of sniff, but she knew Katy's ways and said no more.

"I'm going out to drink tea with Mrs. Hall and attend the evening lecture," she went on. "Be sure that Clover gets her lesson, and if Cecy comes over as usual you must send her home early. All of you must be in bed by nine."

"Yes'm," said Katy; but I fear she was not attending much, but thinking, in her secret soul, how jolly it was to have Aunt Izzie go out for once. Miss Carr was very faithful to her duties, she seldom left the children, even for an evening; so whenever she did they felt a certain sense of novelty and freedom, which was dangerous as well as pleasant.

Still, I am sure that on this occasion Katy meant no mischief. Like all excitable people, she seldom did *mean* to do wrong, she just did it when it came into her head. Supper passed off successfully, and all might have gone well had it not been that after the lessons were learned and Cecy had come in, they fell to talking about "Kikeri."

Kikeri was a game which had been very popular with them a year before. They had invented it themselves, and chosen for it this queer name out of an old fairy story. It was a sort of mixture of blind-man's-buff and tag—only instead of anyone's eyes being bandaged, they all played in the dark. One of the children would stay out in the hall, which was

143

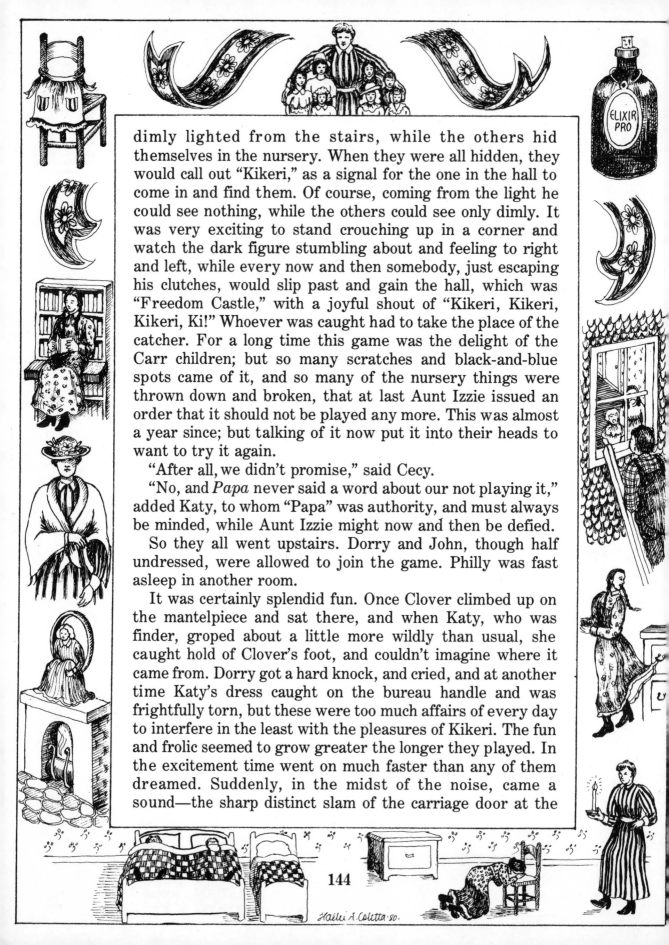

dimly lighted from the stairs, while the others hid themselves in the nursery. When they were all hidden, they would call out "Kikeri," as a signal for the one in the hall to come in and find them. Of course, coming from the light he could see nothing, while the others could see only dimly. It was very exciting to stand crouching up in a corner and watch the dark figure stumbling about and feeling to right and left, while every now and then somebody, just escaping his clutches, would slip past and gain the hall, which was "Freedom Castle," with a joyful shout of "Kikeri, Kikeri, Kikeri, Ki!" Whoever was caught had to take the place of the catcher. For a long time this game was the delight of the Carr children; but so many scratches and black-and-blue spots came of it, and so many of the nursery things were thrown down and broken, that at last Aunt Izzie issued an order that it should not be played any more. This was almost a year since; but talking of it now put it into their heads to want to try it again.

"After all, we didn't promise," said Cecy.

"No, and *Papa* never said a word about our not playing it," added Katy, to whom "Papa" was authority, and must always be minded, while Aunt Izzie might now and then be defied.

So they all went upstairs. Dorry and John, though half undressed, were allowed to join the game. Philly was fast asleep in another room.

It was certainly splendid fun. Once Clover climbed up on the mantelpiece and sat there, and when Katy, who was finder, groped about a little more wildly than usual, she caught hold of Clover's foot, and couldn't imagine where it came from. Dorry got a hard knock, and cried, and at another time Katy's dress caught on the bureau handle and was frightfully torn, but these were too much affairs of every day to interfere in the least with the pleasures of Kikeri. The fun and frolic seemed to grow greater the longer they played. In the excitement time went on much faster than any of them dreamed. Suddenly, in the midst of the noise, came a sound—the sharp distinct slam of the carriage door at the side entrance. Aunt Izzie had returned from her lecture!

The dismay and confusion of that moment! Cecy slipped downstairs like an eel, and fled on the wings of fear along the path which led to her home. Mrs. Hall, as she bade Aunt Izzie good night, and shut Dr. Carr's front door behind her with a bang, might have been struck with the singular fact that a distant bang came from her own front door like a sort of echo. But she was not a suspicious woman; and when she went upstairs there were Cecy's clothes neatly folded on a chair, and Cecy herself in bed, fast asleep, only with a little more colour than usual in her cheeks.

Meantime, Aunt Izzie was on *her* way upstairs, and such a panic prevailed in the nursery! Katy felt it, and basely scuttled off to her own room, where she went to bed with all possible speed. But the others found it much harder to go to bed; there were so many of them, all getting into each other's way, and with no lamp to see by. Dorry and John popped under the clothes half undressed, Elsie disappeared, and Clover, too late for either, and hearing Aunt Izzie's step in the hall, did this horrible thing—fell on her knees, with her face buried in a chair, and began to say her prayers very hard indeed.

Aunt Izzie, coming in with a candle in her hand, stood in the doorway, astonished at the spectacle. She sat down and waited for Clover to get through, while Clover, on her part, didn't dare to get through, but went on repeating, "Now I lay me" over and over again, in a sort of despair. At last Aunt Izzie said very grimly, "That will do, Clover, you can get up!" and Clover rose, feeling like a culprit, which she was, for it was much naughtier to pretend to be praying than to disobey Aunt Izzie and be out of bed after ten o'clock, though I think Clover hardly understood this then.

Aunt Izzie at once began to undress her, and while doing so asked so many questions, that before long she had got at the truth of the whole matter. She gave Clover a sharp scolding, and leaving her to wash her tearful face, she went to the bed where John and Dorry lay, fast asleep, and snoring as

Haili A. Coletta '80.

conspicuously as they knew how. Something strange in the appearance of the bed made her look more closely: she lifted the clothes, and there, sure enough, they were—half dressed, and with their school boots on!

Such a shake as Aunt Izzie gave the little scamps at this discovery would have roused a couple of dormice. Much against their will, John and Dorry were forced to wake up, and be slapped and scolded, and made ready for bed, Aunt Izzie standing over them all the while, like a dragon. She had just tucked them warmly in, when for the first time she missed Elsie.

"Where is my poor little Elsie?" she exclaimed.

"In bed," said Clover meekly.

"In bed!" repeated Aunt Izzie, much amazed. Then, stooping down, she gave a vigorous pull. The trundle-bed came into view and, sure enough, there was Elsie, in full dress, shoes and all, but so fast asleep that not all Aunt Izzie's shakes, and pinches, and calls, were able to rouse her. Her clothes were taken off, her boots unlaced, her nightgown put on; but through it all Elsie slept, and she was the only one of the children who did not get the scolding she deserved that dreadful night.

AND THEIR FAMILIES

Father heard his children scream,
So he threw them in the stream,
Saying, as he drowned the third,
"Children should be seen, not heard!"

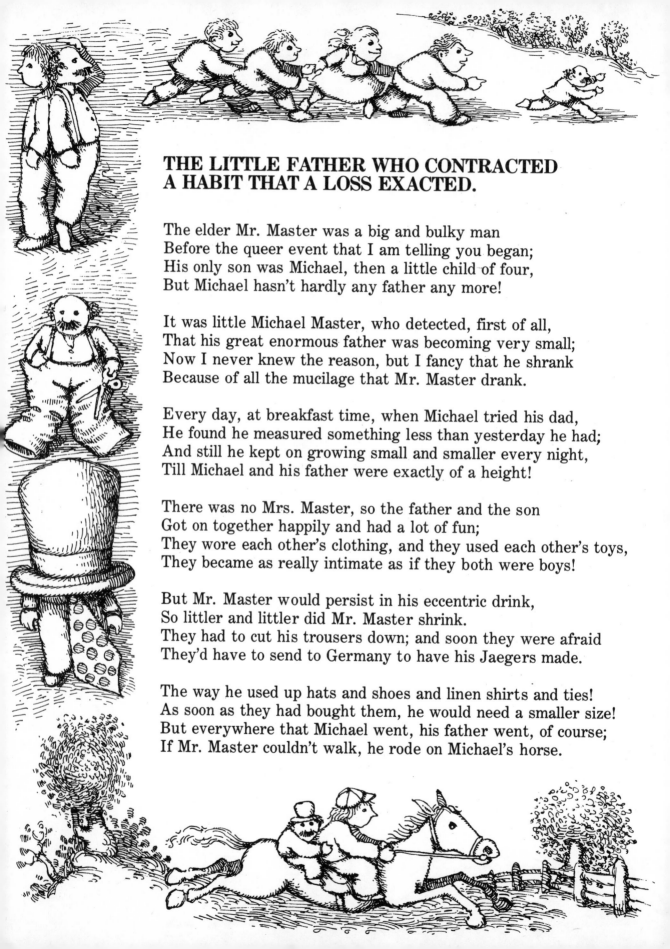

THE LITTLE FATHER WHO CONTRACTED
A HABIT THAT A LOSS EXACTED.

The elder Mr. Master was a big and bulky man
Before the queer event that I am telling you began;
His only son was Michael, then a little child of four,
But Michael hasn't hardly any father any more!

It was little Michael Master, who detected, first of all,
That his great enormous father was becoming very small;
Now I never knew the reason, but I fancy that he shrank
Because of all the mucilage that Mr. Master drank.

Every day, at breakfast time, when Michael tried his dad,
He found he measured something less than yesterday he had;
And still he kept on growing small and smaller every night,
Till Michael and his father were exactly of a height!

There was no Mrs. Master, so the father and the son
Got on together happily and had a lot of fun;
They wore each other's clothing, and they used each other's toys,
They became as really intimate as if they both were boys!

But Mr. Master would persist in his eccentric drink,
So littler and littler did Mr. Master shrink.
They had to cut his trousers down; and soon they were afraid
They'd have to send to Germany to have his Jaegers made.

The way he used up hats and shoes and linen shirts and ties!
As soon as they had bought them, he would need a smaller size!
But everywhere that Michael went, his father went, of course;
If Mr. Master couldn't walk, he rode on Michael's horse.

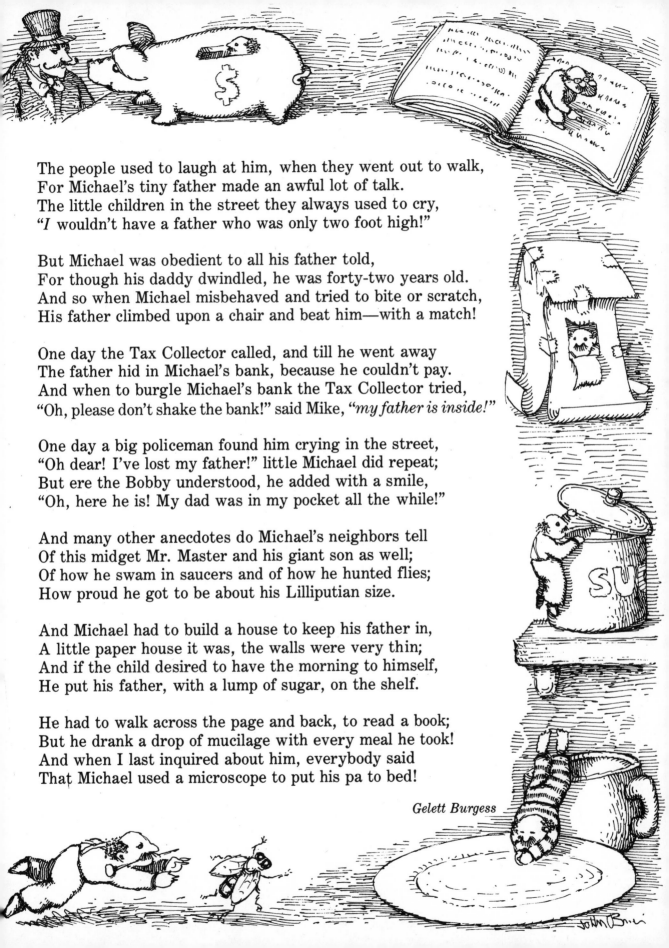

The people used to laugh at him, when they went out to walk,
For Michael's tiny father made an awful lot of talk.
The little children in the street they always used to cry,
"*I* wouldn't have a father who was only two foot high!"

But Michael was obedient to all his father told,
For though his daddy dwindled, he was forty-two years old.
And so when Michael misbehaved and tried to bite or scratch,
His father climbed upon a chair and beat him—with a match!

One day the Tax Collector called, and till he went away
The father hid in Michael's bank, because he couldn't pay.
And when to burgle Michael's bank the Tax Collector tried,
"Oh, please don't shake the bank!" said Mike, *"my father is inside!"*

One day a big policeman found him crying in the street,
"Oh dear! I've lost my father!" little Michael did repeat;
But ere the Bobby understood, he added with a smile,
"Oh, here he is! My dad was in my pocket all the while!"

And many other anecdotes do Michael's neighbors tell
Of this midget Mr. Master and his giant son as well;
Of how he swam in saucers and of how he hunted flies;
How proud he got to be about his Lilliputian size.

And Michael had to build a house to keep his father in,
A little paper house it was, the walls were very thin;
And if the child desired to have the morning to himself,
He put his father, with a lump of sugar, on the shelf.

He had to walk across the page and back, to read a book;
But he drank a drop of mucilage with every meal he took!
And when I last inquired about him, everybody said
That Michael used a microscope to put his pa to bed!

Gelett Burgess

BROTHER'S HASH

To settle a brother's hash, boil his tennis hat for fifteen minutes. Hang in the pantry to cool.

Then lay his four favorite comic books on the kitchen table and spread mustard on page 14 of the first, page 19 of the second, page 28 of the third, and page 35 of the fourth. While the mustard is drying, cut the erasers off all his pencils, place in an ovenproof dish, garnish with his rawhide bootlaces, and bake slowly in a moderate oven until brown.

Place in the cooled but sodden tennis hat, the following:

> *his jackknife*
> *one of the casters from his bed*
> *his rattlesnake skin*
> *his arrowheads*
> *his World War I ammunition pouch*
> *the key to his tin cashbox*
> *the autographed baseball he borrowed from Joe*
> *   Anders*

Stir in the baked erasers and rawhide laces. Set on the window sill to solidify.

Then fry his new sneakers in salad oil until crisp, pour two tablespoons of maple syrup into the toes of his hiking boots, and drop his baseball cards into one quart of lukewarm water to soak. While the cards are melting, eat a slice of cake, guzzle a Coca-Cola, and, stuffing your pockets with nuts and oranges, climb to the top of the maple tree in the backyard. Do not come down until late that night after the whole family, wandering through the fields with flashlights, calling and searching, has become frantic, and your brother, standing under the tree beside your mother (who is sniveling into her apron), says, "Gee, if he'd only come back, I wouldn't even be mad at him for what he did." Then rumple your hair, rip your shirttail, roll up one trouser leg, smudge your cheeks with crumbled bark, and clamber clumsily down.

Thomas Rockwell

The Proper way to Leave a Room
Is not to Plunge it into Gloom;

Just Make a Joke Before you Go,
And Then Escape Before They Know.

Gelett Burgess

BROTHER AND SISTER

"SISTER, sister, go to bed!
Go and rest your weary head."
Thus the prudent brother said.

"Do you want a battered hide,
Or scratches to your face applied?"
Thus his sister calm replied.

"Sister, do not raise my wrath.
I'd make you into mutton broth
As easily as kill a moth!"

The sister raised her beaming eye
And looked on him indignantly
And sternly answered, "Only try!"

Off to the cook he quickly ran.
"Dear Cook, please lend a frying-pan
To me as quickly as you can."

"And wherefore should I lend it you?"
"The reason, Cook, is plain to view.
I wish to make an Irish stew."

"What meat is in that stew to go?"
"My sister'll be the contents!"
                              "Oh!"
"You'll lend the pan to me, Cook?"
                              "No!"

Moral: Never stew your sister.

Lewis Carroll

BROTHER

I had a little brother
And I brought him to my mother
And I said I want another
Little brother for a change.

But she said don't be a bother
So I took him to my father
And I said this little bother
Of a brother's very strange.

But he said one little brother
Is exactly like another
And every little brother
Misbehaves a bit he said.

So I took the little bother
From my mother and father
And I put the little bother
Of a brother back to bed.

Mary Ann Hoberman

CHILDREN WHEN THEY'RE VERY SWEET

Children, when they're very sweet,
Only bite and scratch and kick
A very little. Just enough
To show their parents they're not sick.

After all if children *should*
(By some horrible mistake)
Be entirely good all day
Every parent's heart would ache.

"Our little monsters must be ill:
They're much too well behaved!
Call the doctor! Do it quick!
Maybe they can still be saved!

". . . Wait! They're looking better now.
Johnny just kicked Billy's shin!
Betty just bit Teddy's ear!
Jane just stuck me with a pin!

"There! The little dears are fit
As sharks and crocodiles, you'll find.
No need for the doctor now:
Get a stick and make them mind!"

John Ciardi

ADVICE TO GRANDSONS

When grandma visits you, my dears,
  Be good as you can be;
Don't put hot waffles in her ears,
  Or beetles in her tea.

Don't sew a pattern on her cheek
  With worsted or with silk;
Don't call her naughty names in Greek,
  Or spray her face with milk.

Don't drive a staple in her foot,
  Don't stick pins in her head;
And, oh, I beg you, do not put
  Live embers in her bed.

These things are not considered kind;
  They worry her, and tease—
Such cruelty is not refined
  It always fails to please.

Be good to grandma, little chaps,
  Whatever else you do:
And then she'll grow to be—perhaps—
  More tolerant of you.

OH, NO!

Oh, no!
'Tisn't so!
Papa's watch
Won't go?

It *must* go—
Guess I know!
Last night
I wound it tight,
And greased it nice
With camphor-ice.

Mary Mapes Dodge

THE PARENT

Children aren't happy
    with nothing to ignore,
And that's what parents
    were created for.

Ogden Nash

DADDY FELL INTO THE POND

Everyone grumbled. The sky was grey.
We had nothing to do and nothing to say.
We were nearing the end of a dismal day,
And there seemed to be nothing beyond,

THEN
Daddy fell into the pond!

And everyone's face grew merry and bright,
And Timothy danced for sheer delight.
"Give me the camera, quick, oh quick!
He's crawling out of the duckweed." *Click!*

Then the gardener suddenly slapped his knee,
And doubled up, shaking silently,
And the ducks all quacked as if they were daft,
And it sounded as if the old drake laughed.

O, there wasn't a thing that didn't respond

WHEN
Daddy fell into the pond!

Alfred Noyes

156

Ghoulies and Beasties

From Ghoulies and Ghosties,
And long-leggity Beasties,
And all things that go bump
   in the night,
Good Lord deliver us.

THE KNOCKMANY GIANT

by Sean Kelly

Speaking of Fin McCool, have you heard about himself, his wife Oona and the Giant Cucullin? You haven't?

Well, listen.

They say this Cucullin was a terrific size, at least three times the height of Fin, which would have put his head up about forty feet above the ground, can you believe it?

Me neither.

But the truth of it is, Cucullin must have been big enough, and strong enough, for it's well known that he carried a thunderbolt around in his pocket. He'd flattened the thing out one time with just a blow of his fist. Bam!—like that. Just showing off, he was, which will give you some idea of his character, as well.

For a long time, Cucullin had been bragging and noising it about that he wanted to flatten your man McCool, as well, Fin being the only giant in Ireland he hadn't already fought and beaten.

But Fin kept out of Cucullin's way. As a matter of fact, he and Oona moved their house up to the top of windy and waterless Knockmany, the highest hill in the kingdom, so as to keep a sharp look-out against the coming of Cucullin, the better for Fin to stay out of his way.

Not that Fin McCool was afraid. It was only that he had no wish to go and spoil another fellow's perfect record.

Now, of course, the secret of Fin's great gifts and of his power lay in his thumb; the one he'd scorched as a lad on the Salmon of Wisdom while he was cooking that Fairy Fish for the wizard's breakfast. From that time on, Fin had only to suck his thumb to become clever and far-seeing. But everyone knows that old tale.

Anyway, the day came when Oona found Fin with his thumb stuck in his mouth, and a worried look to him.

"He's coming," said Fin. "I can see him for sure."

"Who's coming, Fin darling?" asked Oona, as if she didn't know.

"Cucullin," said he, and the way he spoke Oona knew that her poor hero of a husband had no idea what to do about it, at all.

"If I fight him, I'm sure to lose," Fin was thinking, "and if I run away, I'll be disgraced in the sight of my people, and me the best man among them. . . ."

"When will he be here?" she asked.

"Tomorrow, at two o'clock," Fin said.

"You just do as I tell you, Fin my love, and leave this Cucullin to me," said his wife. "For haven't I always been the one to get you out of your troubles?"

"You have," said Fin, and he almost gave up his worried shivering and shaking, remembering that his wife, like most women, was well-connected among the Fairy Folk, and could be counted upon for a clever trick or two in time of need.

Then what did she do but make a high smoke on the hilltop, and give out three loud whistles, so Cucullin would know he was invited up, for that was the way the Irish of those days would give a sign to strangers that they were welcome to share a meal, don't you know?

And no sooner had she done that, than she was off, round to the neighbors at the foot of the mountain, borrowing from them no less than one-and-twenty iron griddles! You know the things I mean. Grid-irons, skillets, fry pans, whatever you call them.

When she brought those back up to the house, she went and baked up twenty-four flat cakes, and inside twenty-one of them—listen now— she put one of those hard iron pans!

Then she put them all aside on a shelf to cool, very neatly, so she'd remember which was which.

Just before two o'clock, as Fin's magic thumb had foretold, here comes Cucullin, marching up Knockmany mountain. At the sight of the great bulk of him, Fin nearly commenced his quaking again. But Oona, calm as a sheep, hands her husband a bonnet and a blanket, and points to the cradle she'd brought out, and says, "Now you must pass for your own child, my darling. So lie down there snug, and suck your thumb if you like, and not a word out of you."

As you may imagine, many a brave and angry thought roared 'round Fin's brain as she tucked him in.

Now, here comes Cucullin, stooping low to pass through the door of the house.

"Good day," he says, bold as brass. "Would you be the wife of the great Fin McCool?"

"I am, and proud of it," says she.

"And is himself at home now?" asks the giant.

"He isn't," answers Oona. "Not five minutes ago, he got word that some pitiful wretch of a giant named Cucullin was in the neighborhood, and off he ran in a terrible rage to beat the poor creature to a pulp."

"I am Cucullin," says he, proud as punch.

"Are you now?" says Oona, and begins to laugh to herself, as if to say, "You poor little handful of a man."

"Did you ever see Fin?" she says, changing her manner all at once.

"How could I?" says the giant, "He's never given me the chance."

"Well, it's your bad luck you'll have your chance soon enough," says Oona, "but in the meantime, that's a terrible wind rattling the front door there, and I was wondering if you'd be so kind as to go out for a minute and turn the house around? That's what my Fin always does, when he's at home."

Now, that was a stunner, even for Cucullin. But up he got, and went out of the house. Then he did the strangest thing. Listen to this, now. He pulled the middle finger of his right hand till it cracked three times. Then doesn't he wrap his arms about the house and turn it altogether around, as he'd been asked.

When Fin saw that, he trembled in his cradle, and pulled the blanket up to his eyes. But Oona only smiled.

"My thanks to you," she says, "and if you've a mind to do me another little favor, it's this. After this stretch of dry weather we've been having, we're badly off up here for want of water. Fin tells me there's a fine spring-well under the rocks behind the hill, but before he could tear them apart, this day, he heard of your coming, and off he ran in his fury. I'd take it as a kindness if you were to find it," says she, still smiling her sweet girlish smile.

And she showed Cucullin the spot, there on the mountainside, which was one great piece of solid rock, don't you know? Well, he looks at it a while, and then he cracks his right middle finger no less than nine times, mind you, and doesn't he tear a cleft in the rock about four hundred feet deep and a quarter of a mile in length? And then, of course, the water comes gushing out.

Lumford's Glen, they call that place now. But perhaps you've seen it yourself? Well, you should.

Anyway, by now, Fin's shaking and sweating in his cradle. But then Oona leans over to him, like a mother, and she whispers, "Did you see that business he does with the middle finger of his right hand, darling? It's there that's the secret of this bully-boy's power, and no mistake!"

"Hush, now, little one," she says, for the giant's benefit, who'd just come back in with a pitcher of water. "Sit you down, Cucullin," she turns to him and says, "and eat a bite, won't you? Have one of these little cakes here, while I put the bacon on to boil."

Just like your typical giant, Cucullin was a great greedy guts. So what does he do but stuff a whole one of those cakes—the ones with the iron griddles in them, remember—into his mouth! He takes a huge bite. AAAARRGH!

I'm sorry, did I frighten you? But that's the noise he made, you know.

"What's the matter?" says Oona, cool as the well-known cucumber.

"What class of bread is this at all?" shouts the other. "There's two of my best teeth gone!"

"Why," says she, "that's Fin's bread. Indeed, it's the only bread he'll eat when he's home. And he feeds it to this little fellow in the crib, here, in the hopes that he'll grow up to be a fine figure of a man like his dad. Here," she says kindly, "try another piece. You'll be needing some nourishment if you're to try a bout of strength with the likes of Fin McCool, after he gets back."

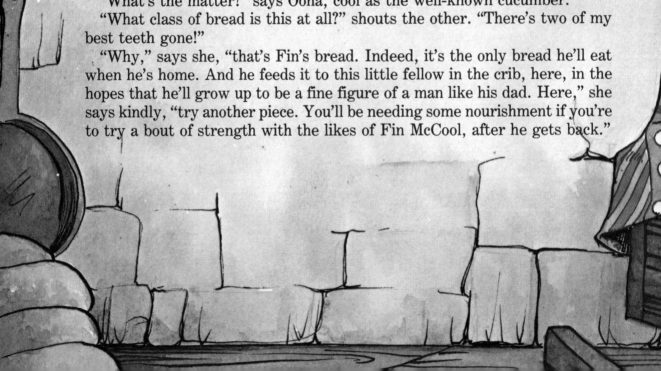

Cucullin was pretty well ravenous, after turning houses 'round and splitting rocks and what not, so he thought he'd have another try. Down he bites on a second cake, and AAAARRGH! again!

I didn't scare you that time, did I? You were expecting it. Aren't you the clever one, though?

"Keep the noise down, man!" says Oona, "and don't be waking the baby! Hush!" Fin must have had his thumb in his mouth that very minute, for he knew just what to do then. He set up a terrible roaring and howling that must have made Cucullin wonder what manner of child this was altogether. "Ma! ma!" Fin was screaming, "Gimme cake!"

Quick as a wink, Oona runs over to the cradle and hands Fin one of those cakes—you remember—that had no griddle in it! And just as quick, the thing disappeared down Fin's throat!

By now, Cucullin was starting to wonder, as well, about the size and strength of a man whose child could easily eat such bread as that. He began to entertain thoughts of leaving in a hurry.

"I think I'll be going now," says he, standing up. "I haven't all day to wait," he says, slowly making his way toward the door.

There in the cradle lay Fin, fairly glowing with delight that Cucullin was taking his leave without discovering the tricks that had been played on him.

"It's well for you that you go," says Oona, "before Fin gets back to make mince-meat of you. But you'll not leave, surely, without having a better look at the little fellow in the cradle there?"

"I would like a good glimpse of him," Cucullin admits, "if only to see the class of teeth he has to eat cakes like those ones."

"Please yourself," says she, "but his cutest little grinders are far back in his head, so you'd best put your finger a good way in to appreciate them."

"I will," says Cucullin and imagine his surprise when he brings his hand back out of Fin's mouth, and discovers that he's left behind him the very finger upon which his whole strength depended!

That was fine with Fin, who leapt from the cradle, and commenced flinging griddle-cakes at the weak and foolish Cucullin, who took to his heels, and was never seen again in the length and breadth of Ireland.

After that time, people still talked of the great strength of men, and the little strength of women. But they didn't talk that way in front of Fin McCool.

THE TROLL

Be wary of the loathsome troll
that slyly lies in wait
to drag you to his dingy hole
and put you on his plate.

His blood is black and boiling hot,
he gurgles ghastly groans.
He'll cook you in his dinner pot,
your skin, your flesh, your bones.

He'll catch your arms and clutch your legs
and grind you to a pulp,
then swallow you like scrambled eggs—
gobble! gobble! gulp!

So watch your steps when next you go
upon a pleasant stroll,
or you might end in the pit below
as supper for the troll.

Jack Prelutsky

KIND LITTLE EDMUND

by E. Nesbit

Edmund was a boy. The people who did not like him said that he was the most tiresome boy that ever lived, but his grandmother and his other friends said that he had an inquiring mind. And his granny often added that he was the best of boys. But she was very kind and very old.

Edmund loved to find out about things. Perhaps you will think that in that case he was constant in his attendance at school, since there, if anywhere, we may learn whatever there is to be learned. But Edmund did not want to learn things: he wanted to find things out, which is quite different. His inquiring mind led him to take clocks to pieces to see what made them go, to take locks off doors to see what made them stick. It was Edmund who cut open the india-rubber ball to see what made it bounce, and he never *did* see, any more than you did when you tried the same experiment.

Edmund lived with his grandmother. She loved him very much, in spite of his inquiring mind, and hardly scolded him at all when he frizzled up her tortoiseshell comb in his anxiety to find out whether it was made of real tortoiseshell or of something that would burn. Edmund went to school, of course, now and then, and sometimes he could not prevent

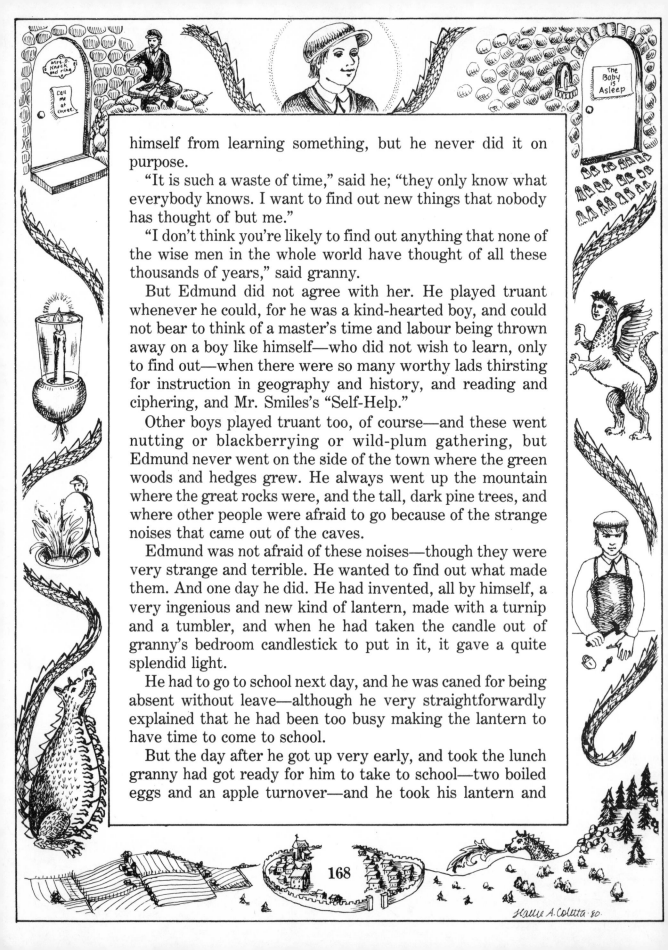

himself from learning something, but he never did it on purpose.

"It is such a waste of time," said he; "they only know what everybody knows. I want to find out new things that nobody has thought of but me."

"I don't think you're likely to find out anything that none of the wise men in the whole world have thought of all these thousands of years," said granny.

But Edmund did not agree with her. He played truant whenever he could, for he was a kind-hearted boy, and could not bear to think of a master's time and labour being thrown away on a boy like himself—who did not wish to learn, only to find out—when there were so many worthy lads thirsting for instruction in geography and history, and reading and ciphering, and Mr. Smiles's "Self-Help."

Other boys played truant too, of course—and these went nutting or blackberrying or wild-plum gathering, but Edmund never went on the side of the town where the green woods and hedges grew. He always went up the mountain where the great rocks were, and the tall, dark pine trees, and where other people were afraid to go because of the strange noises that came out of the caves.

Edmund was not afraid of these noises—though they were very strange and terrible. He wanted to find out what made them. And one day he did. He had invented, all by himself, a very ingenious and new kind of lantern, made with a turnip and a tumbler, and when he had taken the candle out of granny's bedroom candlestick to put in it, it gave a quite splendid light.

He had to go to school next day, and he was caned for being absent without leave—although he very straightforwardly explained that he had been too busy making the lantern to have time to come to school.

But the day after he got up very early, and took the lunch granny had got ready for him to take to school—two boiled eggs and an apple turnover—and he took his lantern and went off as straight as a dart to the mountains to explore the caves.

The caves were very dark, but his lantern lighted them up beautifully; and they were most interesting caves, with stalactites and stalagmites and fossils, and all the things you read about in the instructive books for the young. But Edmund did not care for any of these things just then. He wanted to find out what made the noises that people were afraid of, and there was nothing in the caves to tell him.

Presently he sat down in the biggest cave and listened very carefully, and it seemed to him that he could distinguish three different sorts of noises. There was a heavy, rumbling sound, like a very large old gentleman asleep after dinner; and there was a smaller sort of rumble going on at the same time; and there was a sort of crowing, clucking sound, such as a chicken might make if it happened to be as big as a haystack.

"It seems to me," said Edmund to himself, "that the clucking is nearer than the others." So he started up again and explored the caves once more. He found out nothing, only, about half-way up the wall of the cave, he saw a hole. And, being a boy, he climbed up to it and crept in; and it was the entrance to a rocky passage. And now the clucking sounded more plainly than before, and he could hardly hear the rumbling at all.

"I am going to find out something at last," said Edmund, and on he went. The passage wound and twisted, and twisted and turned, and turned and wound, but Edmund kept on.

"My lantern's burning better and better," said he presently, but the next minute he saw that all the light did not come from his lantern. It was a pale yellow light, and it shone down the passage far ahead of him through what looked like the chink of a door.

"I expect it's the fire in the middle of the earth," said Edmund, who had not been able to help learning about that at school.

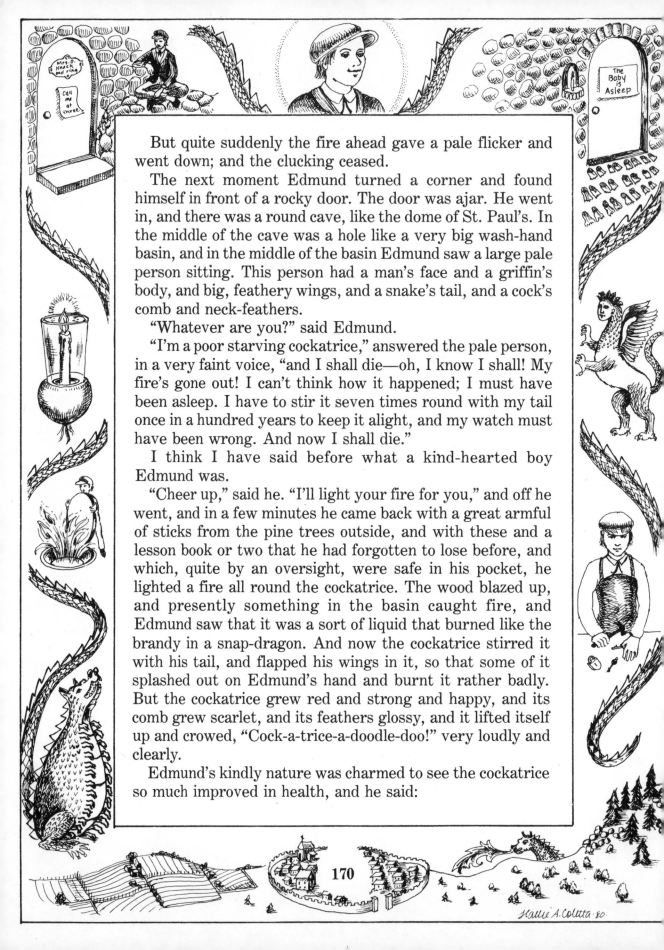

But quite suddenly the fire ahead gave a pale flicker and went down; and the clucking ceased.

The next moment Edmund turned a corner and found himself in front of a rocky door. The door was ajar. He went in, and there was a round cave, like the dome of St. Paul's. In the middle of the cave was a hole like a very big wash-hand basin, and in the middle of the basin Edmund saw a large pale person sitting. This person had a man's face and a griffin's body, and big, feathery wings, and a snake's tail, and a cock's comb and neck-feathers.

"Whatever are you?" said Edmund.

"I'm a poor starving cockatrice," answered the pale person, in a very faint voice, "and I shall die—oh, I know I shall! My fire's gone out! I can't think how it happened; I must have been asleep. I have to stir it seven times round with my tail once in a hundred years to keep it alight, and my watch must have been wrong. And now I shall die."

I think I have said before what a kind-hearted boy Edmund was.

"Cheer up," said he. "I'll light your fire for you," and off he went, and in a few minutes he came back with a great armful of sticks from the pine trees outside, and with these and a lesson book or two that he had forgotten to lose before, and which, quite by an oversight, were safe in his pocket, he lighted a fire all round the cockatrice. The wood blazed up, and presently something in the basin caught fire, and Edmund saw that it was a sort of liquid that burned like the brandy in a snap-dragon. And now the cockatrice stirred it with his tail, and flapped his wings in it, so that some of it splashed out on Edmund's hand and burnt it rather badly. But the cockatrice grew red and strong and happy, and its comb grew scarlet, and its feathers glossy, and it lifted itself up and crowed, "Cock-a-trice-a-doodle-doo!" very loudly and clearly.

Edmund's kindly nature was charmed to see the cockatrice so much improved in health, and he said:

"Don't mention it; delighted, I'm sure," when the cockatrice began to thank him.

"But what can I do for you?" said the creature.

"Tell me stories," said Edmund.

"What about?" said the cockatrice.

"About true things that they don't know at school," said Edmund.

So the cockatrice began, and it told him about mines and treasures, and geological formations, and about gnomes and fairies and dragons, and glaciers and the stone age, and the beginning of the world, and about the unicorn and the phoenix, and about Magic, black and white.

And Edmund ate his eggs and his turnover, and listened. And when he got hungry again he said goodbye and went home. But he came again next day for more stories, and the next day, and the next, for a long time.

He told the boys at school about the cockatrice and its wonderful true tales, and the boys liked the stories; but when he told the master he was caned for untruthfulness.

"But it's true," said Edmund; "just you look where the fire burnt my hand."

"I see you've been playing with fire—in mischief as usual," said the master, and he caned Edmund harder than ever. The master was ignorant and unbelieving: but I am told that some schoolmasters are not like that.

Now, one day Edmund made a new lantern out of something chemical which he sneaked from the school laboratory. And with it he went exploring again to see if he could find the things that made the other sorts of noises. And in quite another part of the mountain he found a dark passage, all lined with brass, so that it was like the inside of a huge telescope, and at the very end of it he found a bright green door. There was a brass plate on the door which said: "Mrs. D. Knock and ring," and a white label which said: "Call me at three." Edmund had a watch: it had been given to him on his birthday two days before, and he had not yet had time

Hallie A. Coletta '80

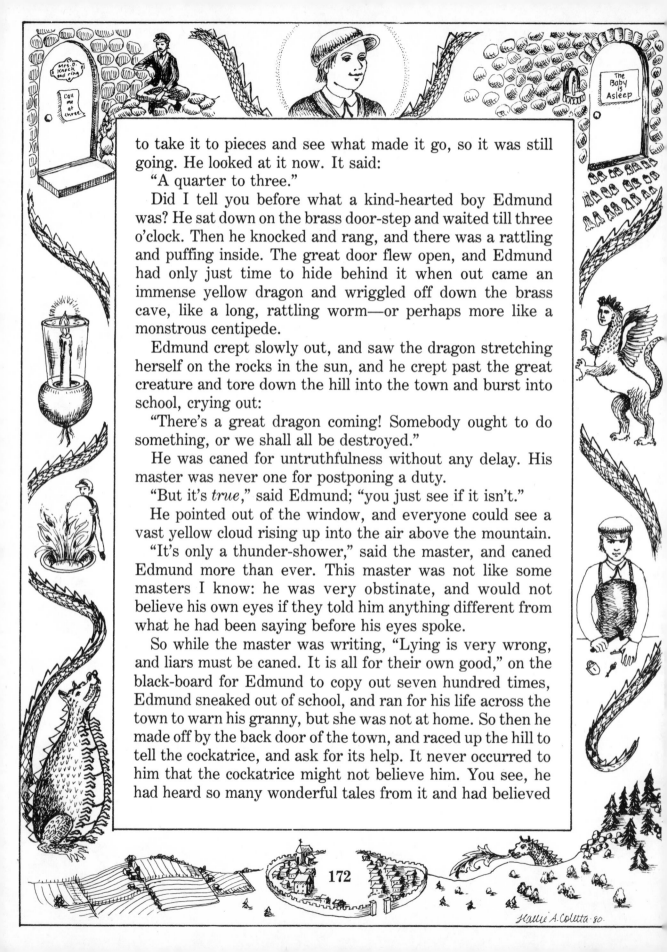

to take it to pieces and see what made it go, so it was still going. He looked at it now. It said:

"A quarter to three."

Did I tell you before what a kind-hearted boy Edmund was? He sat down on the brass door-step and waited till three o'clock. Then he knocked and rang, and there was a rattling and puffing inside. The great door flew open, and Edmund had only just time to hide behind it when out came an immense yellow dragon and wriggled off down the brass cave, like a long, rattling worm—or perhaps more like a monstrous centipede.

Edmund crept slowly out, and saw the dragon stretching herself on the rocks in the sun, and he crept past the great creature and tore down the hill into the town and burst into school, crying out:

"There's a great dragon coming! Somebody ought to do something, or we shall all be destroyed."

He was caned for untruthfulness without any delay. His master was never one for postponing a duty.

"But it's *true*," said Edmund; "you just see if it isn't."

He pointed out of the window, and everyone could see a vast yellow cloud rising up into the air above the mountain.

"It's only a thunder-shower," said the master, and caned Edmund more than ever. This master was not like some masters I know: he was very obstinate, and would not believe his own eyes if they told him anything different from what he had been saying before his eyes spoke.

So while the master was writing, "Lying is very wrong, and liars must be caned. It is all for their own good," on the black-board for Edmund to copy out seven hundred times, Edmund sneaked out of school, and ran for his life across the town to warn his granny, but she was not at home. So then he made off by the back door of the town, and raced up the hill to tell the cockatrice, and ask for its help. It never occurred to him that the cockatrice might not believe him. You see, he had heard so many wonderful tales from it and had believed them all—and when you believe all a person's stories they ought to believe yours. This is only fair.

At the mouth of the cockatrice's cave Edmund stopped, very much out of breath, to look back at the town. As he ran he had felt his little legs tremble and shake, while the shadows of the great yellow cloud fell upon him. Now he stood once more between warm earth and blue sky, and looked down on the green plain, dotted with fruit trees and red-roofed farms and plots of gold corn. In the middle of that plain the grey town lay, with its strong walls, with the holes pierced for the archers, and its square towers with holes in for dropping melted lead on the heads of strangers, its bridges, and its steeples, the quiet river edged with willow and alder, and the pleasant green garden-place in the middle of the town, where people sat on holidays to smoke their pipes and listen to the band.

Edmund saw it all; and he saw, too, creeping across the plain, marking her way by a black line, as everything withered at her touch, the great yellow dragon—and he saw that she was many times bigger than the whole town.

"Oh, my poor, dear granny," said Edmund, for he had a feeling heart, as I ought to have told you before.

The yellow dragon crept nearer and nearer, licking her greedy lips with her long, red tongue, and Edmund knew that in the school his master was still teaching earnestly, and still not believing Edmund's tale the least little bit.

"He'll jolly well *have* to believe it soon, anyhow," said Edmund to himself, and though he was a very tender-hearted boy—I think it only fair to tell you that he was this—I am afraid he was not so sorry as he ought to have been to think of the way in which his master was going to learn how to believe what Edmund said. Then the dragon opened her jaws wider and wider and wider. Edmund shut his eyes close, for though his master *was* in the town, yet the amiable Edmund shrank from beholding the awful sight.

When he opened his eyes again there was no town—only a

bare place where it had stood, and the dragon licking her lips and curling herself up to go to sleep, just as pussy does when she has quite finished with a mouse. Edmund gasped once or twice, and then ran into the cave to tell the cockatrice.

"Well," said the cockatrice, thoughtfully, when the tale had been told, "what then?"

"I don't think you quite understand," said Edmund, gently; "the dragon has swallowed up the town."

"Does it matter?" said the cockatrice.

"But I live there," said Edmund, blankly.

"Never mind," said the cockatrice, turning over in the pool of fire to warm its other side, which was chilly, because Edmund had, as usual, forgotten to close the cave door, "you can live here with me."

"I'm afraid I haven't made my meaning clear," said Edmund, patiently. "You see, my granny is in the town, and I can't bear to lose my granny like this."

"I don't know what a granny may be," said the cockatrice, who seemed to be growing weary of the subject; "but if it's a possession to which you attach any importance—"

"Of course it is," said Edmund, losing patience at last. "Oh—do help me. What can I do?"

"If I were you," said his friend, stretching itself out in the pool of flame so that the waves covered it up to the chin, "I should find the drakling and bring it here."

"But why?" said Edmund. He had got into the habit of asking why at school, and the master had always found it trying. As for the cockatrice, it was not going to stand that sort of thing for a moment.

"Oh, don't talk to me!" it said, splashing angrily in the flames. "I give you advice; take it or leave it—I shan't bother about you any more. If you bring the drakling here to me, I'll tell you what to do next. If not, not."

And the cockatrice drew the fire up close round its shoulders, tucked itself up in it, and went to sleep.

Now this was exactly the right way to manage Edmund,

174

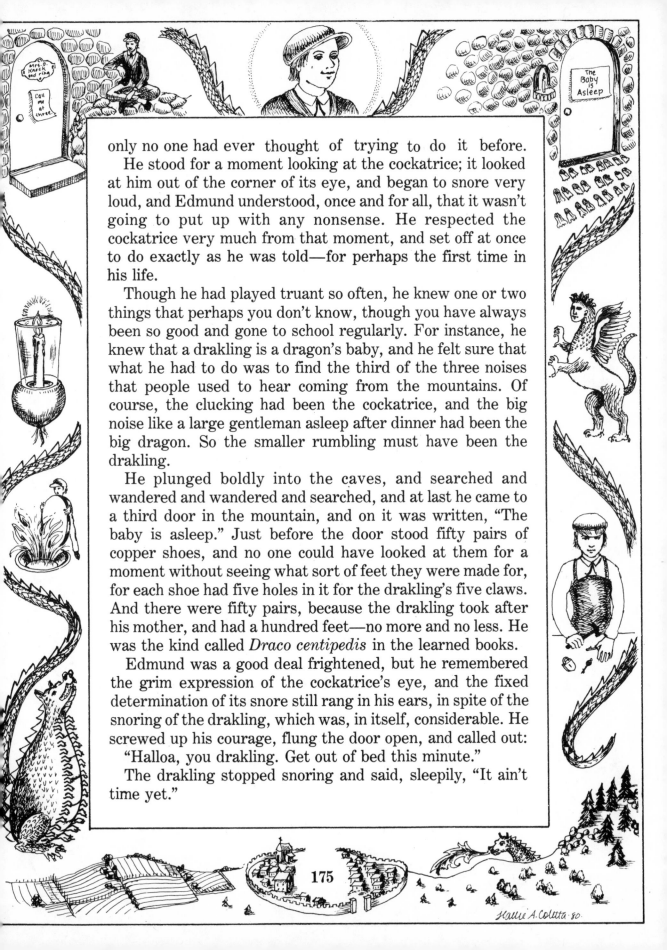

only no one had ever thought of trying to do it before.

He stood for a moment looking at the cockatrice; it looked at him out of the corner of its eye, and began to snore very loud, and Edmund understood, once and for all, that it wasn't going to put up with any nonsense. He respected the cockatrice very much from that moment, and set off at once to do exactly as he was told—for perhaps the first time in his life.

Though he had played truant so often, he knew one or two things that perhaps you don't know, though you have always been so good and gone to school regularly. For instance, he knew that a drakling is a dragon's baby, and he felt sure that what he had to do was to find the third of the three noises that people used to hear coming from the mountains. Of course, the clucking had been the cockatrice, and the big noise like a large gentleman asleep after dinner had been the big dragon. So the smaller rumbling must have been the drakling.

He plunged boldly into the caves, and searched and wandered and wandered and searched, and at last he came to a third door in the mountain, and on it was written, "The baby is asleep." Just before the door stood fifty pairs of copper shoes, and no one could have looked at them for a moment without seeing what sort of feet they were made for, for each shoe had five holes in it for the drakling's five claws. And there were fifty pairs, because the drakling took after his mother, and had a hundred feet—no more and no less. He was the kind called *Draco centipedis* in the learned books.

Edmund was a good deal frightened, but he remembered the grim expression of the cockatrice's eye, and the fixed determination of its snore still rang in his ears, in spite of the snoring of the drakling, which was, in itself, considerable. He screwed up his courage, flung the door open, and called out:

"Halloa, you drakling. Get out of bed this minute."

The drakling stopped snoring and said, sleepily, "It ain't time yet."

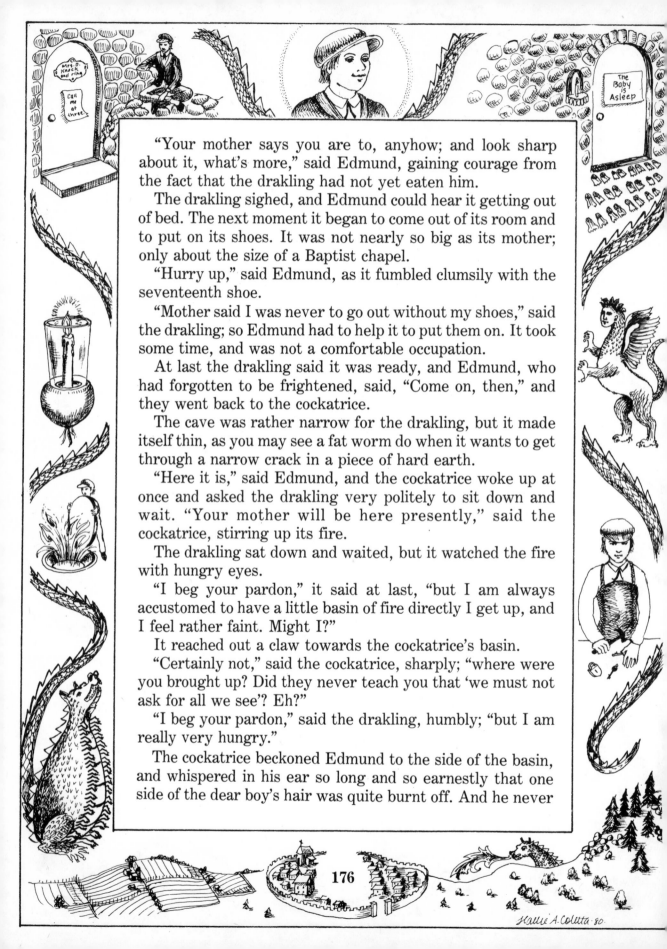

"Your mother says you are to, anyhow; and look sharp about it, what's more," said Edmund, gaining courage from the fact that the drakling had not yet eaten him.

The drakling sighed, and Edmund could hear it getting out of bed. The next moment it began to come out of its room and to put on its shoes. It was not nearly so big as its mother; only about the size of a Baptist chapel.

"Hurry up," said Edmund, as it fumbled clumsily with the seventeenth shoe.

"Mother said I was never to go out without my shoes," said the drakling; so Edmund had to help it to put them on. It took some time, and was not a comfortable occupation.

At last the drakling said it was ready, and Edmund, who had forgotten to be frightened, said, "Come on, then," and they went back to the cockatrice.

The cave was rather narrow for the drakling, but it made itself thin, as you may see a fat worm do when it wants to get through a narrow crack in a piece of hard earth.

"Here it is," said Edmund, and the cockatrice woke up at once and asked the drakling very politely to sit down and wait. "Your mother will be here presently," said the cockatrice, stirring up its fire.

The drakling sat down and waited, but it watched the fire with hungry eyes.

"I beg your pardon," it said at last, "but I am always accustomed to have a little basin of fire directly I get up, and I feel rather faint. Might I?"

It reached out a claw towards the cockatrice's basin.

"Certainly not," said the cockatrice, sharply; "where were you brought up? Did they never teach you that 'we must not ask for all we see'? Eh?"

"I beg your pardon," said the drakling, humbly; "but I am really very hungry."

The cockatrice beckoned Edmund to the side of the basin, and whispered in his ear so long and so earnestly that one side of the dear boy's hair was quite burnt off. And he never

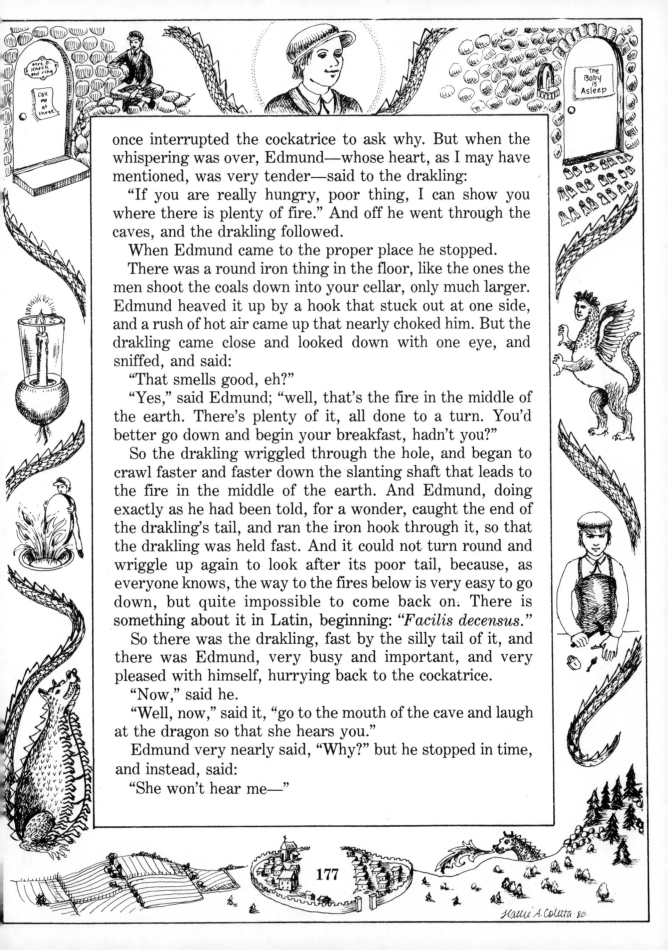

once interrupted the cockatrice to ask why. But when the whispering was over, Edmund—whose heart, as I may have mentioned, was very tender—said to the drakling:

"If you are really hungry, poor thing, I can show you where there is plenty of fire." And off he went through the caves, and the drakling followed.

When Edmund came to the proper place he stopped.

There was a round iron thing in the floor, like the ones the men shoot the coals down into your cellar, only much larger. Edmund heaved it up by a hook that stuck out at one side, and a rush of hot air came up that nearly choked him. But the drakling came close and looked down with one eye, and sniffed, and said:

"That smells good, eh?"

"Yes," said Edmund; "well, that's the fire in the middle of the earth. There's plenty of it, all done to a turn. You'd better go down and begin your breakfast, hadn't you?"

So the drakling wriggled through the hole, and began to crawl faster and faster down the slanting shaft that leads to the fire in the middle of the earth. And Edmund, doing exactly as he had been told, for a wonder, caught the end of the drakling's tail, and ran the iron hook through it, so that the drakling was held fast. And it could not turn round and wriggle up again to look after its poor tail, because, as everyone knows, the way to the fires below is very easy to go down, but quite impossible to come back on. There is something about it in Latin, beginning: *Facilis decensus.*

So there was the drakling, fast by the silly tail of it, and there was Edmund, very busy and important, and very pleased with himself, hurrying back to the cockatrice.

"Now," said he.

"Well, now," said it, "go to the mouth of the cave and laugh at the dragon so that she hears you."

Edmund very nearly said, "Why?" but he stopped in time, and instead, said:

"She won't hear me—"

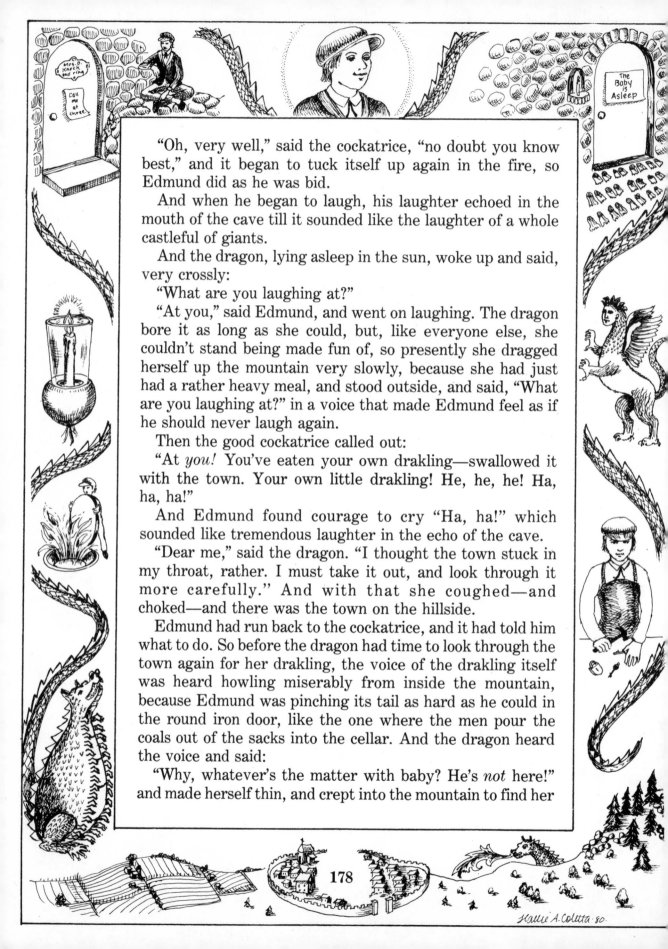

"Oh, very well," said the cockatrice, "no doubt you know best," and it began to tuck itself up again in the fire, so Edmund did as he was bid.

And when he began to laugh, his laughter echoed in the mouth of the cave till it sounded like the laughter of a whole castleful of giants.

And the dragon, lying asleep in the sun, woke up and said, very crossly:

"What are you laughing at?"

"At you," said Edmund, and went on laughing. The dragon bore it as long as she could, but, like everyone else, she couldn't stand being made fun of, so presently she dragged herself up the mountain very slowly, because she had just had a rather heavy meal, and stood outside, and said, "What are you laughing at?" in a voice that made Edmund feel as if he should never laugh again.

Then the good cockatrice called out:

"At *you!* You've eaten your own drakling—swallowed it with the town. Your own little drakling! He, he, he! Ha, ha, ha!"

And Edmund found courage to cry "Ha, ha!" which sounded like tremendous laughter in the echo of the cave.

"Dear me," said the dragon. "I thought the town stuck in my throat, rather. I must take it out, and look through it more carefully." And with that she coughed—and choked—and there was the town on the hillside.

Edmund had run back to the cockatrice, and it had told him what to do. So before the dragon had time to look through the town again for her drakling, the voice of the drakling itself was heard howling miserably from inside the mountain, because Edmund was pinching its tail as hard as he could in the round iron door, like the one where the men pour the coals out of the sacks into the cellar. And the dragon heard the voice and said:

"Why, whatever's the matter with baby? He's *not* here!" and made herself thin, and crept into the mountain to find her

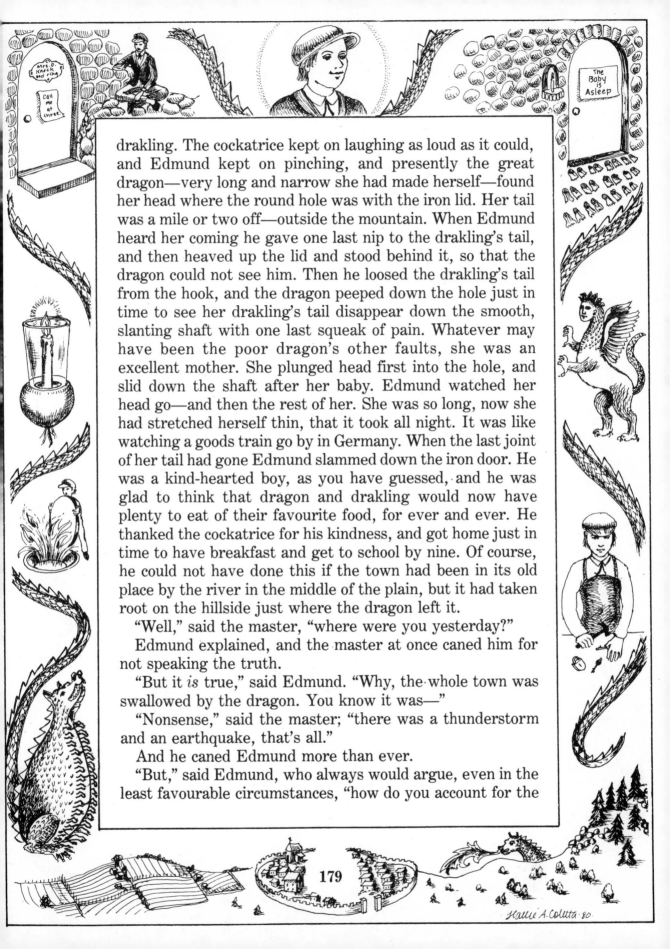

drakling. The cockatrice kept on laughing as loud as it could, and Edmund kept on pinching, and presently the great dragon—very long and narrow she had made herself—found her head where the round hole was with the iron lid. Her tail was a mile or two off—outside the mountain. When Edmund heard her coming he gave one last nip to the drakling's tail, and then heaved up the lid and stood behind it, so that the dragon could not see him. Then he loosed the drakling's tail from the hook, and the dragon peeped down the hole just in time to see her drakling's tail disappear down the smooth, slanting shaft with one last squeak of pain. Whatever may have been the poor dragon's other faults, she was an excellent mother. She plunged head first into the hole, and slid down the shaft after her baby. Edmund watched her head go—and then the rest of her. She was so long, now she had stretched herself thin, that it took all night. It was like watching a goods train go by in Germany. When the last joint of her tail had gone Edmund slammed down the iron door. He was a kind-hearted boy, as you have guessed, and he was glad to think that dragon and drakling would now have plenty to eat of their favourite food, for ever and ever. He thanked the cockatrice for his kindness, and got home just in time to have breakfast and get to school by nine. Of course, he could not have done this if the town had been in its old place by the river in the middle of the plain, but it had taken root on the hillside just where the dragon left it.

"Well," said the master, "where were you yesterday?"

Edmund explained, and the master at once caned him for not speaking the truth.

"But it *is* true," said Edmund. "Why, the whole town was swallowed by the dragon. You know it was—"

"Nonsense," said the master; "there was a thunderstorm and an earthquake, that's all."

And he caned Edmund more than ever.

"But," said Edmund, who always would argue, even in the least favourable circumstances, "how do you account for the

179

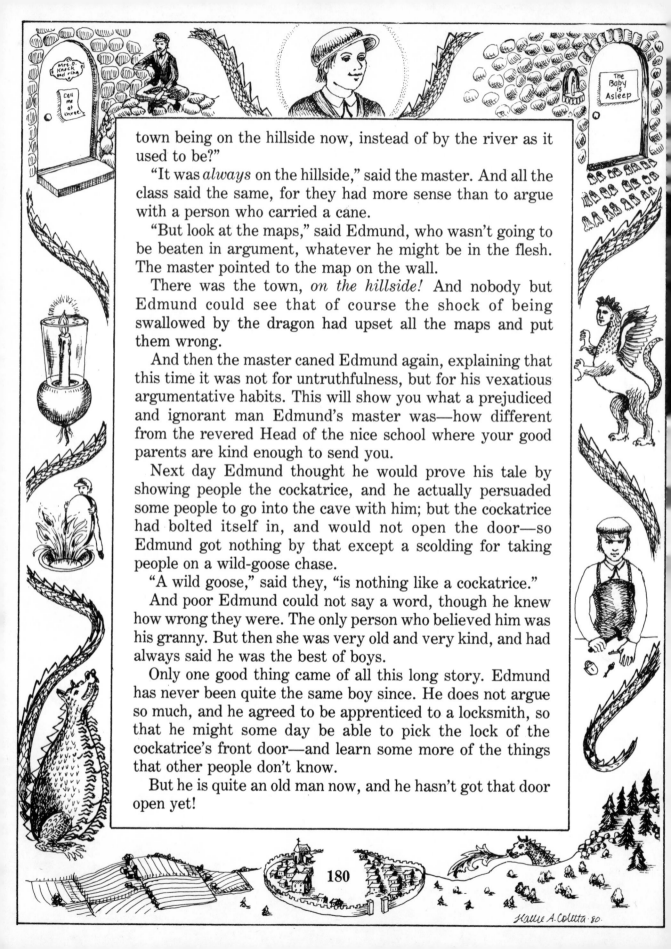

town being on the hillside now, instead of by the river as it used to be?"

"It was *always* on the hillside," said the master. And all the class said the same, for they had more sense than to argue with a person who carried a cane.

"But look at the maps," said Edmund, who wasn't going to be beaten in argument, whatever he might be in the flesh. The master pointed to the map on the wall.

There was the town, *on the hillside!* And nobody but Edmund could see that of course the shock of being swallowed by the dragon had upset all the maps and put them wrong.

And then the master caned Edmund again, explaining that this time it was not for untruthfulness, but for his vexatious argumentative habits. This will show you what a prejudiced and ignorant man Edmund's master was—how different from the revered Head of the nice school where your good parents are kind enough to send you.

Next day Edmund thought he would prove his tale by showing people the cockatrice, and he actually persuaded some people to go into the cave with him; but the cockatrice had bolted itself in, and would not open the door—so Edmund got nothing by that except a scolding for taking people on a wild-goose chase.

"A wild goose," said they, "is nothing like a cockatrice."

And poor Edmund could not say a word, though he knew how wrong they were. The only person who believed him was his granny. But then she was very old and very kind, and had always said he was the best of boys.

Only one good thing came of all this long story. Edmund has never been quite the same boy since. He does not argue so much, and he agreed to be apprenticed to a locksmith, so that he might some day be able to pick the lock of the cockatrice's front door—and learn some more of the things that other people don't know.

But he is quite an old man now, and he hasn't got that door open yet!

JABBERWOCKY

'Twas brillig, and the slithy toves
　　Did gyre and gimble in the wabe;
All mimsy were the borogoves,
　　And the mome raths outgrabe.

"Beware the Jabberwock, my son!
　　The jaws that bite, the claws that catch!
Beware the Jubjub bird, and shun
　　The frumious Bandersnatch!"

He took his vorpal sword in hand:
　　Long time the manxome foe he sought.
So rested he by the Tumtum tree,
　　And stood awhile in thought.

And as in uffish thought he stood,
　　The Jabberwock with eyes of flame,
Came whiffling through the tulgey wood,
　　And burbled as it came!

One, two! One, two! And through, and through
　　The vorpal blade went snicker-snack!
He left it dead, and with its head
　　He went galumphing back.

"And has thou slain the Jabberwock?
　　Come to my arms, my beamish boy!"
"Oh, frabjous day! Callooh! callay!"
　　He chortled in his joy.

'Twas brillig, and the slithy toves
　　Did gyre and gimble in the wabe;
All mimsy were the borogoves
　　And the mome raths outgrabe.

Lewis Carroll

THE CATIPOCE

"O Harry, Harry! hold me close—
 I fear some animile.
It is the horny Catipoce
 With her outrageous smile!"

Thus spoke the maiden in alarm;
 She had good cause to fear:
The Catipoce can do great harm,
 If any come too near.

Despite her looks, do not presume
 The creature's ways are mild;
For many have gone mad on whom
 The Catipoce has smiled.

She lurks in woods at close of day
 Among the toadstools soft,
Or sprawls on musty sacks and hay
 In cellar, barn, or loft.

Behind neglected rubbish-dumps
   At dusk your blood will freeze
Only to glimpse her horny humps
   And hear her fatal sneeze.

Run, Run! adventurous boy or girl—
   Run home, and do not pause
To feel her breath around you curl,
   And tempt her carrion claws.

Avoid her face: for underneath
   That gentle, fond grimace
Lie four-and-forty crooked teeth—
   My dears, avoid her face!

"O Harry, Harry! hold me close,
   And hold me close a while;
It is the odious Catipoce
   With her devouring smile!"

James Reeves

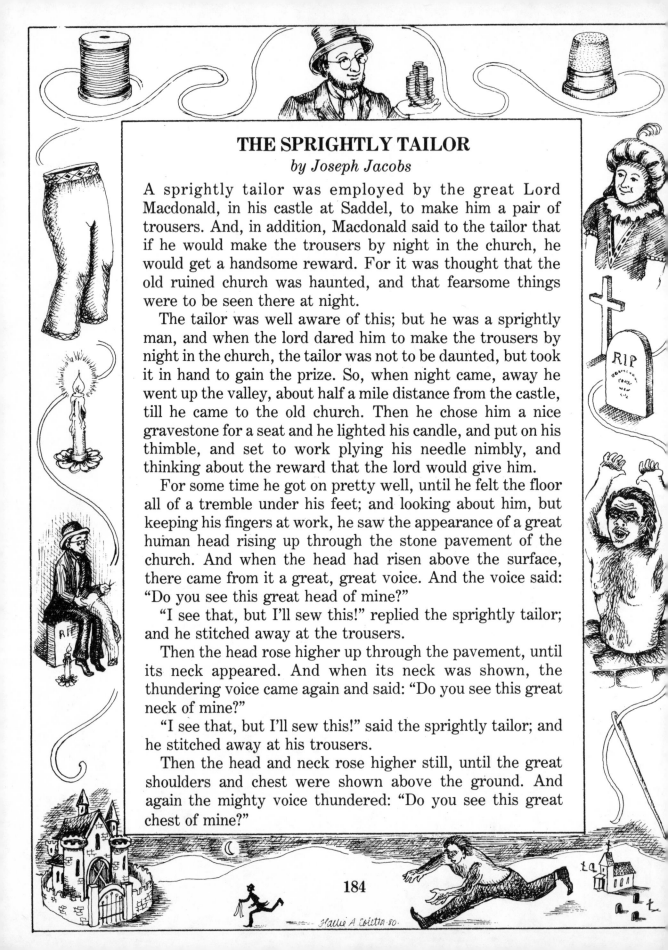

THE SPRIGHTLY TAILOR

by Joseph Jacobs

A sprightly tailor was employed by the great Lord Macdonald, in his castle at Saddel, to make him a pair of trousers. And, in addition, Macdonald said to the tailor that if he would make the trousers by night in the church, he would get a handsome reward. For it was thought that the old ruined church was haunted, and that fearsome things were to be seen there at night.

The tailor was well aware of this; but he was a sprightly man, and when the lord dared him to make the trousers by night in the church, the tailor was not to be daunted, but took it in hand to gain the prize. So, when night came, away he went up the valley, about half a mile distance from the castle, till he came to the old church. Then he chose him a nice gravestone for a seat and he lighted his candle, and put on his thimble, and set to work plying his needle nimbly, and thinking about the reward that the lord would give him.

For some time he got on pretty well, until he felt the floor all of a tremble under his feet; and looking about him, but keeping his fingers at work, he saw the appearance of a great human head rising up through the stone pavement of the church. And when the head had risen above the surface, there came from it a great, great voice. And the voice said: "Do you see this great head of mine?"

"I see that, but I'll sew this!" replied the sprightly tailor; and he stitched away at the trousers.

Then the head rose higher up through the pavement, until its neck appeared. And when its neck was shown, the thundering voice came again and said: "Do you see this great neck of mine?"

"I see that, but I'll sew this!" said the sprightly tailor; and he stitched away at his trousers.

Then the head and neck rose higher still, until the great shoulders and chest were shown above the ground. And again the mighty voice thundered: "Do you see this great chest of mine?"

184

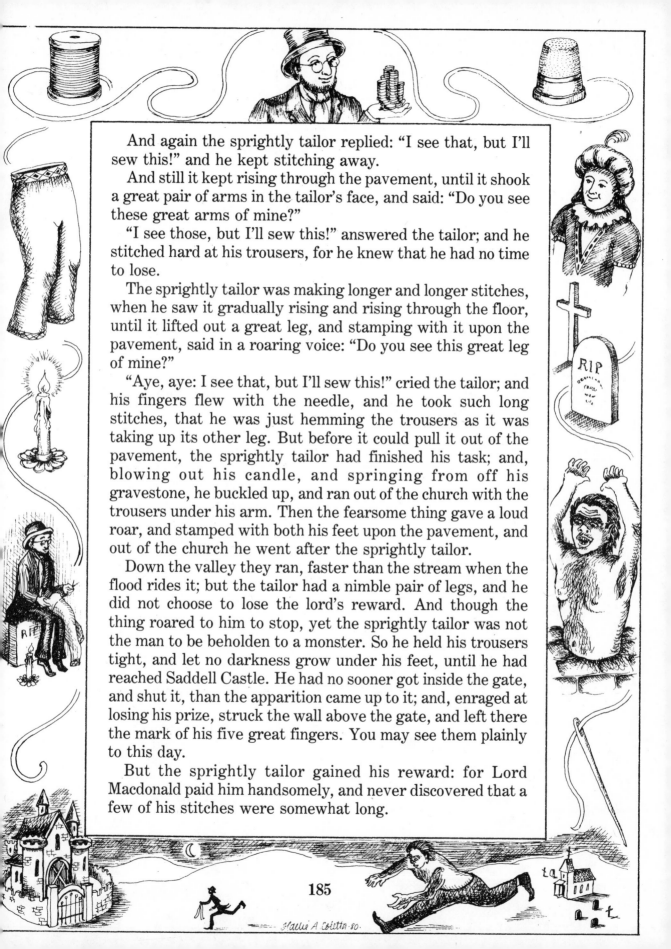

And again the sprightly tailor replied: "I see that, but I'll sew this!" and he kept stitching away.

And still it kept rising through the pavement, until it shook a great pair of arms in the tailor's face, and said: "Do you see these great arms of mine?"

"I see those, but I'll sew this!" answered the tailor; and he stitched hard at his trousers, for he knew that he had no time to lose.

The sprightly tailor was making longer and longer stitches, when he saw it gradually rising and rising through the floor, until it lifted out a great leg, and stamping with it upon the pavement, said in a roaring voice: "Do you see this great leg of mine?"

"Aye, aye: I see that, but I'll sew this!" cried the tailor; and his fingers flew with the needle, and he took such long stitches, that he was just hemming the trousers as it was taking up its other leg. But before it could pull it out of the pavement, the sprightly tailor had finished his task; and, blowing out his candle, and springing from off his gravestone, he buckled up, and ran out of the church with the trousers under his arm. Then the fearsome thing gave a loud roar, and stamped with both his feet upon the pavement, and out of the church he went after the sprightly tailor.

Down the valley they ran, faster than the stream when the flood rides it; but the tailor had a nimble pair of legs, and he did not choose to lose the lord's reward. And though the thing roared to him to stop, yet the sprightly tailor was not the man to be beholden to a monster. So he held his trousers tight, and let no darkness grow under his feet, until he had reached Saddell Castle. He had no sooner got inside the gate, and shut it, than the apparition came up to it; and, enraged at losing his prize, struck the wall above the gate, and left there the mark of his five great fingers. You may see them plainly to this day.

But the sprightly tailor gained his reward: for Lord Macdonald paid him handsomely, and never discovered that a few of his stitches were somewhat long.

As I was going up the stair
I met a man who wasn't there.
He wasn't there again today—
I wish, I wish, he'd go away!

There were three ghostesses
Sitting on postesses
Eating buttered toastesses
And greasing their fistesses
Right up to their wristesses.
Weren't they beastesses
To make such feastesses!

THE CARNIVORISTICOUS OUNCE

There once was a beast called an Ounce,
Who went with a spring and a bounce.
    His head was as flat
    As the head of a cat,
This quadrupedantical Ounce,
            'tical Ounce,
This quadrupedantical Ounce.

You'd think from his name he was small,
But that was not like him at all;—
    He weighed, I'll be bound,
    Three or four hundred pound,
And he looked most uncommonly tall,
           'monly tall,
He looked most uncommonly tall.

He sprang on his prey with a pounce,
And he gave it a jerk and a trounce;
    Then crunched up its bones
    Or the grass or the stones,
This carnivoristicous Ounce,
        'ticous Ounce!
This carnivoristicous Ounce!

When a hunter he'd meet on the shore,
He'd give a wild rush and a roar—
    His claws he'd unsheath,
    And he'd show all his teeth,—
But the man would be seen nevermore,
         Nevermore!
The man would be seen nevermore!

I'd rather—I'm telling you true—
Meet with three hundred weight of a Gnu,
    A Sea-Horse or Whale,
    Or a Cow with a tail,
Than an Ounce of this kind—wouldn't *you?*
        Wouldn't you?
Than an Ounce of this kind—*wouldn't* you?

Mrs. M. E. Blake

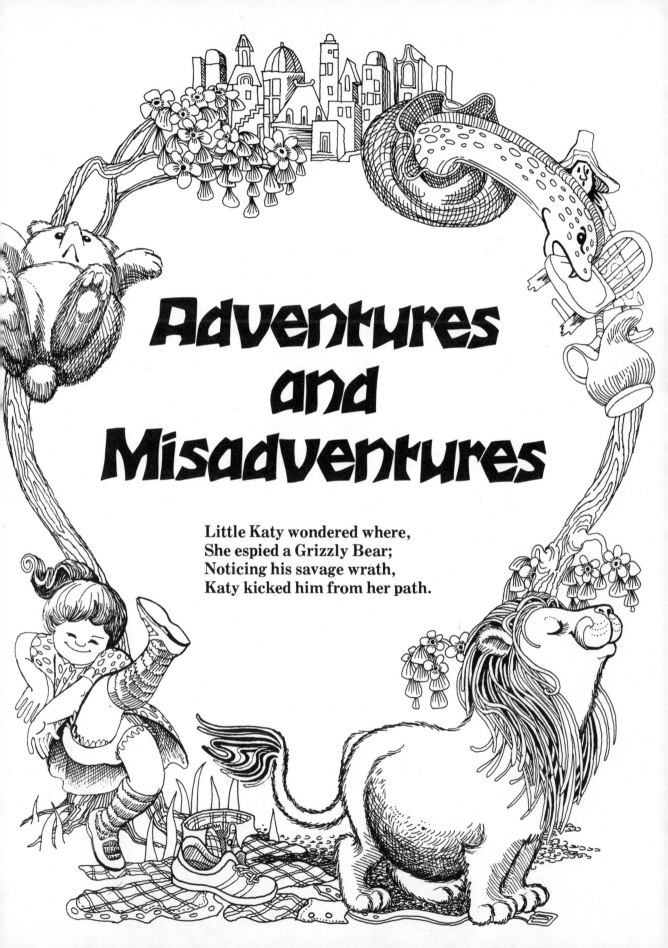

Adventures and Misadventures

Little Katy wondered where,
She espied a Grizzly Bear;
Noticing his savage wrath,
Katy kicked him from her path.

JIMMY JET AND HIS TV SET

I'll tell you the story of Jimmy Jet—
And you know what I tell you is true.
He loved to watch his TV set
Almost as much as you.

He watched all day, he watched all night
Till he grew pale and lean,
From "The Early Show" to "The Late Late Show"
And all the shows between.

He watched till his eyes were frozen wide,
And his bottom grew into his chair.
And his chin turned into a tuning dial,
And antennae grew out of his hair.

And his brains turned into TV tubes,
And his face to a TV screen.
And two knobs saying "VERT" and "HORIZ"
Grew where his ears had been.

And he grew a plug that looked like a tail
So we plugged in little Jim.
And now instead of him watching TV
We all sit around and watch him.

Shel Silverstein

THE SAD STORY OF A LITTLE BOY WHO CRIED

Once a little boy, Jack, was, oh! ever so good,
Till he took a strange notion to cry all he could.

So he cried all the day, and he cried all the night,
He cried in the morning and in the twilight;

He cried till his voice was as hoarse as a crow,
And his mouth grew so large it looked like a great O.

It grew at the bottom, and grew at the top;
It grew till they thought that it never would stop.

Each day his great mouth grew taller and taller,
And his dear little self grew smaller and smaller.

At last, that same mouth grew so big that—alack!—
It was only a mouth with a border of Jack.

A LOVE STORY

He was a Wizard's son,
  She an Enchanter's daughter;
He dabbled in Spells for fun,
  Her father some magic had taught her.

They loved—but alas! to agree
  Their parents they couldn't persuade,
An Enchanter and Wizard, you see,
  Were natural rivals in trade—
And the market for magic was poor—
  There was scarce enough business for two
So what started rivalry pure
  Into hatred and jealousy grew.

Now the lovers were dreadfully good;
  But when there was really no hope,
After waiting as long as they could,
  What else could they do but elope?
They eloped in a hired coupé;
  And the youth, with what magic he knew—
Made it go fully five miles a day.
  (Such wonders can sorcery do!)

Then the maiden her witcheries plied,
  And enchanted the cabman so much,
When they got to the end of their ride
  Not a cent of his fare would he touch!
Now they're married and live to this day
  In a nice little tower, alone,
For the building of which, by the way,
  Their parents provided the stone.

Then the parents relented? Oh, no!
  They pursued with the fury of brutes,
But arrived just too late for the show,
  Through a leak in their seven-league boots;
And finding their children were wed,
  Into such a wild rage they were thrown,
They rushed on each other instead
  And each turned the other to stone.

Then the lovers, since lumber was high,
  And bricks were as then quite unknown,
As soon as their tears were quite dry—
  They quarried their parents for stone.

And now in a nice little tower,
  In Blissfulness tinged with Remorse,
They live like as not to this hour—
  (Unless they have got a divorce).

MORAL

Crime, Wickedness, Villainy, Vice,
  And sin only misery bring;
If you want to be Happy and Nice,
  Be good and all that sort of thing.

Oliver Herford

THE STORY OF FLYING ROBERT

When the rain comes tumbling down
In the country or the town,
All good little girls and boys
Stay at home and mind their toys.
Robert thought—"No, when it pours,
It is better out of doors."
Rain it *did*, and in a minute
Bob was in it.

What a wind! Oh! how it whistles
Through the trees and flow'rs and thistles!
It has caught his red umbrella;
It has caught him, silly fellow;
Up he flies
To the skies.
No one heard his screams and cries,
Through the clouds the rude wind bore him,
And his hat flew on before him.
Soon they got to such a height,
There were nearly out of sight!
And the hat went up so high,
That it really touch'd the sky.
No one ever yet could tell
Where they stopp'd, or where they fell:
Only, this one thing is plain,
Bob was never seen again!

Heinrich Hoffman

THE LITTLE PEACH

A little peach in the orchard grew,
A little peach of emerald hue;
Warmed by the sun and wet by the
    dew,
  It grew.

One day, passing that orchard
    through,
That little peach dawned on the
    view
Of Johnny Jones and his sister Sue,
  Them two.
Up at that peach a club they threw,

Down from the stem on which it
    grew
Fell that peach of emerald hue.
  Mon Dieu!

John took a bite and Sue took a
    chew,
And then the trouble began to brew,
Trouble the doctor couldn't subdue.
  Too true!

Under the turf where the daisies
    grew
They planted John and his sister
    Sue,
And their little souls to the angels
    flew,
  Boo hoo!

What of that peach of the emerald
    hue;
Warmed by the sun and wet by the
    dew?
Ah, well, its mission on earth is
    through.
  Adieu!

Eugene Field

THE UPS AND DOWNS OF THE ELEVATOR CAR

The elevator car in the elevator shaft,
Complained of the buzzer, complained of the draught.
It said it felt carsick as it rose and fell,
It said it had a headache from the ringing of the bell.

"There is spring in the air," sighed the elevator car.
Said the elevator man, "You are well-off where you are."
The car paid no attention but it frowned an ugly frown
when
up   it
going   should
started   be
it   going
And   down.

Down flashed the signal, but *up* went the car.
The elevator man cried, "You are going much too far!"
Said the elevator car, "I'm doing no such thing.
I'm through with buzzers buzzing. I'm looking for the spring!"

Then the elevator man began to shout and call
And all the people came running through the hall.

The elevator man began to call and shout.
"The car won't stop! Let me out! Let me out!"

On went the car past the penthouse door.
On went the car up one flight more.
On went the elevator till it came to the top.
On went the elevator, and it would not stop!

Right through the roof went the man and the car.
And nobody knows where the two of them are!
(Nobody knows but everyone cares,
Wearily, drearily climbing the stairs!)

Now on a summer evening when you see a shooting star
Fly through the air, perhaps it *is*—that elevator car!

Caroline D. Emerson

Here are some thoughts of archy, the famous cockroach, who lives with his friend mehitabel, the alley cat, in New York City.

prudence

i do not think a prudent one
will ever aim too high
a cockroach seldom whips a dog
and seldom should he try

and should a locust take a vow
to eat a pyramid
he likely would wear out his teeth
before he ever did

i do not think the prudent one
hastes to initiate
a sequence of events which he
lacks power to terminate

for should i kick the woolworth tower
so hard i laid it low
it probably might injure me
if it fell on my toe

i do not think the prudent one
will be inclined to boast
lest circumstances unforeseen
should get him goat and ghost

for should i tell my friends i d drink
the hudson river dry
a tidal wave might come and turn
my statements to a lie

> archy
> *(don marquis)*

AN ACCOMMODATING LION

An athlete, one vacation,
Met a lion in privation
On a desert where the lion-food was rare.
The lion was delighted
That the athlete he had sighted,
But the athlete wished that he had been elsewhere.

The athlete dared not fight him,
And he recalled an item
That was published in some journal he had read,
Of a lion that retreated,
Disheartened and defeated,
When an unarmed hunter stood upon his head.

On this hint from print extracted
The athlete promptly acted,
And brandished both his shoe-heels in the air.
Upon this feat amazing
The lion sat a-gazing,
And studied the phenomenon with care.

Said the lion, "This position
Is quite against tradition,
But I'll gladly eat you any way you choose.
Inverted perpendicular
Will do—I'm not particular!"
He finished him, beginning with his shoes.

Tudor Jenks

OLD HOGAN'S GOAT

Old Hogan's goat was feeling fine,
Ate six red shirts from off the line;
Old Hogan grabbed him by the back
And tied him to the railroad track.
Now when the train came into sight,
That goat grew pale and green with fright;
He heaved a sigh, as if in pain,
Coughed up those shirts and flagged the train!

THE TERMITE

Some primal termite knocked on wood
And tasted it, and found it good,
And that is why your Cousin May
Fell through the parlor floor today.

Ogden Nash

THE EEL

There was an old person of Dover
Who called on his sister in Deal
With a sack hanging over his shoulder
In which was a whopping great eel.
It leapt down the area, scuttled upstairs,
It golloped up bolsters and wash-jugs and chairs,
Her boots, shoes, and slippers, in singles and pairs;
And alas! when this Ogre
Had finished its meal,
There was no-one of Dover
With a sister in Deal.

Walter de la Mare

THE TABLE AND THE CHAIR

Said the Table to the Chair,
"You can hardly be aware
How I suffer from the heat
And from chilblains on my feet.
If we took a little walk,
We might have a little talk;
Pray let us take the air."
Said the Table to the Chair.

Said the Chair unto the Table,
"Now, you *know* we are not able:
How foolishly you talk,
When you know we *cannot* walk!"
Said the Table with a sigh,
"It can do no harm to try.
I've as many legs as you:
Why can't we walk on two?"

So they both went slowly down,
And walked about the town
With a cheerful bumpy sound
As they toddled round and round
And everybody cried,
As they hastened to their side,
"See! the Table and the Chair
Have come to take the air!"

But in going down an alley,
To a castle in a valley,
They completely lost their way,
And wandered all the day;
Till, to see them safely back,
They paid a Ducky-quack,
And a Beetle, and a Mouse
Who took them to their house.

Then they whispered to each other,
"O delightful little brother,
What a lovely walk we've taken!
Let us dine on beans and bacon."
So the Ducky and the leetle
Browny-Mousy and the Beetle
Dined, and danced upon their heads
Till they toddled to their beds.

Edward Lear

LIMERICKS

There was a young man from the city,
Who met what he thought was a kitty.
   He gave it a pat.
   And said, "Nice little cat!"
And they buried his clothes, out of pity.

A mouse in her room woke Miss Dowd;
She was frightened and screamed very loud,
   Then a happy thought hit her—
   To scare off the critter,
She sat up in bed and meowed.

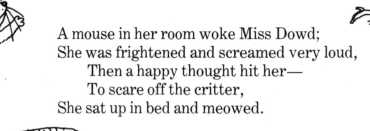

A Boston boy went out to Yuma
And there he encountered a puma—
   And later they found
   Just a spot on the ground
And a puma in very good huma.

There was a young lady of Lynn,
Who was so uncommonly thin
   That when she essayed
   To drink lemonade,
She slipped through the straw and fell in.

There was a young man of Bengal
Who went to a fancy-dress ball,
   He went, just for fun,
   Dressed up as a bun,
And a dog ate him up in the hall.

An epicure dining at Crewe
Once found a large mouse in his stew.
   Said the waiter, "Don't shout
   And wave it about,
Or the rest will be wanting one, too."

Elders... and Betters?

After the Ball was over
The lady took out her glass eye,
Put her false teeth in water,
Hung out her hair to dry;
Then she removed her cork leg,
Stood it against the wall;
Now we know what became of the lady
After the Ball.

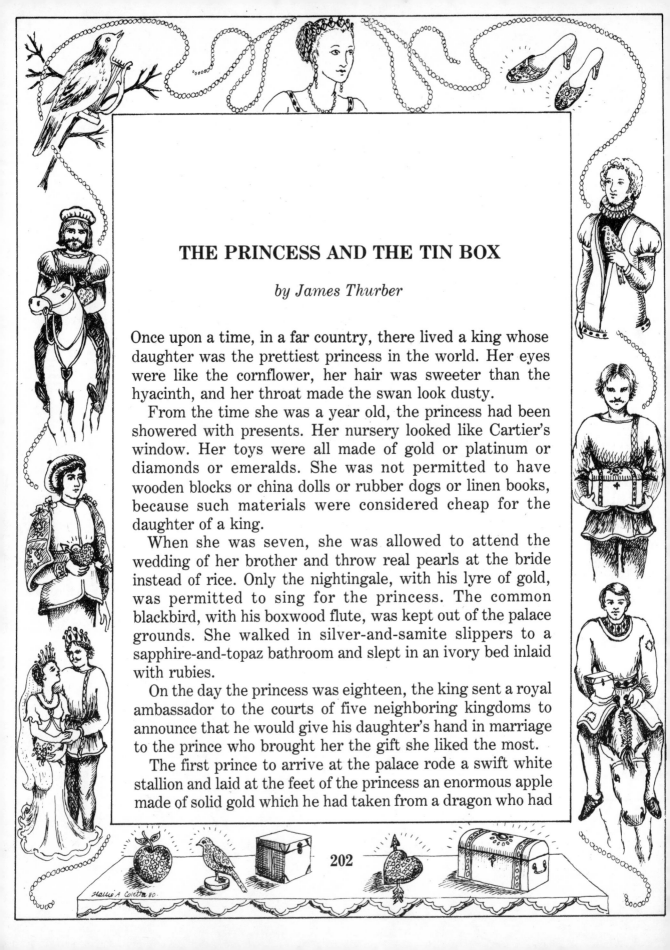

THE PRINCESS AND THE TIN BOX

by James Thurber

Once upon a time, in a far country, there lived a king whose daughter was the prettiest princess in the world. Her eyes were like the cornflower, her hair was sweeter than the hyacinth, and her throat made the swan look dusty.

From the time she was a year old, the princess had been showered with presents. Her nursery looked like Cartier's window. Her toys were all made of gold or platinum or diamonds or emeralds. She was not permitted to have wooden blocks or china dolls or rubber dogs or linen books, because such materials were considered cheap for the daughter of a king.

When she was seven, she was allowed to attend the wedding of her brother and throw real pearls at the bride instead of rice. Only the nightingale, with his lyre of gold, was permitted to sing for the princess. The common blackbird, with his boxwood flute, was kept out of the palace grounds. She walked in silver-and-samite slippers to a sapphire-and-topaz bathroom and slept in an ivory bed inlaid with rubies.

On the day the princess was eighteen, the king sent a royal ambassador to the courts of five neighboring kingdoms to announce that he would give his daughter's hand in marriage to the prince who brought her the gift she liked the most.

The first prince to arrive at the palace rode a swift white stallion and laid at the feet of the princess an enormous apple made of solid gold which he had taken from a dragon who had

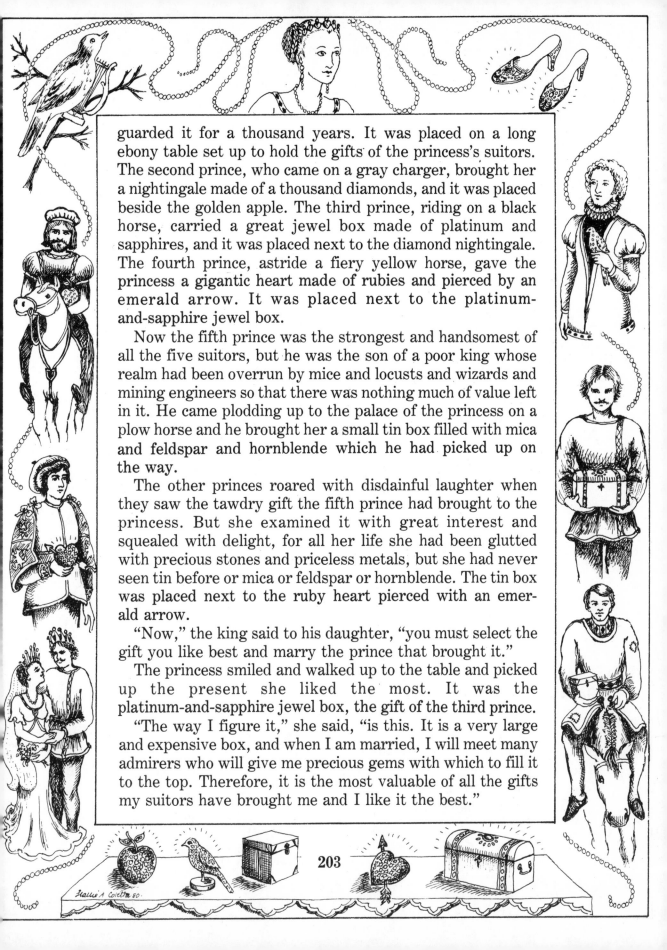

guarded it for a thousand years. It was placed on a long ebony table set up to hold the gifts of the princess's suitors. The second prince, who came on a gray charger, brought her a nightingale made of a thousand diamonds, and it was placed beside the golden apple. The third prince, riding on a black horse, carried a great jewel box made of platinum and sapphires, and it was placed next to the diamond nightingale. The fourth prince, astride a fiery yellow horse, gave the princess a gigantic heart made of rubies and pierced by an emerald arrow. It was placed next to the platinum-and-sapphire jewel box.

Now the fifth prince was the strongest and handsomest of all the five suitors, but he was the son of a poor king whose realm had been overrun by mice and locusts and wizards and mining engineers so that there was nothing much of value left in it. He came plodding up to the palace of the princess on a plow horse and he brought her a small tin box filled with mica and feldspar and hornblende which he had picked up on the way.

The other princes roared with disdainful laughter when they saw the tawdry gift the fifth prince had brought to the princess. But she examined it with great interest and squealed with delight, for all her life she had been glutted with precious stones and priceless metals, but she had never seen tin before or mica or feldspar or hornblende. The tin box was placed next to the ruby heart pierced with an emerald arrow.

"Now," the king said to his daughter, "you must select the gift you like best and marry the prince that brought it."

The princess smiled and walked up to the table and picked up the present she liked the most. It was the platinum-and-sapphire jewel box, the gift of the third prince.

"The way I figure it," she said, "is this. It is a very large and expensive box, and when I am married, I will meet many admirers who will give me precious gems with which to fill it to the top. Therefore, it is the most valuable of all the gifts my suitors have brought me and I like it the best."

203

The princess married the third prince that very day in the midst of great merriment and high revelry. More than a hundred thousand pearls were thrown at her and she loved it.

Moral: All those who thought the princess was going to select the tin box filled with worthless stones instead of one of the other gifts will kindly stay after class and write one hundred times on the blackboard "I would rather have a hunk of aluminum silicate than a diamond necklace."

A TRAGIC STORY

There lived a sage in days of yore,
And he a handsome pigtail wore;
But wondered much, and sorrowed more,
    Because it hung behind him.

He mused upon this curious case,
And swore he'd change the pigtail's place,
And have it hanging at his face,
    Not dangling there behind him.

Says he, "The mystery I've found—
I'll turn me round,"—he turned him round;
    But still it hung behind him.

Then round and round and out and in,
All day the puzzled sage did spin,
In vain—it mattered not a pin—
    The pigtail hung behind him.

And right, and left, and round about,
And up, and down, and in, and out,
He turned; but still the pigtail stout
    Hung steadily behind him.

And though his efforts never slack,
And though he twist, and twirl, and spin,
Alas! still faithful to his back,
    The pigtail hangs behind him.

William Makepeace Thackeray

A MOST DELIGHTFUL DAY

A man possessed
    Of common sense
Need not invest
    At great expense—

It does not call
    For pockets deep
These jokes are all
    Extremely cheap.

No fun compares with easy chairs
whose seats are stuffed with needles—

Live shrimps their patience tax
When put down people's backs.

Surprising, too, what one can do with
a pint of fat black beetles—

Then sharp tin tacks
    And pocket squirts—
And cobblers' wax
    For ladies' skirts—

And slimy slugs
    On bedroom floors—
And water jugs
    On open doors—

Prepared with these cheap properties,
    amusing tricks to play
Upon a friend a man may spend
    a most delightful day.

W. S. Gilbert

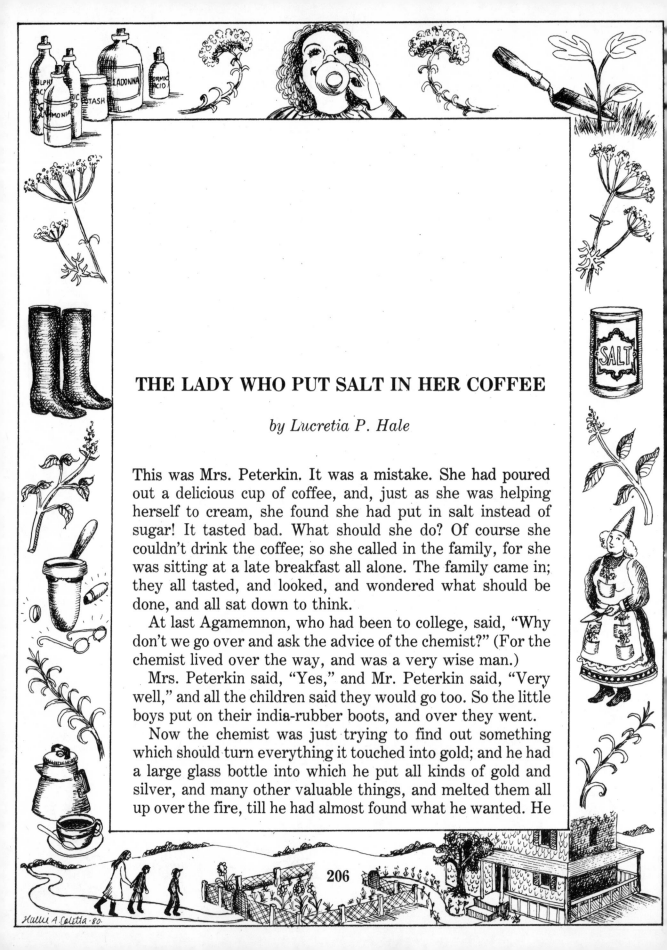

THE LADY WHO PUT SALT IN HER COFFEE

by Lucretia P. Hale

This was Mrs. Peterkin. It was a mistake. She had poured out a delicious cup of coffee, and, just as she was helping herself to cream, she found she had put in salt instead of sugar! It tasted bad. What should she do? Of course she couldn't drink the coffee; so she called in the family, for she was sitting at a late breakfast all alone. The family came in; they all tasted, and looked, and wondered what should be done, and all sat down to think.

At last Agamemnon, who had been to college, said, "Why don't we go over and ask the advice of the chemist?" (For the chemist lived over the way, and was a very wise man.)

Mrs. Peterkin said, "Yes," and Mr. Peterkin said, "Very well," and all the children said they would go too. So the little boys put on their india-rubber boots, and over they went.

Now the chemist was just trying to find out something which should turn everything it touched into gold; and he had a large glass bottle into which he put all kinds of gold and silver, and many other valuable things, and melted them all up over the fire, till he had almost found what he wanted. He

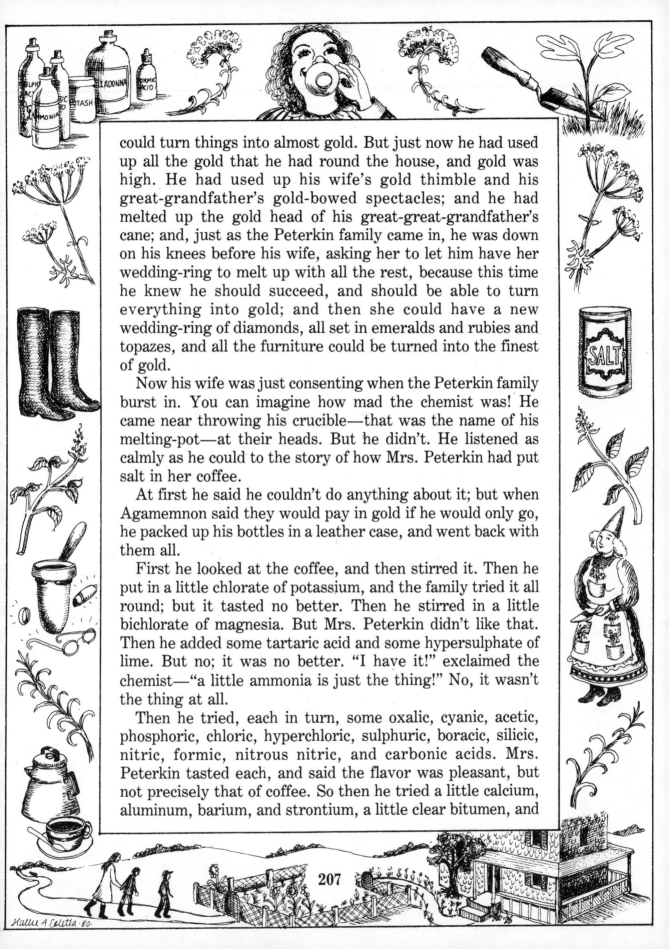

could turn things into almost gold. But just now he had used up all the gold that he had round the house, and gold was high. He had used up his wife's gold thimble and his great-grandfather's gold-bowed spectacles; and he had melted up the gold head of his great-great-grandfather's cane; and, just as the Peterkin family came in, he was down on his knees before his wife, asking her to let him have her wedding-ring to melt up with all the rest, because this time he knew he should succeed, and should be able to turn everything into gold; and then she could have a new wedding-ring of diamonds, all set in emeralds and rubies and topazes, and all the furniture could be turned into the finest of gold.

Now his wife was just consenting when the Peterkin family burst in. You can imagine how mad the chemist was! He came near throwing his crucible—that was the name of his melting-pot—at their heads. But he didn't. He listened as calmly as he could to the story of how Mrs. Peterkin had put salt in her coffee.

At first he said he couldn't do anything about it; but when Agamemnon said they would pay in gold if he would only go, he packed up his bottles in a leather case, and went back with them all.

First he looked at the coffee, and then stirred it. Then he put in a little chlorate of potassium, and the family tried it all round; but it tasted no better. Then he stirred in a little bichlorate of magnesia. But Mrs. Peterkin didn't like that. Then he added some tartaric acid and some hypersulphate of lime. But no; it was no better. "I have it!" exclaimed the chemist—"a little ammonia is just the thing!" No, it wasn't the thing at all.

Then he tried, each in turn, some oxalic, cyanic, acetic, phosphoric, chloric, hyperchloric, sulphuric, boracic, silicic, nitric, formic, nitrous nitric, and carbonic acids. Mrs. Peterkin tasted each, and said the flavor was pleasant, but not precisely that of coffee. So then he tried a little calcium, aluminum, barium, and strontium, a little clear bitumen, and

207

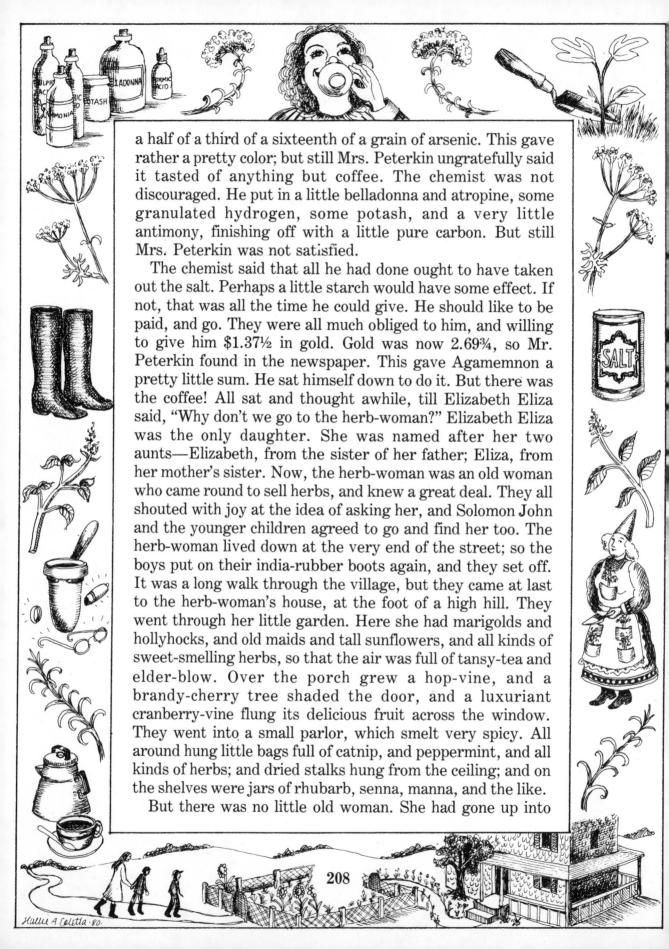

a half of a third of a sixteenth of a grain of arsenic. This gave rather a pretty color; but still Mrs. Peterkin ungratefully said it tasted of anything but coffee. The chemist was not discouraged. He put in a little belladonna and atropine, some granulated hydrogen, some potash, and a very little antimony, finishing off with a little pure carbon. But still Mrs. Peterkin was not satisfied.

The chemist said that all he had done ought to have taken out the salt. Perhaps a little starch would have some effect. If not, that was all the time he could give. He should like to be paid, and go. They were all much obliged to him, and willing to give him $1.37½ in gold. Gold was now 2.69¾, so Mr. Peterkin found in the newspaper. This gave Agamemnon a pretty little sum. He sat himself down to do it. But there was the coffee! All sat and thought awhile, till Elizabeth Eliza said, "Why don't we go to the herb-woman?" Elizabeth Eliza was the only daughter. She was named after her two aunts—Elizabeth, from the sister of her father; Eliza, from her mother's sister. Now, the herb-woman was an old woman who came round to sell herbs, and knew a great deal. They all shouted with joy at the idea of asking her, and Solomon John and the younger children agreed to go and find her too. The herb-woman lived down at the very end of the street; so the boys put on their india-rubber boots again, and they set off. It was a long walk through the village, but they came at last to the herb-woman's house, at the foot of a high hill. They went through her little garden. Here she had marigolds and hollyhocks, and old maids and tall sunflowers, and all kinds of sweet-smelling herbs, so that the air was full of tansy-tea and elder-blow. Over the porch grew a hop-vine, and a brandy-cherry tree shaded the door, and a luxuriant cranberry-vine flung its delicious fruit across the window. They went into a small parlor, which smelt very spicy. All around hung little bags full of catnip, and peppermint, and all kinds of herbs; and dried stalks hung from the ceiling; and on the shelves were jars of rhubarb, senna, manna, and the like.

But there was no little old woman. She had gone up into

the woods to get some more wild herbs, so they all thought they would follow her—Elizabeth Eliza, Solomon John, and the little boys. They had to climb up over high rocks, and in among huckleberry-bushes and blackberry-vines. But the little boys had their india-rubber boots. At last they discovered the little old woman. They knew her by her hat. It was steeple-crowned, without any vane. They saw her digging with her trowel round a sassafras bush. They told her their story—how their mother had put salt in her coffee, and how the chemist had made it worse instead of better, and how their mother couldn't drink it, and wouldn't she come and see what she could do? And she said she would, and took up her little old apron, with pockets all round, all filled with everlasting and pennyroyal, and went back to her house.

There she stopped, and stuffed her huge pockets with some of all the kinds of herbs. She took some tansy and peppermint, and caraway-seed and dill, spearmint and cloves, pennyroyal and sweet marjoram, basil and rosemary, wild thyme and some of the other time—such as you have in clocks—sappermint and oppermint, catnip, valerian, and hop; indeed, there isn't a kind of herb you can think of that the little old woman didn't have done up in her little paper bags, that had all been dried in her little Dutch-oven. She packed these all up, and then went back with the children, taking her stick.

Meanwhile Mrs. Peterkin was getting quite impatient for her coffee.

As soon as the little old woman came she had it set over the fire, and began to stir in the different herbs. First she put in a little hop for the bitter. Mrs. Peterkin said it tasted like hop-tea, and not at all like coffee. Then she tried a little flagroot and snakeroot, then some spruce gum, and some caraway and some dill, some rue and rosemary, some sweet marjoram and sour, some oppermint and sappermint, a little spearmint and peppermint, some wild thyme, and some of the other tame time, some tansy and basil, and catnip and valerian, and sassafras, ginger, and pennyroyal. The children

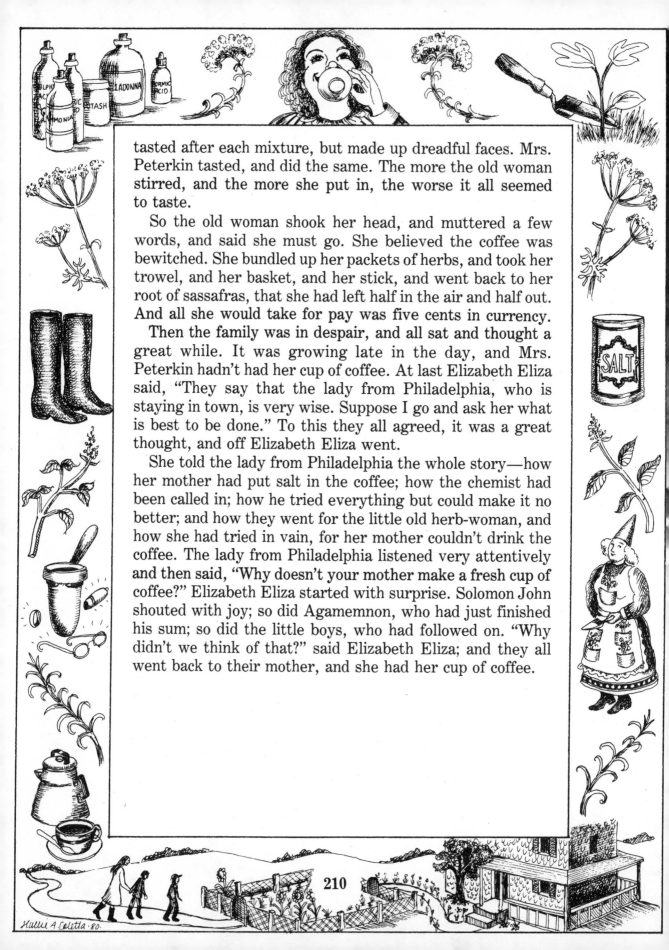

tasted after each mixture, but made up dreadful faces. Mrs. Peterkin tasted, and did the same. The more the old woman stirred, and the more she put in, the worse it all seemed to taste.

So the old woman shook her head, and muttered a few words, and said she must go. She believed the coffee was bewitched. She bundled up her packets of herbs, and took her trowel, and her basket, and her stick, and went back to her root of sassafras, that she had left half in the air and half out. And all she would take for pay was five cents in currency.

Then the family was in despair, and all sat and thought a great while. It was growing late in the day, and Mrs. Peterkin hadn't had her cup of coffee. At last Elizabeth Eliza said, "They say that the lady from Philadelphia, who is staying in town, is very wise. Suppose I go and ask her what is best to be done." To this they all agreed, it was a great thought, and off Elizabeth Eliza went.

She told the lady from Philadelphia the whole story—how her mother had put salt in the coffee; how the chemist had been called in; how he tried everything but could make it no better; and how they went for the little old herb-woman, and how she had tried in vain, for her mother couldn't drink the coffee. The lady from Philadelphia listened very attentively and then said, "Why doesn't your mother make a fresh cup of coffee?" Elizabeth Eliza started with surprise. Solomon John shouted with joy; so did Agamemnon, who had just finished his sum; so did the little boys, who had followed on. "Why didn't we think of that?" said Elizabeth Eliza; and they all went back to their mother, and she had her cup of coffee.

SOMEBODY SAID THAT IT COULDN'T BE DONE

Somebody said that it couldn't be done—
But he, with a grin, replied
He'd never be one to say it couldn't be done—
Leastways, not 'til he'd tried.
So he buckled right in, with a trace of a grin;
By golly, he went right to it.
He tackled The Thing That Couldn't Be Done!
And he couldn't do it.

FATHER WILLIAM

"You are old, Father William," the young man said
    "And your hair has become very white;
And yet you incessantly stand on your head—
    Do you think, at your age, it is right?"

"In my youth," Father William replied to his son,
    "I feared it might injure the brain;
But now that I'm perfectly sure I have none,
    Why, I do it again and again."

"You are old," said the youth, "as I mentioned before,
    And have grown most uncommonly fat;
Yet you turned a back somersault in at the door—
    Pray, what is the reason of that?"

"In my youth," said the sage, as he shook his gray locks,
    "I kept all my limbs very supple
By the use of this ointment—one shilling the box—
    Allow me to sell you a couple."

"You are old," said the youth, "and your jaws are too weak
   For anything tougher than suet;
Yet you finished the goose, with the bones and the beak—
   Pray, how did you manage to do it?"

"In my youth," said his father, "I took to the law,
   And argued each case with my wife;
And the muscular strength, which it gave to my jaw,
   Has lasted the rest of my life."

"You are old," said the youth, "one would hardly suppose
   That your eye was as steady as ever;
Yet you balanced an eel on the end of your nose—
   What made you so awfully clever?"

"I have answered three questions, and that is enough,"
   Said his father, "don't give yourself airs!
Do you think I can listen all day to such stuff?
   Be off, or I'll kick you downstairs!"

Lewis Carroll

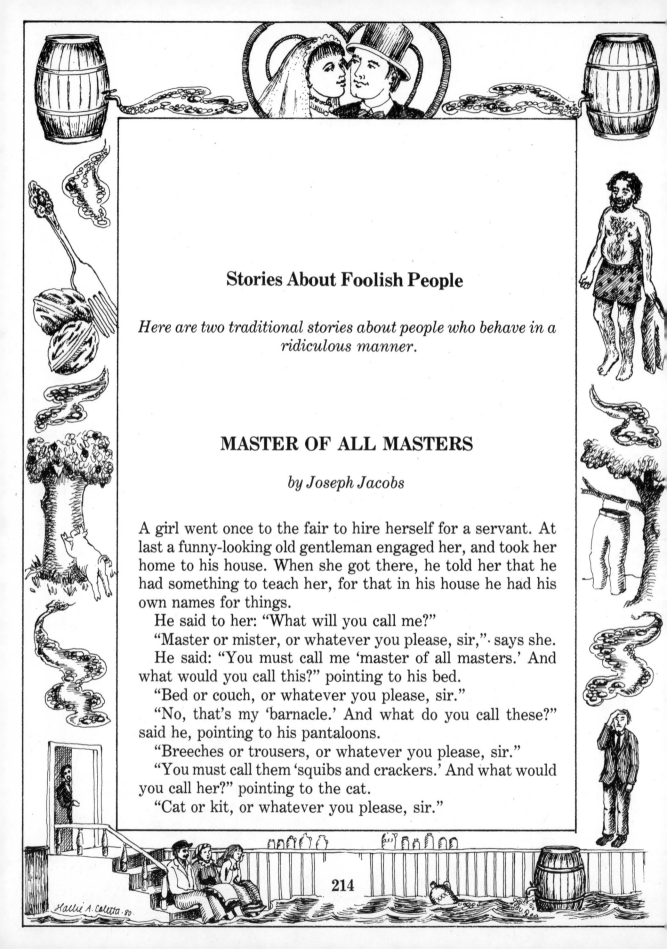

Stories About Foolish People

Here are two traditional stories about people who behave in a ridiculous manner.

MASTER OF ALL MASTERS

by Joseph Jacobs

A girl went once to the fair to hire herself for a servant. At last a funny-looking old gentleman engaged her, and took her home to his house. When she got there, he told her that he had something to teach her, for that in his house he had his own names for things.

He said to her: "What will you call me?"

"Master or mister, or whatever you please, sir," says she.

He said: "You must call me 'master of all masters.' And what would you call this?" pointing to his bed.

"Bed or couch, or whatever you please, sir."

"No, that's my 'barnacle.' And what do you call these?" said he, pointing to his pantaloons.

"Breeches or trousers, or whatever you please, sir."

"You must call them 'squibs and crackers.' And what would you call her?" pointing to the cat.

"Cat or kit, or whatever you please, sir."

Hallie A. Coletta · 80

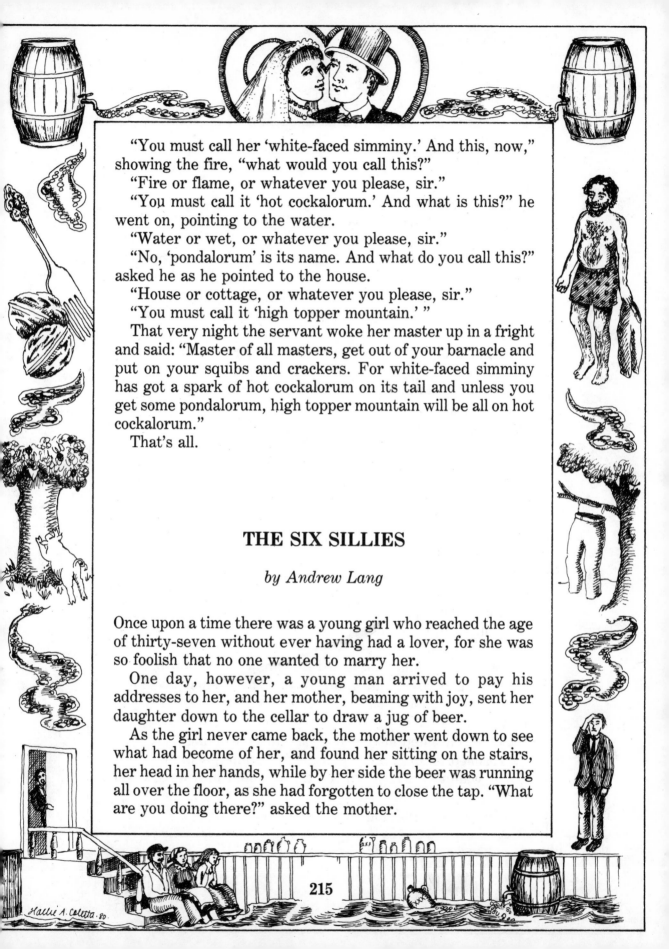

"You must call her 'white-faced simminy.' And this, now," showing the fire, "what would you call this?"

"Fire or flame, or whatever you please, sir."

"You must call it 'hot cockalorum.' And what is this?" he went on, pointing to the water.

"Water or wet, or whatever you please, sir."

"No, 'pondalorum' is its name. And what do you call this?" asked he as he pointed to the house.

"House or cottage, or whatever you please, sir."

"You must call it 'high topper mountain.' "

That very night the servant woke her master up in a fright and said: "Master of all masters, get out of your barnacle and put on your squibs and crackers. For white-faced simminy has got a spark of hot cockalorum on its tail and unless you get some pondalorum, high topper mountain will be all on hot cockalorum."

That's all.

THE SIX SILLIES

by Andrew Lang

Once upon a time there was a young girl who reached the age of thirty-seven without ever having had a lover, for she was so foolish that no one wanted to marry her.

One day, however, a young man arrived to pay his addresses to her, and her mother, beaming with joy, sent her daughter down to the cellar to draw a jug of beer.

As the girl never came back, the mother went down to see what had become of her, and found her sitting on the stairs, her head in her hands, while by her side the beer was running all over the floor, as she had forgotten to close the tap. "What are you doing there?" asked the mother.

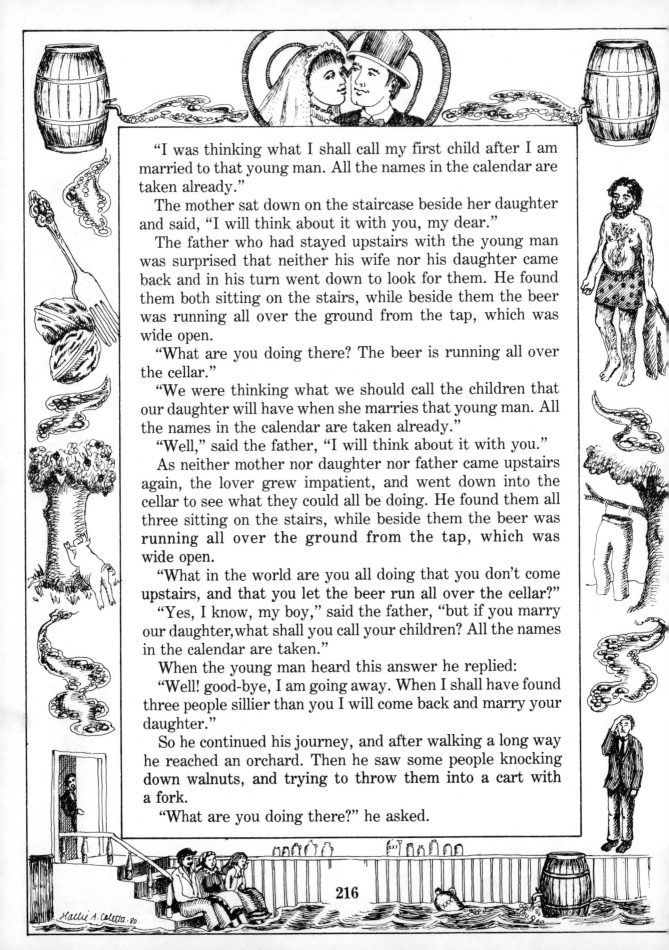

"I was thinking what I shall call my first child after I am married to that young man. All the names in the calendar are taken already."

The mother sat down on the staircase beside her daughter and said, "I will think about it with you, my dear."

The father who had stayed upstairs with the young man was surprised that neither his wife nor his daughter came back and in his turn went down to look for them. He found them both sitting on the stairs, while beside them the beer was running all over the ground from the tap, which was wide open.

"What are you doing there? The beer is running all over the cellar."

"We were thinking what we should call the children that our daughter will have when she marries that young man. All the names in the calendar are taken already."

"Well," said the father, "I will think about it with you."

As neither mother nor daughter nor father came upstairs again, the lover grew impatient, and went down into the cellar to see what they could all be doing. He found them all three sitting on the stairs, while beside them the beer was running all over the ground from the tap, which was wide open.

"What in the world are you all doing that you don't come upstairs, and that you let the beer run all over the cellar?"

"Yes, I know, my boy," said the father, "but if you marry our daughter, what shall you call your children? All the names in the calendar are taken."

When the young man heard this answer he replied:

"Well! good-bye, I am going away. When I shall have found three people sillier than you I will come back and marry your daughter."

So he continued his journey, and after walking a long way he reached an orchard. Then he saw some people knocking down walnuts, and trying to throw them into a cart with a fork.

"What are you doing there?" he asked.

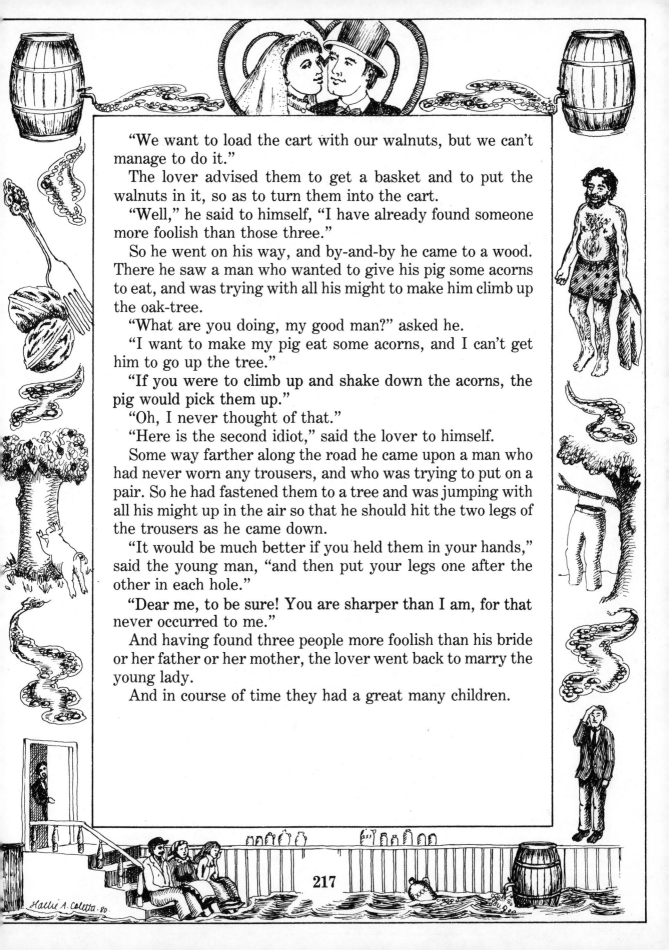

"We want to load the cart with our walnuts, but we can't manage to do it."

The lover advised them to get a basket and to put the walnuts in it, so as to turn them into the cart.

"Well," he said to himself, "I have already found someone more foolish than those three."

So he went on his way, and by-and-by he came to a wood. There he saw a man who wanted to give his pig some acorns to eat, and was trying with all his might to make him climb up the oak-tree.

"What are you doing, my good man?" asked he.

"I want to make my pig eat some acorns, and I can't get him to go up the tree."

"If you were to climb up and shake down the acorns, the pig would pick them up."

"Oh, I never thought of that."

"Here is the second idiot," said the lover to himself.

Some way farther along the road he came upon a man who had never worn any trousers, and who was trying to put on a pair. So he had fastened them to a tree and was jumping with all his might up in the air so that he should hit the two legs of the trousers as he came down.

"It would be much better if you held them in your hands," said the young man, "and then put your legs one after the other in each hole."

"Dear me, to be sure! You are sharper than I am, for that never occurred to me."

And having found three people more foolish than his bride or her father or her mother, the lover went back to marry the young lady.

And in course of time they had a great many children.

217

SIR SMASHAM UPPE

Good afternoon, Sir Smasham Uppe!
We're having tea: do take a cup.
Sugar and milk? Now let me see—
Two lumps, I think? . . . Good gracious me!
The silly thing slipped off your knee!
Pray don't apologize, old chap:
A very trivial mishap!
So clumsy of you? How absurd!
My dear Sir Smasham, not a word!
Now do sit down and have another,
And tell us all about your brother—
You know, the one who broke his head.
Is the poor fellow still in bed?—
A chair—allow me, sir! . . . Great Scott!
That *was* a nasty smash! Eh, what?
Oh, not at all; the chair was old—
Queen Anne, or so we have been told.
We've got at least a dozen more:
Just leave the pieces on the floor.
I want you to admire our view:
Come nearer to the window, do;
And look how beautiful . . . Tut, tut!
You didn't see that it was shut?
I hope you are not badly cut!
Not hurt? A fortunate escape!
Amazing! Not a single scrape!
And now, if you have finished tea,
I fancy you might like to see
A little thing or two I've got.
That china plate? Yes, worth a lot:
A beauty, too . . . Ah, there it goes!
I trust it didn't hurt your toes?
Your elbow brushed it off the shelf?
Of course: I've done the same myself.
And now my dear Sir Smasham—Oh,
You surely don't intend to go?
You *must* be off? Well, come again.
So glad you're fond of porcelain!

E. V. Rieu

MONTEZUMA

Montezuma
Met a puma
Coming through the rye;
Montezuma
Made the puma
Into apple-pie.

Invitation
To the nation
Everyone to come.
Montezuma
And the puma
Give a kettle-drum.

Acceptation
Of the nation,
One and all invited.
Montezuma
And the puma
Equally delighted.

Preparation,
Ostentation,
Dresses rich prepared:
Feathers—jewels—
Work in crewels—
No expense is spared.

Congregation
Of the nation
Round the palace wall.
Awful rumour
That the puma
Won't be served at all.

Deputation
From the nation,
Audience they gain.
"What's this rumour?
Montezuma,
If you please, explain."

Montezuma
(Playful humour
Very well sustained)
Answers "Pie-dish,
And it's my dish,
Is for me retained."

Exclamation!
Indignation!
Feeling running high.
Montezuma
Joins the puma
In the apple-pie.

D. F. Alderson

220

What Nonsense!

Say, did you say, or did you not say
What I said you said?
For it is said that you said
That you did not say
What I said you said.
Now if you say that you did not say
What I said you said,
Then what do you say you did say instead
Of what I said you said?

THE QUANGLE WANGLE'S HAT

On the top of the Crumpetty Tree
    The Quangle Wangle sat,
But his face you could not see,
    On account of his Beaver Hat.
For his Hat was a hundred and two feet wide,
With ribbons and bibbons on every side,
And bells, and buttons, and loops, and lace,
So that nobody ever could see the face
        Of the Quangle Wangle Quee.

The Quangle Wangle said
  To himself on the Crumpetty Tree,
  "Jam, and jelly, and bread
  Are the best of food for me!
But the longer I live on this Crumpetty Tree
The plainer than ever it seems to me
That very few people come this way
And that life on the whole is far from gay!"
    Said the Quangle Wangle Quee.

But there came to the Crumpetty Tree
  Mr. and Mrs. Canary;
And they said, "Did ever you see
  Any spot so charmingly airy?
May we build a nest on your lovely Hat?
Mr. Quangle Wangle, grant us that!
O please let us come and build a nest
Of whatever material suits you best,
    Mr. Quangle Wangle Quee!"

And besides, to the Crumpetty Tree
   Came the Stork, the Duck, and the Owl;
The Snail and the Bumble-Bee,
   The Frog and the Fimble Fowl
(The Fimble Fowl, with a Corkscrew leg);
And all of them said, "We humbly beg
We may build our homes on your lovely Hat—
Mr. Quangle Wangle, grant us that!
   Mr. Quangle Wangle Quee!"

And the Golden Grouse came there,
  And the Pobble who has no toes,
And the small Olympian bear,
  And the Dong with a luminous nose.
And the Blue Baboon who played the flute,
And the Orient Calf from the Land of Tute,
And the Attery Squash, and the Bisky Bat—
All came and built on the lovely Hat
    Of the Quangle Wangle Quee.

And the Quangle Wangle said
  To himself on the Crumpetty Tree,
"When all these creatures move,
  What a wonderful noise there'll be!"
And at night by the light of the Mulberry moon
They danced to the Flute of the Blue Baboon,
On the broad green leaves of the Crumpetty Tree,
And all were as happy as happy could be,
    With the Quangle Wangle Quee.

Edward Lear

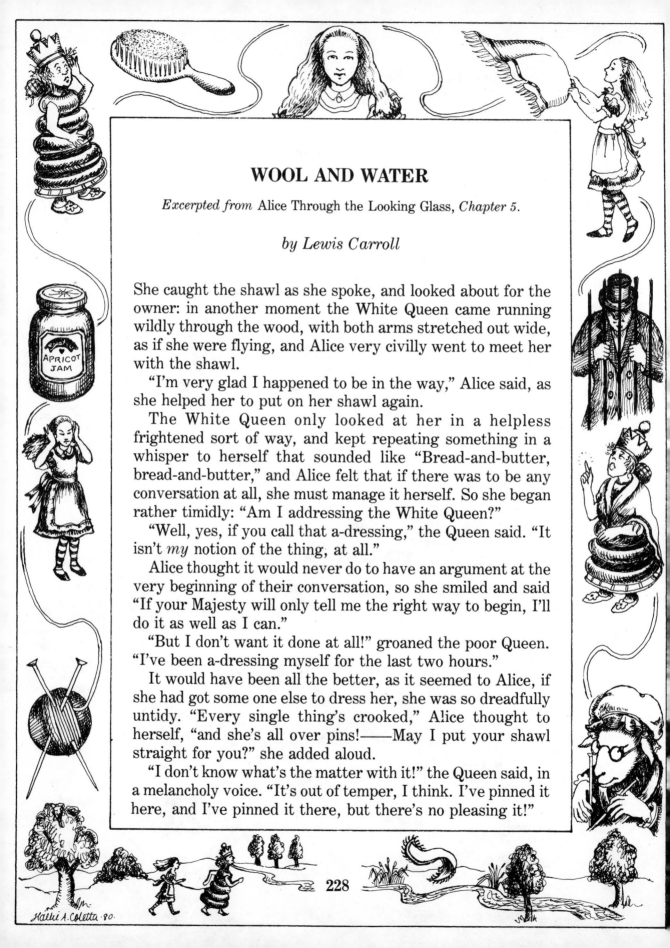

WOOL AND WATER

Excerpted from Alice Through the Looking Glass, *Chapter 5.*

by Lewis Carroll

She caught the shawl as she spoke, and looked about for the owner: in another moment the White Queen came running wildly through the wood, with both arms stretched out wide, as if she were flying, and Alice very civilly went to meet her with the shawl.

"I'm very glad I happened to be in the way," Alice said, as she helped her to put on her shawl again.

The White Queen only looked at her in a helpless frightened sort of way, and kept repeating something in a whisper to herself that sounded like "Bread-and-butter, bread-and-butter," and Alice felt that if there was to be any conversation at all, she must manage it herself. So she began rather timidly: "Am I addressing the White Queen?"

"Well, yes, if you call that a-dressing," the Queen said. "It isn't *my* notion of the thing, at all."

Alice thought it would never do to have an argument at the very beginning of their conversation, so she smiled and said "If your Majesty will only tell me the right way to begin, I'll do it as well as I can."

"But I don't want it done at all!" groaned the poor Queen. "I've been a-dressing myself for the last two hours."

It would have been all the better, as it seemed to Alice, if she had got some one else to dress her, she was so dreadfully untidy. "Every single thing's crooked," Alice thought to herself, "and she's all over pins!——May I put your shawl straight for you?" she added aloud.

"I don't know what's the matter with it!" the Queen said, in a melancholy voice. "It's out of temper, I think. I've pinned it here, and I've pinned it there, but there's no pleasing it!"

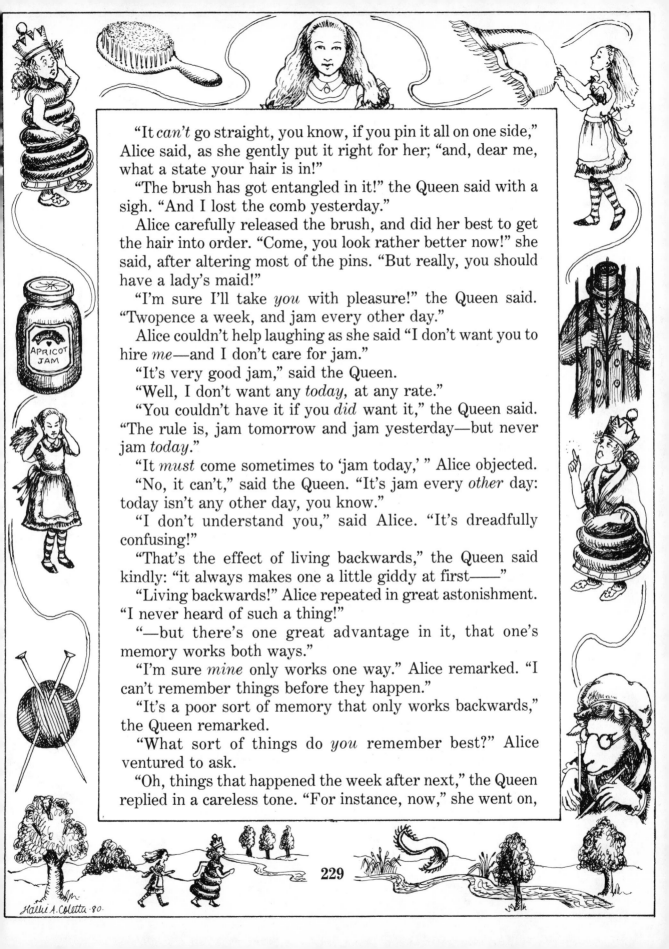

"It *can't* go straight, you know, if you pin it all on one side," Alice said, as she gently put it right for her; "and, dear me, what a state your hair is in!"

"The brush has got entangled in it!" the Queen said with a sigh. "And I lost the comb yesterday."

Alice carefully released the brush, and did her best to get the hair into order. "Come, you look rather better now!" she said, after altering most of the pins. "But really, you should have a lady's maid!"

"I'm sure I'll take *you* with pleasure!" the Queen said. "Twopence a week, and jam every other day."

Alice couldn't help laughing as she said "I don't want you to hire *me*—and I don't care for jam."

"It's very good jam," said the Queen.

"Well, I don't want any *today*, at any rate."

"You couldn't have it if you *did* want it," the Queen said. "The rule is, jam tomorrow and jam yesterday—but never jam *today*."

"It *must* come sometimes to 'jam today,' " Alice objected.

"No, it can't," said the Queen. "It's jam every *other* day: today isn't any other day, you know."

"I don't understand you," said Alice. "It's dreadfully confusing!"

"That's the effect of living backwards," the Queen said kindly: "it always makes one a little giddy at first——"

"Living backwards!" Alice repeated in great astonishment. "I never heard of such a thing!"

"—but there's one great advantage in it, that one's memory works both ways."

"I'm sure *mine* only works one way." Alice remarked. "I can't remember things before they happen."

"It's a poor sort of memory that only works backwards," the Queen remarked.

"What sort of things do *you* remember best?" Alice ventured to ask.

"Oh, things that happened the week after next," the Queen replied in a careless tone. "For instance, now," she went on,

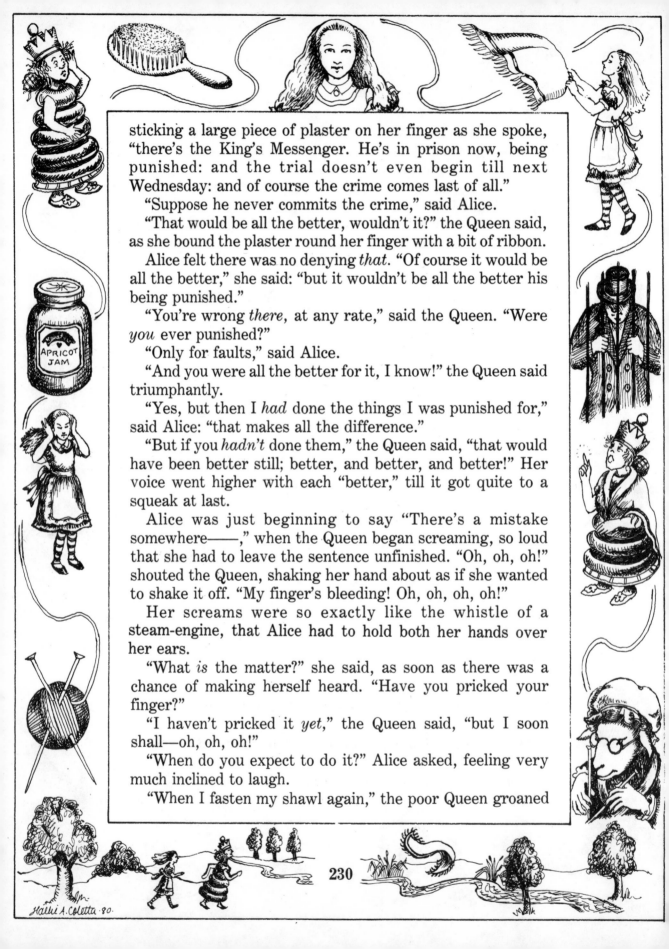

sticking a large piece of plaster on her finger as she spoke, "there's the King's Messenger. He's in prison now, being punished: and the trial doesn't even begin till next Wednesday: and of course the crime comes last of all."

"Suppose he never commits the crime," said Alice.

"That would be all the better, wouldn't it?" the Queen said, as she bound the plaster round her finger with a bit of ribbon.

Alice felt there was no denying *that*. "Of course it would be all the better," she said: "but it wouldn't be all the better his being punished."

"You're wrong *there*, at any rate," said the Queen. "Were *you* ever punished?"

"Only for faults," said Alice.

"And you were all the better for it, I know!" the Queen said triumphantly.

"Yes, but then I *had* done the things I was punished for," said Alice: "that makes all the difference."

"But if you *hadn't* done them," the Queen said, "that would have been better still; better, and better, and better!" Her voice went higher with each "better," till it got quite to a squeak at last.

Alice was just beginning to say "There's a mistake somewhere——," when the Queen began screaming, so loud that she had to leave the sentence unfinished. "Oh, oh, oh!" shouted the Queen, shaking her hand about as if she wanted to shake it off. "My finger's bleeding! Oh, oh, oh, oh!"

Her screams were so exactly like the whistle of a steam-engine, that Alice had to hold both her hands over her ears.

"What *is* the matter?" she said, as soon as there was a chance of making herself heard. "Have you pricked your finger?"

"I haven't pricked it *yet*," the Queen said, "but I soon shall—oh, oh, oh!"

"When do you expect to do it?" Alice asked, feeling very much inclined to laugh.

"When I fasten my shawl again," the poor Queen groaned

Hallie A. Coletta '80.

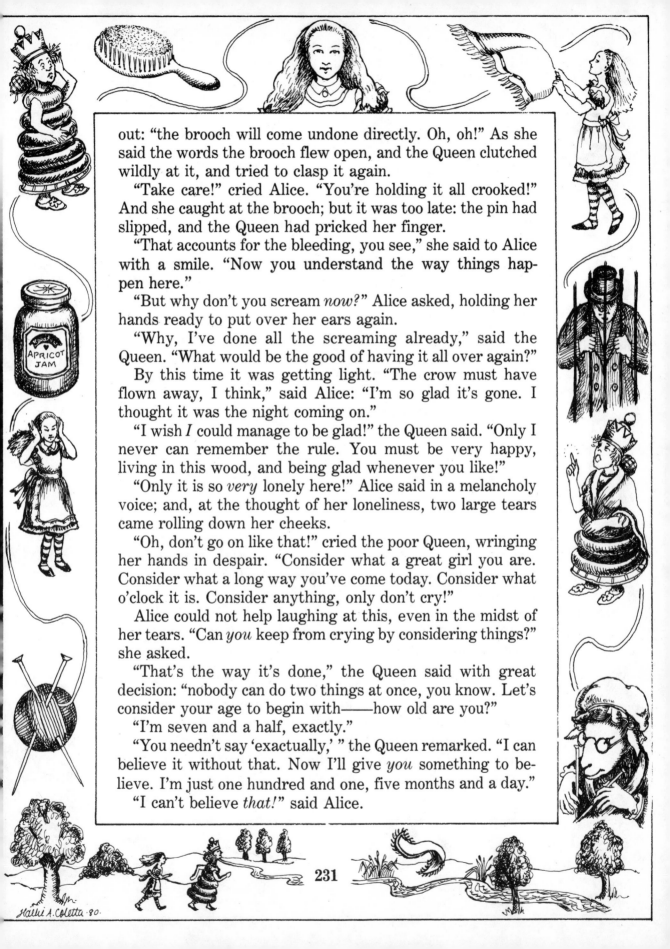

out: "the brooch will come undone directly. Oh, oh!" As she said the words the brooch flew open, and the Queen clutched wildly at it, and tried to clasp it again.

"Take care!" cried Alice. "You're holding it all crooked!" And she caught at the brooch; but it was too late: the pin had slipped, and the Queen had pricked her finger.

"That accounts for the bleeding, you see," she said to Alice with a smile. "Now you understand the way things happen here."

"But why don't you scream *now?*" Alice asked, holding her hands ready to put over her ears again.

"Why, I've done all the screaming already," said the Queen. "What would be the good of having it all over again?"

By this time it was getting light. "The crow must have flown away, I think," said Alice: "I'm so glad it's gone. I thought it was the night coming on."

"I wish *I* could manage to be glad!" the Queen said. "Only I never can remember the rule. You must be very happy, living in this wood, and being glad whenever you like!"

"Only it is so *very* lonely here!" Alice said in a melancholy voice; and, at the thought of her loneliness, two large tears came rolling down her cheeks.

"Oh, don't go on like that!" cried the poor Queen, wringing her hands in despair. "Consider what a great girl you are. Consider what a long way you've come today. Consider what o'clock it is. Consider anything, only don't cry!"

Alice could not help laughing at this, even in the midst of her tears. "Can *you* keep from crying by considering things?" she asked.

"That's the way it's done," the Queen said with great decision: "nobody can do two things at once, you know. Let's consider your age to begin with——how old are you?"

"I'm seven and a half, exactly."

"You needn't say 'exactually,' " the Queen remarked. "I can believe it without that. Now I'll give *you* something to believe. I'm just one hundred and one, five months and a day."

"I can't believe *that!*" said Alice.

"Can't you?" the Queen said in a pitying tone. "Try again: draw a long breath, and shut your eyes."

Alice laughed. "There's no use trying," she said: "one *can't* believe impossible things."

"I daresay you haven't had much practice," said the Queen. "When I was your age, I always did it for half-an-hour a day. Why, sometimes I've believed as many as six impossible things before breakfast. There goes the shawl again!"

The brooch had come undone as she spoke, and a sudden gust of wind blew the Queen's shawl across a little brook. The Queen spread out her arms again and went flying after it, and this time she succeeded in catching it for herself. "I've got it!" she cried in a triumphant tone. "Now you shall see me pin it on again, all by myself!"

"Then I hope your finger is better now?" Alice said very politely, as she crossed the little brook after the Queen.

*   *   *   *   *

  *   *   *   *

*   *   *   *   *

"Oh, much better!" cried the Queen, her voice rising into a squeak as she went on. "Much be-etter! Be-etter! Be-e-e-etter! Be-e-ehh!" The last word ended in a long bleat, so like a sheep that Alice quite started.

She looked at the Queen, who seemed to have suddenly wrapped herself up in wool. Alice rubbed her eyes, and looked again. She couldn't make out what had happened at all. Was she in a shop? And was that really—was it really a *sheep* that was sitting on the other side of the counter? Rub as she would, she could make nothing more of it: she was in a little dark shop, leaning with her elbows on the counter, and opposite to her was an old Sheep, sitting in an arm-chair, knitting, and every now and then leaving off to look at her through a great pair of spectacles.

CALICO PIE

Calico Pie,
The little Birds fly
Down to the calico tree,
Their wings were blue,
And they sang "Tilly-loo!"
Till away they flew—
And they never came back to me!
They never came back!
They never came back!
They never came back to me!

233

Calico Jam,
The little Fish swam,
Over the syllabub sea,
He took off his hat,
To the Sole and the Sprat,
And the Willeby-wat—
But he never came back to me!
He never came back!
He never came back!
He never came back to me!

Calico Ban,
The little Mice ran,
To be ready in time for tea,
Flippity flup,
They drank it all up,
And danced in the cup—
But they never came back to me!
They never came back!
They never came back!
They never came back to me!

Calico Drum,
The Grasshoppers come,
The Butterfly, Beetle, and Bee,
Over the ground,
Around and round,
With a hop and a bound—
But they never came back!
They never came back!
They never came back!
They never came back to me!

Edward Lear

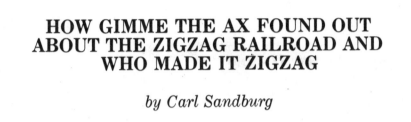

HOW GIMME THE AX FOUND OUT
ABOUT THE ZIGZAG RAILROAD AND
WHO MADE IT ZIGZAG

by Carl Sandburg

One day Gimme the Ax said to himself, "Today I go to the post office and around, looking around. Maybe I will hear about something happening last night when I was sleeping. Maybe a policeman began laughing and fell in a cistern and came out with a wheelbarrow full of goldfish wearing new jewelry. How do I know? Maybe the man in the moon going down a cellar stairs to get a pitcher of buttermilk for the woman in the moon to drink and stop crying, maybe he fell down the stairs and broke the pitcher and laughed and picked up the broken pieces and said to himself, 'One, two, three, four, accidents happen in the best-regulated families.' How do I know?"

So with his mind full of simple and refreshing thoughts, Gimme the Ax went out into the backyard garden and looked at the different necktie poppies growing early in the summer. Then he picked one of the necktie poppies to wear for a necktie scarf going downtown to the post office and around looking around.

"It is a good speculation to look nice around looking around in a necktie scarf," said Gimme the Ax. "It is a necktie with a

Hallie A. Coutts 80

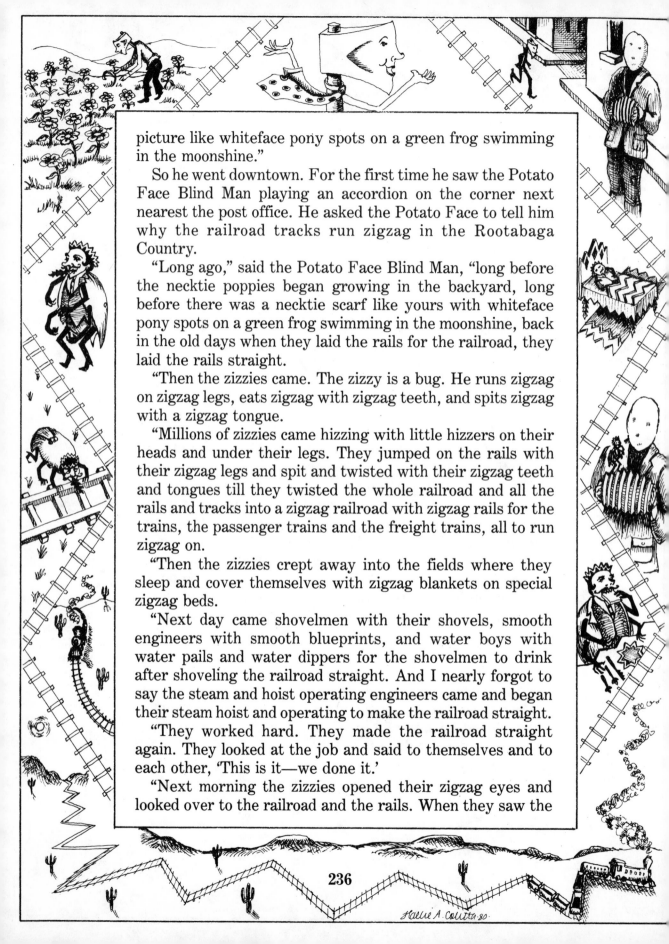

picture like whiteface pony spots on a green frog swimming in the moonshine."

So he went downtown. For the first time he saw the Potato Face Blind Man playing an accordion on the corner next nearest the post office. He asked the Potato Face to tell him why the railroad tracks run zigzag in the Rootabaga Country.

"Long ago," said the Potato Face Blind Man, "long before the necktie poppies began growing in the backyard, long before there was a necktie scarf like yours with whiteface pony spots on a green frog swimming in the moonshine, back in the old days when they laid the rails for the railroad, they laid the rails straight.

"Then the zizzies came. The zizzy is a bug. He runs zigzag on zigzag legs, eats zigzag with zigzag teeth, and spits zigzag with a zigzag tongue.

"Millions of zizzies came hizzing with little hizzers on their heads and under their legs. They jumped on the rails with their zigzag legs and spit and twisted with their zigzag teeth and tongues till they twisted the whole railroad and all the rails and tracks into a zigzag railroad with zigzag rails for the trains, the passenger trains and the freight trains, all to run zigzag on.

"Then the zizzies crept away into the fields where they sleep and cover themselves with zigzag blankets on special zigzag beds.

"Next day came shovelmen with their shovels, smooth engineers with smooth blueprints, and water boys with water pails and water dippers for the shovelmen to drink after shoveling the railroad straight. And I nearly forgot to say the steam and hoist operating engineers came and began their steam hoist and operating to make the railroad straight.

"They worked hard. They made the railroad straight again. They looked at the job and said to themselves and to each other, 'This is it—we done it.'

"Next morning the zizzies opened their zigzag eyes and looked over to the railroad and the rails. When they saw the

railroad all straight again, and the rails and the ties and the spikes all straight again, the zizzies didn't even eat breakfast that morning.

"They jumped out of their zigzag beds, jumped onto the rails with their zigzag legs, and spit and twisted till they spit and twisted all the rails and the ties and the spikes back into a zigzag like the letter Z and the letter Z at the end of the alphabet.

"After that the zizzies went to breakfast. And they said to themselves and to each other, the same as the shovelmen, the smooth engineers, and the steam hoist and operating engineers, 'This is it—we done it.' "

"So that is the how of the which—it was the zizzies," said Gimme the Ax.

"Yes, it was the zizzies," said the Potato Face Blind Man. "That is the story told to me."

"Who told it to you?"

"*Two little zizzies.* They came to me one cold winter night and slept in my accordion where the music keeps it warm in winter. In the morning I said, 'Good morning, zizzies. Did you have a good sleep last night and pleasant dreams?' And after they had breakfast, they told me the story. Both told it zigzag, but it was the same kind of zigzag each had together."

INDEX OF TITLES

INDEX OF FIRST LINES

INDEX OF AUTHORS